Innovative Activities of Multinational Enterprises in Austria

AF756915

Strukturwandel und Strukturpolitik

Herausgegeben von Prof. Dr. Wolfram Elsner

Band 19

PETER LANG
Frankfurt am Main · Berlin · Bern · Bruxelles · New York · Oxford · Wien

Bernhard Dachs

Innovative Activities of Multinational Enterprises in Austria

PETER LANG
Internationaler Verlag der Wissenschaften

Bibliographic Information published by the Deutsche Nationalbibliothek
The Deutsche Nationalbibliothek lists this publication in the Deutsche Nationalbibliografie; detailed bibliographic data is available in the internet at <http://www.d-nb.de>.

Zugl.: Bremen, Univ., Diss., 2008

D 46
ISSN 1438-2644
ISBN 978-3-631-59094-2

© Peter Lang GmbH
Internationaler Verlag der Wissenschaften
Frankfurt am Main 2009
All rights reserved.

All parts of this publication are protected by copyright. Any utilisation outside the strict limits of the copyright law, without the permission of the publisher, is forbidden and liable to prosecution. This applies in particular to reproductions, translations, microfilming, and storage and processing in electronic retrieval systems.

Printed in Germany 1 2 3 4 5 7

www.peterlang.de

Zur Reihe "Strukturwandel und Strukturpolitik"

"Strukturwandel", vor allem "globaler" Strukturwandel, ist in aller Munde. Er ist in der Tat das wichtigste Phänomen, in dem sich die Dynamik des Wirtschaftens äußert und das dem Wachstum der Wirtschaft zugrunde liegt. Auch Wirtschaftspolitik ist seit mehr als zwei Jahrzehnten weit eher "Strukturpolitik" (im weitesten Sinne, also institutionelle Strukturen eingeschlossen) als "Globalsteuerung".

Statisch-statistisch gesehen haben Struktur und Strukturwandel mit ökonomischen Phänomenen auf *"mittlerer" Aggregationsebene* und ihrem Wandel zu tun: Sektoren, Branchen, sektorale Cluster und Netzwerke, ferner Regionen, regionale Cluster und Netzwerke sowie schließlich Betriebsgrößenklassen (wie z. B. der "Mittelstand" oder Kleinstunternehmen und Existenzgründer). Diese strukturelle Dimension der Wirtschaft beschreibt zugleich das moderne Feld der *Meso-Ökonomik.* Zur Strukturpolitik zählen dementsprechend die sektorale Strukturpolitik (industrial policy), die heutzutage auch *cluster- und netzwerkorientiert* ist, einschließlich der Technologiepolitik, die *regionale* Strukturpolitik, einschließlich der Humankapitalförderung i. w. S., sowie die *Mittelstands- und Existenzgründungsförderpolitik.*

Dynamisch und *ökonomisch-theoretisch* betrachtet haben Strukturwandel und Strukturpolitik etwas mit unmittelbaren (d. h. nicht nur indirekten, preisvermittelten) *Interaktionen* von Akteuren zu tun. Diese finden i. d. R. in komplexen und mit Unsicherheit behafteten Entscheidungssituationen statt und induzieren Prozesse, deren Ergebnisse nicht nur in Mengen und Preisen beschreibbar sind. Sie sind bedingt durch funktional und räumlich fragmentierte Wertschöpfungsketten, die zugleich technologisch höchst interdependent sind und insbesondere durch Netztechnologien und Netzexternalitäten die Akteure in ihren Entscheidungen voneinander abhängig machen. Diese neue Realität der New Economy verlangt hochgradig abgestimmte individuelle Entscheidungen und dichte Interaktionen. Solche Interaktionen wiederum verlangen vielfältige *Koordinierungs- und Kooperationsleistungen* von den Akteuren einschließlich der öffentlichen Akteure. Diese Leistungen lassen sich nach aller Erfahrung und theoretisch erhärtet vor allem in *"mittelgroßen" Gruppen* effektiv erbringen. Dort finden *soziale Lernprozesse* relativ leicht statt, und private Akteure können in diesem Rahmen im evolutionären Prozeß soziale Institutionen der Koordination und Kooperation herausbilden. Netzwerke, als fortgeschrittene Kooperationsformen, bewirken dann nach empirischen Erkenntnissen erhebliche Effizienzsteigerungen, z. B. oft erhebliche Beschleunigungen des Innovationsprozesses zwischen kleinen und mittleren Unternehmen. Solche spontanen dezentralen Prozesse sind jedoch zugleich – sowohl in der sozialökonomischen Realität wie in sozialen Experimenten, erhärtet durch theoretische Forschung – oft *blockiert*, anhaltend *fragil* und/oder sehr *zeitaufwendig*.

Wenn Global Player vor diesem Hintergrund ihre Macht einsetzen und globale Zuliefernetzwerke hierarchisch organisieren und kommandieren ("Hub & Spoke Netzwerke"), dann finden dezentrale Lernprozesse i. d. R. ebenfalls in suboptimaler Weise statt. Die Koordinations- und Kooperationsleistungen der privaten Akteure lassen sich jedoch *initiieren*, *stabilisieren* und/oder *beschleunigen* durch eine moderne Wirtschafts(struktur)politik, die die Anreize, Motive und Leistungen der Privaten nicht (etwa im Sinne der traditionellen Kollektivguttheorie) ersetzt, sondern sich wiederum interaktiv mit diesen koordiniert, um die Privaten zu Beiträgen im eigenen, aber auch im strukturpolitischen Interesse zu motivieren. Zu dem damit angedeuteten Paradigma einer "*interaktiven*“ (und damit zugleich "schlankeren") *Wirtschafts- und Strukturpolitik* soll diese Buchreihe ebenfalls Beiträge liefern.

Insgesamt soll mit dieser Reihe der Anspruch verfolgt werden, eine moderne, interaktive *Meso-Ökonomik* zu repräsentieren. Diese kann die vielfältigen Insuffizienzen reiner Mikro- und reiner Makro-Ökonomik und die vielfältigen, oft unbeabsichtigten (wenngleich oft systematischen) strukturellen Effekte von mikro- und makroökonomischen Vorgängen und mikro- und makropolitischen Aktionen aufdecken helfen und schließlich die Probleme durch adäquate privat-private und privat-öffentliche Interaktionsstrukturen einer Lösung näherbringen.

Wolfram Elsner, Bremen

To Eveline and Alexander

Acknowledgements

Like any other doctoral student, I owe a lot to a number of people. First, I thank my academic supervisor, Andreas Pyka, for his support and encouragement and his comments on previous versions of the text.

At Austrian Research Centers (ARC), I benefited from discussions with Susanne Giesecke, Karl-Heinz Leitner, Sami Mahroum, Thomas Roediger-Schluga, and Doris Schartinger. In particular, I am indebted to Matthias Weber and Josef Fröhlich for giving me the opportunity to develop my ideas in various projects. I also thank Karin Bichler and Silvia Steinbrunner for administrative assistance. Financial support from ARC's "All-around excellence" mobility programme is gratefully acknowledged.

I also wish to thank the people at the Centre for Policy Research in Science and Technology (CPROST) at Simon Fraser University, Vancouver, for their hospitality, in particular Florence Chee, Adam Holbrook, Jane McCarthy, and Brian Wixted. Special thanks are due to Angela Paloubis who helped to improve the readability of the text considerably in its final stage.

This thesis includes research conducted over a period of more than four years in different national and international projects. I want to express my gratitude to the Anniversary Fund of the Austrian National Bank for its financial support of the project "Innovative Activities of Multinational Enterprises in Austria". I thank the co-ordinator of the project, Christian Bellak (Vienna University of Economics and Business Administration), for his critical comments which considerably increased the quality of the text.

Moreover, I want to thank my collaborators in various projects of the TIP programme, in particular Martin Falk (Austrian Institute for Economic Research - WIFO), Rahel Falk (WIFO), Brigitte Nones (Joanneum) and Andreas Schibany (Joanneum), and my collaborators at MERIT and EIIW in the project "Internationalisation of European ICT activities" funded by the European Commission.

Special thanks for their support are also due to Bernd Ebersberger (MCI Innsbruck), Norbert Knoll (AWS), Jörg Mahlich (Austrian Federal Chamber of Commerce), and Michael Peneder (WIFO). Finally, I thank Wolfram Elsner, University of Bremen, for giving me the opportunity to publish my book in the series "Strukturwandel und Strukturpolitik".

Table of Contents

List of Figures

List of Tables

Deutsche Kurzfassung

Technologischer Wandel und die zunehmende Internationalisierung von Gesellschaft und Wirtschaft sind in mehrfacher Hinsicht eng miteinander verbunden. Ein Aspekt dieser Beziehung ist der Umstand, dass neues Wissen und neue Technologien nicht mehr national, sondern zunehmend durch grenzüberschreitende Forschung, Entwicklung, und Innovation (FE&I) geschaffen werden.

Diese Internationalisierung von FE&I ist, genauso wie die Internationalisierung anderer wirtschaftlicher Aktivitäten, kein neues Phänomen. In den letzten Jahrzehnten lässt sich allerdings eine deutliche Intensivierung und Beschleunigung des Prozesses feststellen. Diese Intensivierung kann zu einem Gutteil auf die Aktivitäten multinationaler Unternehmen zurückgeführt werden, die FE&I-Einrichtungen zunehmend außerhalb ihrer Heimatländer ansiedeln.

Österreich ist innerhalb der OECD eines jener Länder, die von der Internationalisierung von FE&I am stärksten berührt sind. Unternehmen im ausländischen Eigentum vereinigen 45% der F&E-Ausgaben des österreichischen Unternehmenssektors auf sich. Dieser – auch im internationalen Vergleich – außerordentlich hohe Anteil weckt das Interesse der Wirtschaftspolitik. Welche Vor- oder Nachteile hat das österreichische Innovationssystem aus der Präsenz ausländischer multinationaler Unternehmen? Wie nachhaltig ist das Engagement dieser ausländischer Unternehmen?

Die Analyse zeigt, dass Unternehmen im ausländischen Eigentum im Durchschnitt häufiger Innovationen einführen, mehr Mittel für diese Innovationen ausgeben, mehr F&E-Personal beschäftigen und häufiger Innovationskooperationen eingehen als Unternehmen im inländischen Eigentum. Überproportional häufig entwickeln Unternehmen im ausländischen Eigentum auch Marktneuheiten für überregionale Märkte. Weiters zeigen Unternehmen im deutschen, Schweizer oder liechtensteinischen Eigentum eine höhere Innovationsleistung als Unternehmen im Eigentum von Gesellschaften aus anderen Ländern.

Die bessere Innovationsleistung ist allerdings kein Ergebnis der Eigentümerstruktur. Vielmehr sind Unternehmen im ausländischen Eigentum im Innovationsprozess erfolgreicher, weil sie durchschnittlich größer sind, mehr Mitarbeiter mit Universitätsabschluss beschäftigen, häufiger in Hochtechnologiesektoren tätig sind und eine höhere Exportintensität aufweisen. Diese Eigenschaften beeinflussen wiederum das Innovationsverhalten. Korrigiert man um diese Faktoren, lässt sich in den meisten Fällen kein signifikanter Einfluss der Eigentümerstruktur auf die Innovationsleistung entdecken.

Die Wiederholung der Analyse mit einem internationalen Sample zeigt, dass die österreichischen Ergebnisse auch für andere Länder gültig sind. Wiederum sind

Unterschiede in der Innovationsleistung hauptsächlich durch andere Firmencharakteristika als die Eigentümerstruktur erklärbar. Weiters haben die gesamtwirtschaftlichen Bedingungen des jeweiligen Gastlandes signifikanten Einfluss auf das Innovationsverhalten von Unternehmen im ausländischen Eigentum. Im Vergleich zu anderen Ländern haben ausländische Unternehmen in Österreich eine höhere Bereitschaft, neues Wissen zu schaffen.

Einen Grund für diesen Umstand illustriert eine Fallstudie. Tochtergesellschaften multinationaler Unternehmen in Österreich besitzen vielfach Produkt- und Technologiemandate und einen hohen Grad an Autonomie innerhalb ihres Konzerns. Diese Autonomie ist das Ergebnis des Wechselspiels von Standortvorteilen in Österreich, der Initiative des Managements der Tochtergesellschaft und der Bereitschaft der Konzernmutter, Verantwortung abzugeben.

Die Arbeit zeigt deutlich, dass die Internationalisierung dem österreichischen Innovationssystem mehr Vor- als Nachteile gebracht hat. Österreich konnte mithilfe ausländischer Mittel seine gesamtwirtschaftlichen FE&I-Aufwendungen beträchtlich steigern. Weitere positive Effekte sind Wissensflüsse zu österreichischen Organisationen, eine Beschleunigung des Strukturwandels hin zu Hochtechnologiebranchen sowie eine stärkere Nachfrage nach wissenschaftlichem Personal.

Die österreichischen FE&I-Politik sollte versuchen, diese Vorteile weiter zu maximieren. Die Bevorzugung von multinationalen Unternehmen (sofern rechtlich überhaupt zulässig) ist dafür allerdings kein geeignetes Mittel. Vielmehr sollte die Politik Maßnahmen setzten, um die innovativen Kapazitäten von Unternehmen im in- *und* ausländischen Eigentum zu stärken. Weiters kann die Förderung der Einbindung von Unternehmen im ausländischen Eigentum in das österreichische Innovationssystem Wissensflüsse zu inländischen Organisationen erhöhen und so die Vorteile aus der Präsenz ausländischer Unternehmen weiter steigern. Eine starke Einbindung erscheint auch als geeignetes Mittel, um Abwanderungen zu verhindern.

Die österreichische Politik sollte aber auch aufmerksam gegenüber den Problemen des hohen Auslandsanteils sein. Auslandskontrollierte FE&I-Aktivitäten in Österreich konzentrieren sich auf einige wenige Unternehmen. Damit sind die sektoralen und gesamtwirtschaftlichen F&E-Ausgaben sensibel gegenüber Entscheidungen einzelner Akteure. Die positiven Effekte der Internationalisierung könnten auch erheblich getrübt werden, wenn multinationale Unternehmen in Österreich zwar forschen, die Ergebnisse der FE&I-Aktivitäten aber an anderen Standorten in Produkte und damit Beschäftigung umgesetzt werden. Innovationspolitik kann hier nur im Zusammenspiel mit der allgemeinen Wirtschafts- und Standortpolitik zu einer positiven gesamtwirtschaftlichen Entwicklung beitragen.

Abstract

An important aspect of the ongoing internationalisation of the world economy is the internationalisation of innovative activities. Multinational enterprises (MNEs) are the main drivers of this process - by locating research and development activities outside of their home countries. Subsidiaries of foreign-owned MNEs account for a rising share on national research, development and innovation expenditure in almost all OECD countries. MNE investments in innovation have supported national efforts to increase domestic R&D expenditure in a number of countries, including Austria. The presence of MNE subsidiaries, however, has also raised concerns of a loss of control over national innovative capacity.

This book contributes to the ongoing policy discussion on the effects of the internationalisation of innovation. We examine the innovative activities of the subsidiaries of MNEs in Austria and tackle two questions: First, are there systematic differences in innovative activities between foreign-owned and domestically owned enterprises in Austria? Second, if differences exist, are they related to foreign ownership or other firm characteristics such as size? The two questions have a high relevance for policy: a superior or inferior performance due to ownership may give reason to treat foreign-owned and domestically owned enterprises differently.

The literature discusses various reasons for performance differences between foreign-owned and domestically owned enterprises. First, subsidiaries of multinational enterprises usually differ from domestically owned enterprises in a number of variables that are positively associated with innovation. They are, for example, larger, employ more staff with tertiary education, have a higher export intensity and operate more frequently in high-technology sectors.

But there is also reason to believe that both groups differ after controlling for these factors. Economic theory regards multinational enterprises as a mean to exploit superior assets such as technology, brands, or superior managerial capabilities at international markets; MNEs that pursue such an exploitation strategy concentrate R&D and other innovative activities in their home countries. The innovative activities of subsidiaries abroad are restricted to the adaptation of existing products to the host markets. If the majority of foreign-owned enterprises in Austria pursue such a strategy, this would lead to a different innovative behaviour of MNE subsidiaries compared to domestically owned enterprises. Foreign-owned enterprises would exhibit less R&D and less radical innovation, more adaptation of existing technologies, and more knowledge transfer within the MNE group as compared to their domestically owned counterparts.

The quantitative analysis draws on data from the Community Innovation Survey (CIS). In a descriptive comparison between the two groups, we observe that the average foreign-owned enterprise is more likely to be innovative, spends more on its innovative activities, yields a higher turnover from new products, and is more often engaged in co-operative arrangements than the average domestically owned enterprise. These findings, however, are not sufficient to conclude that foreign-owned enterprises are superior to their domestically owned counterparts because the two groups also differ in some important characteristics that determine innovative performance. They are larger, operate more frequently in high-technology sectors, employ more university graduates, and have a stronger export orientation than domestically owned enterprises.

Multivariate analysis reveals that a superior performance of foreign-owned enterprises is not the result of the ownership status. It can be explained by taking factors such as different size, sectoral affiliation and higher investments in physical and human capital into consideration. Once we control for these factors, the impact of foreign ownership on innovative behaviour is statistically not significant for most indicators. A high degree of foreign ownership, therefore, does not weaken or increase national innovative capacity, all other things equal. Foreign ownership is not associated with a higher or lower degree of co-operation and embeddedness in the domestic innovation system, either.

A similar result can be observed with a larger CIS sample from 15 European countries. In general, performance differences between foreign-owned and domestically owned enterprises are rather related to enterprise characteristics such as size, sector, absorptive capacity or the propensity to do R&D than to the ownership status. Foreign ownership makes a significant difference in a number of cases. The coefficients of the ownership variables, however, are considerably smaller than those for other firm characteristics. This indicates that other variables accounting for enterprise characteristics are more decisive.

The analysis shows a considerable degree of heterogeneity within the groups of foreign-owned and domestically owned enterprises, indicating that foreign or domestic ownership are too broad categories for the analysis. Foreign-owned enterprises are - in many respect - more similar to domestically owned enterprises affiliated to an enterprises group than to domestically owned non-group enterprises. We also observe differences between foreign-owned enterprises of different home countries.

Our results provide no support for a positive or negative discrimination of foreign-owned enterprises with respect to innovation. Special investment incentives to foreign-owned enterprises are indeed only rarely in place in OECD countries. Rather, governments should try to maintain good economic fundamentals and provide a "healthy business environment" to attract foreign R&D. Another key determinant of attractiveness is the quality and specialisation of the knowledge base of the host country. Hence, all measures to improve the scientific and technological capabilities of an economy are also increasing the country's attractiveness for MNE R&D investment. Science and innovation policy should promote the development of innovative capabilities of both, foreign-owned and domestically owned enterprises. This includes 'supply policies' intended to support the creation of knowledge (funding, basic research and education at universities, public infrastructure), as well as the 'adoption policies' that foster the capabilities of enterprises to absorb and utilize new technology (information services, technology transfer, standards, promotion of technology diffusion). Policies that aim to strengthen the ties between different actors in the innovation system further increase the embeddedness of foreign-owned enterprises and therefore the possibility of knowledge spillovers to the domestic economy.

1. Introduction

1.1 Internationalisation of Innovation: A Challenge for Economic Policy

An important characteristic of the modern world economy is the intensified division of labour in the generation of scientific and technological knowledge between countries and regions. This 'internationalisation' of science and technology is not a new phenomenon; scientists, knowledge and artefacts have always crossed borders easily in economic history (Burke 2001). What is new, however, is the fact that the process has gained momentum in recent years. We see a higher number of trans-border technological alliances, a rising share of joint scientific publications involving authors from different countries, an increasing international mobility of researchers and higher trans-border financial flows related to science and technology (UNCTAD 2005; Veugelers 2005).

The internationalisation of research, development and innovation is driven by three principal forces (Zitt and Bassecoulard 2004). The first one is the scientific community itself, which regards the self-organisation of science, including border-free publication activity, co-operation and competition as essential. Advances in communication technologies, such as the internet, and decreasing travel cost have fostered the internationalisation of science.

A second driving force towards internationalisation is policy. National governments and international organisations such as the European Union (EU) aim to strengthen top-down international co-operation in science, innovation and technology. Examples are large-scale research programs such as the European Organization for Nuclear Research (CERN) or the European Southern Observatory (ESO). Other measures facilitate the mobility of researchers across countries and strengthen international networking via the promotion of joint research projects. An important example of such activities is the 7th Framework Programme for Research and Technology Development (FP7) of the European Union (EU). Moreover, EU member states increasingly try to co-ordinate national science and technology policies and promotion activities via the 'European Research Area' initiative and other activities (European Commission 2007).

Finally, a third important actor is the enterprise sector. Multinational enterprises (MNEs) increasingly locate research, development and design facilities outside of their home countries to support overseas production and tap into foreign sources of knowledge. In 2001, foreign-owned subsidiaries accounted for 15% to 20% of total research and development (R&D) expenditure in manufacturing in France, Germany and the United States; between 30% and 50% in Portugal, the Netherlands, Spain, Sweden and the United Kingdom; and between 50 and 70% in the Czech Republic, Hungary and Ireland (OECD 2004b, p. 172).

The internationalisation of research, development and innovation gives rise to both, hopes and concerns. Austrian politics is aware that attracting R&D facilities of MNEs has substantially increased Austria's gross domestic expenditure for research and development (GERD) in the past and can further promote the country's technological capabilities in the future. The financial contribution of foreign sources to Austria's GERD soared from 107 Mio Euro (1994) to 1.05 bn Euro in 2006. Today, every fifth Euro spent on R&D in Austria comes from sources from abroad, mainly from MNEs to support R&D activities at their Austrian subsidiaries. Without foreign financing, Austria's GERD as percentage of GDP would be only 2.15% compared to 2.54% predicted by Statistics Austria for 2007 (Statistik Austria 2007b).

However, there are also fears that foreign ownership could have negative consequences for the country. Critics argue that a strong presence of MNEs may result in a loss of control over domestic innovative capacity, and less radical innovation. In the long run, foreign-owned enterprises may tend to concentrate R&D activities in their home country and reduce these activities at locations abroad.

A frequently cited example to support this claim is the case of the Austrian tyre manufacturer Semperit. In 1985, the German MNE Continental acquired its Austrian competitor Semperit. Continental subsequently reduced production and employment at Semperit from 3,030 employees (1992) to 2,411 (1994) and 1,350 employees at the end of 2001. In the same year, Continental closed down the production of tyres in Austria.

The transfer of all research and development activities of Semperit to the German head office in 1994 has been regarded by many observers as the crucial point for the end of Semperit as an independent enterprise (DIE PRESSE 1997, June 17th, 1997). This point was raised, among others, by Austrian trade unions[1] (Artmäuer et al. 2003; ÖGB 2003). The argument appeared again in discussions about the privatisation of the state-owned minority share of Austrian steel producer VOEST in 2003[2] and has been present in Austrian policy discussions ever since.

1 The former chairman of the Austrian Trade Union, Fritz Verzetnitsch, wrote in the preface of a book on Semperit "Semperit shows that the sell-out of Austrian key enterprises to investors from aboard has countless number of negative consequences for the employees of these firms, their suppliers and in the whole region. A number of studies show that the vast majority of the head offices of multinational enterprises are located in the owner's country. This is associated with a loss of domestic know-how."

2 A number of examples for this line of argument can be found in the protocol of a session of Austria's national council (Nationalrat) on privatisation on September 2nd, 2003

1.2 Outline

This book contributes to this discussion by investigating the innovative behaviour of MNE subsidiaries in Austria.

The basic questions can be stated as follows:

- Are there systematic differences in innovative activities between foreign-owned and domestically owned enterprises in Austria?
- If differences exist, are they related to foreign ownership?

An answer to these questions will contribute to the ongoing discussion in two ways:

First, a better understanding of MNE strategies and behaviour with respect to the international organisation of their innovative activities will contribute to the formulation of research, technology and innovation policy.

Second, the book will also increase our understanding of how MNEs spread their innovative activities across countries. The empirical literature has concentrated so far on large countries which have a relatively small share of foreign-financed innovative activities. We will enlarge this picture with empirical evidence from a small, open economy.

The book is structured as follows: after the introduction and a chapter to define key terms and concepts, we present stylized facts on innovative activities of foreign-owned enterprises in Austria in chapter 3. Chapter 4 develops a framework to understand the determinants of innovative activity and the motives of multinational enterprises to engage in innovative activities abroad. Moreover, we derive two alternative hypotheses about the innovative activities of foreign-owned enterprises in Austria.

The empirical part starts in chapter 5 with a description of the dataset. The analysis employs the Austrian results of the Community Innovation Survey (CIS) as the main data source. Chapter 6 examines differences between foreign-owned and domestically owned enterprises in a descriptive analysis of CIS data. We proceed with a multivariate analysis in chapter 7 to test if the differences between the two groups found in the previous chapter are associated with foreign ownership or other enterprise characteristics.

Chapter 8 puts the Austrian results in an international perspective. Results from the CIS are available for a number of EU member states and for in Norway and Iceland. We rerun selected regressions with a dataset of nearly 50,000 observations from 15 countries to see if the Austrian results are an exception or part of a common story across countries.

The econometric exercise of chapters 7 and 8 will be complemented in chapter 9 with a case study on the emergence of subsidiary mandates in selected foreign-owned enterprises in Austria.

The final chapter 10 deals with policy issues. We first examine the relevant literature on the effects of the internationalisation of innovative activities on host and home countries. We then turn to the international policy framework for the internationalisation of innovation. Finally, the chapter discusses what countries can actually do to maximise the benefits from the internationalisation of MNE innovative activities. Here, the results of the empirical part and the survey of international policy will be used to derive recommendations for policy.

2. Key Terms and Concepts

Terms such as knowledge, innovation or multinational enterprises are ubiquitous in today's discussions of economic policy. Nevertheless – and even because of their frequent use – it is important to clarify what these terms mean in the context of this study. This section will therefore provide definitions for the main terms and concepts.

This thesis looks at the internationalisation of corporate research and development from a Neo-Schumpeterian point of view. The concepts are examined in more detail in Hanusch and Pyka (2007), Freeman and Soete (1997), and Fagerberg et al. (2005). Neo-Schumpeterian economics puts knowledge, innovation and entrepreneurship at the center of the analysis to understand change at the micro, meso and macro level. Innovation is seen as the major driving force of economic dynamics in particular (Pyka and Hanusch 2007). We will discuss this approach in section 2.2, 2.3, 2.4 and chapter 4.

2.1 Multinational Enterprises and Foreign Ownership

A second body of literature relevant for the questions addressed in this book is the literature on foreign direct investment (FDI) and MNEs. According to Barba Navaretti and Venables (2004, p. 2),

> *"MNEs are firms that own a significant equity share (typically 50% or more) of another company (henceforth subsidiary or affiliate) operating in a foreign country."*

The OECD (1996) recommends a lower threshold and regards an enterprise as foreign-owned if a foreign investor owns 10 per cent or more of the ordinary shares or voting power of an enterprise.

A multinational enterprise therefore consists of at least two entities[3]. We will call the enterprise that controls the other one(s) parent enterprise. The controlled enterprise will be called subsidiary. Subsidiaries are, by definition, members of a group of enterprises. We distinguish them from non-group enterprises which are not affiliated to a group.

If an enterprise is the subsidiary of a parent enterprise located outside of Austria, we speak of a foreign-owned group enterprise, or simply of a foreign-owned

3 The analysis of MNEs does not necessarily have to take place at the level of enterprises. A perspective from the firm, plant or establishment level is better suited for some questions regarding multinationals (Bellak 2004, p. 490). Data on innovative behaviour, however, is rarely collected for individual plants, establishments or even firms, but mostly for the whole enterprise. Therefore, the analysis will concentrate on the enterprise level.

enterprise, since these enterprises are by definition part of a group. In contrast, enterprises which are member of an enterprise group located in Austria are referred to as domestically owned group enterprises. These two distinctions lead to three types of enterprises:

Table 1: Types of enterprises according to ownership and group membership

Type of ownership	No group member	Group member
Domestic ownership	Domestically owned non-group enterprise	Domestically owned group enterprise
Foreign ownership		Foreign-owned (group) enterprise

The distinction between group members and non-group members on the one hand and foreign-owned and domestically owned enterprises on the other hand is essential for answering the questions of the study. Moreover, since we are only interested in the behaviour of enterprises located in Austria, we leave all foreign-owned enterprises not domiciled in Austria out of the analysis.

There is a close linkage between technology and the MNE. This linkage can be seen in enterprise and industry characteristics: according to Markusen (2002, p. 6), "multinationals tend to be important in industries and firms that (a) have high levels of R&D relative to sales, (b) employ large numbers of professional and technical workers as a percentage of their total workforces, (c) produce new and / or technically complex products, and (d) have high levels of product differentiation and advertising."

Theory suggests that it is not by chance that MNEs predominantly exhibit these firm characteristics. The existence of multinational enterprises is closely related to knowledge and technology. MNEs exist because they possess firm-specific intangible assets such as technological knowledge, well-known products and brands, design or management capabilities (Dunning 1973; Markusen 1995; Navaretti Barba and Venables 2004). An enterprise producing for its own domestic market has various alternatives for growth: it can diversify (horizontally) into new products, or vertically into new activities; including the production of knowledge; it can acquire existing enterprises; or it can exploit foreign markets. According to Dunning (1981; 1995), enterprises will prefer foreign investment over other modes of international expansion and exploitation of firm-specific assets when three conditions are met:

- *Ownership* advantage: The asset must provide some advantages over incumbent competitors that allows the MNE to enter foreign markets.

- *Location* advantage: Foreign production must be advantageous compared to a concentration of production in the home country.
- *Internalisation* advantage: Enterprises must see an advantage in exploiting the asset internally, compared to licensing. This may reflect the transferability and some public good characteristics of knowledge, as well as principal-agent problems or other forms of asymmetric information.

We will discuss in section 4.2 how different strategies regarding the creation of these assets can influence innovation behaviour of foreign-owned enterprises.

2.2 Information and Knowledge

The assets that distinguish multinational enterprises from their competitors can be regarded as information and knowledge. Today, it is widely accepted that knowledge and information are important driving forces of productivity growth at the firm level and of aggregate economic growth and welfare (OECD 2004c; Wieser 2005).

Knowledge and information are frequently used synonymous throughout the literature. It is, however, important to distinguish between the two categories (Cohendet and Steinmueller 2000; Cowan et al. 2000; Foray 2004):

Information, according to Foray (2004, p. 4), "... takes the shape of structured and formatted data". Examples are scientific publications, weather forecasts or stock prices. Information can be reproduced at very low marginal cost (although its production may be costly). The main economic problem of information is its protection and disclosure, because information has some public good characteristics (Foray 2004, p. 5).

Knowledge, in contrast to information, "... empowers its possessors with the capacity for intellectual or physical action" (Foray 2004, p. 4). Knowledge is therefore needed to put information into action; it is not structured and formatted data, but enables us to interpret this data. Stock prices, for example, are pieces of information readers can pick from any newspaper. However, it requires specific knowledge to make sense of it and recognize if a certain stock is undervalued or not. Without this knowledge, the economic benefit one derives from information on stock prices will be very limited.

Knowledge, like information, has some public good characteristics. It is partly non-rival and non-excludable (Foray 2004, p. 91 ff). This makes knowledge difficult to control: "Knowledge continuously escapes from the entities producing it" (Foray 2004, p. 15). As a consequence, knowledge and information spill over between agents. Spillovers of knowledge and information are an externality, because the sender is usually not adequately compensated for. Moreover, they diminish with distance between sender and receiver, and are therefore locally bound (see also section 2.5).

The differences between information and knowledge and their specific characteristics have various consequences for the topics of this book. Despite its public good characteristics, the main economic problem associated with knowledge is its transfer and reproduction (Foray 2004, p. 5). The transfer and reproduction of knowledge is a far more expensive process than the reproduction of information for two reasons; first, it involves learning, which is time-consuming and often needs proximity and interaction between people. Second, knowledge is 'tacit' to some extent. Tacitness results from the fact that cognitive capabilities and abstract concepts are not easy to articulate explicitly and to transfer between people. Moreover, knowledge is context-specific and often produced for a local context and for a specific purpose (Cowan et al. 2000; Breschi and Lissoni 2001a). This relates to new knowledge in particular.

Tacitness both allows and limits the transferability of knowledge. It makes the transfer and reproduction of knowledge easy within a group of people ('epistemic community') who share a common vocabulary or 'codebook', but increases the cost of transferring it to outsiders (Cowan et al. 2000). The creation of such an epistemic community is a long process and involves mutual learning, for example, in master-apprentice relations. Tacitness is considered to be larger in new fields of knowledge, where epistemic communities are still small.

The locally bound and tacit characteristics of knowledge are related to the topics discussed here in two ways. First, they force MNEs to be present where new knowledge occurs if they want to absorb it. This corresponds to the description of foreign-owned subsidiaries as 'antennas' provided by Florida (1997). Second, the tacit nature of some types of knowledge may also affect the transferability of knowledge within multinational enterprises (Gupta and Govindarajanan 2000; Criscuolo and Narula 2005, p. 8).

2.3 The Innovation Process

Innovation in enterprises can be described as the accumulation of competencies – knowledge and information – in a complex, cumulative, path-dependent process (Dosi 1988; Patel and Pavitt 1997; Pavitt 2005). The process of innovation is highly industry-specific, and therefore differs considerably between sectors. The level of technological opportunity, expectations of future demand and the conditions to appropriate the returns from innovation have been identified as key determinants for the level of innovative activity at the sectoral level (Cohen and Levin 1989; Cohen 1995).

According to Pavitt (2005, p. 88), enterprises have to fulfil three principal tasks in the innovation process: a) producing scientific and technological knowledge; b) translating this knowledge into working artefacts; c) influencing and responding to market demand.

The *creation of new scientific and technological knowledge* often takes place in designated R&D or design departments. But also other departments (production, marketing) can contribute to the stock of knowledge of the enterprise because they have different experiences with technologies or market demand. Moreover, the enterprise draws on knowledge from universities, competitors, specialised suppliers and the general knowledge base. We will come back later to this point.

The main challenge in *transferring knowledge into products* is the fact that a scientific principle does not necessarily lead to a working product. The number of possible design configurations of a product is limited by a number of factors, such as available materials and production technologies, complementary technologies (displays and batteries in the case of mobile phones), necessary infrastructure (gas stations for hydrogen cars) and others. As a consequence, enterprises are faced with a fundamental technological uncertainty when developing products. One strategy to master this uncertainty is to broaden the knowledge base to cover many different technologies. Modern enterprises – in particular producers of complex products including many different parts – are multi-technological (Granstrand and Sjölander 1994). Their technological competences are much wider than their range of products.

A final principal task in the innovation process is to *match the product with changing market demand.* This is easier during periods where technological change moves along stable trajectories and basic characteristics of the product develop in a fairly predictable way (Dosi 1982). The task becomes very difficult for the enterprise when technologies emerge that rival its main product. The rise of competing technologies is often associated with the market entrance of new competitors. One example is digital photography, which has completely replaced chemical photography in the mass consumer market but also many professional application areas. As a consequence, the technological competencies of enterprises in chemical photography became obsolete, and new entrants from the computer industry compete with incumbent producers of cameras. In such a situation, enterprises can become victims of their own (past) success and yesterday's core competencies turn into today's core rigidities (Leonard-Barton 1998). A possible solution to this threat is to maintain very broad search processes and the acquisition of knowledge in fields well ahead of practical industrial application.

A constant exchange of knowledge and information between different parts of the enterprise and between the enterprise and its environment is essential to master the three tasks of the innovation process (Figure 1). This exchange also includes feedback loops between various states of the innovation process. People in R&D, for example, are usually not aware of changes in consumer preferences. Moreover, innovation also requests the combination of different knowledge bases from inside and outside of the enterprise. These knowledge bases can be accessed by s co-operation with partners in science and within and outside the own industry.

Figure 1: Innovation as an interactive process

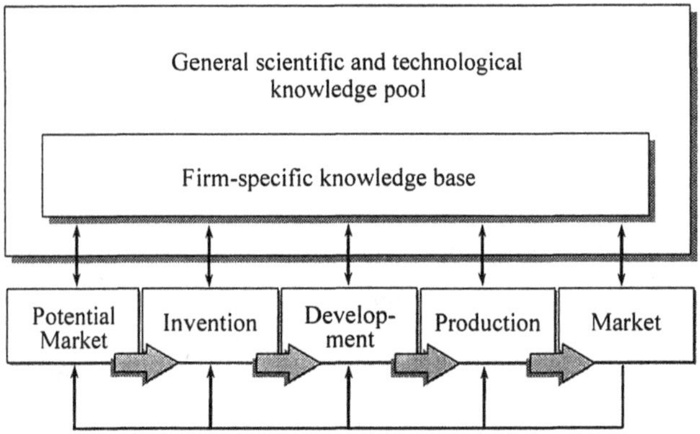

Source: Adapted with minor changes from Kline and Rosenberg (1986)

2.4 Distinguishing between Innovation, Research and Development

New knowledge and information can be created by enterprises in various ways. We focus at two of them, innovation and research and development (R&D). We use the OECD definitions of innovation and R&D as published in two documents, the Frascati Manual (latest edition: OECD 2002) and the Oslo Manual (latest edition: OECD 2005c). These definitions are commonly accepted and serve in some countries, for example Austria and Canada, as the legal criteria for the eligibility of R&D tax credits.

Research and development is defined in the Frascati Manual as:

> *"creative work undertaken on a systematic basis in order to increase the stock of knowledge, including knowledge of man, culture and society, and the use of this stock of knowledge to devise new applications."(OECD 2002, p. 30)*

R&D comprises of three activities (OECD 2002, p. 30): *basic research* (without any particular application or use in view), *applied research* (directed primarily towards a specific practical aim or objective), and *experimental development* (directed to produce new materials, products and devices, new processes, systems and services; or to improve substantially those already produced or installed).

The basic criterion for distinguishing R&D from other related activities such as product design is the presence of novelty and the solution of scientific and/or technological problems (OECD 2002, p. 34). An activity cannot be regarded as R&D when the solution to a problem is readily apparent to someone familiar with the topic. Therefore, a routine application of scientific methods, such as technical testing, is not an R&D activity. Another definition problem refers to software development which has become an important activity in a number of industries. The Frascati Manual tends to regard software development as an R&D activity if it meets the novelty criteria: "... its completion must be dependent on the development of a scientific and/or technological advance, and the aim of the project must be resolution of a scientific and/or technological uncertainty" (OECD 2002, p. 46). Similar criteria have to be applied to R&D in social sciences and to R&D in the service sector.

Closely related to R&D is innovation. The OECD defines innovation as:

> *"... the implementation of a new or significantly improved product (good or service), or process, a new marketing method, or a new organisational method in business practices, workplace organisation or external relations."(OECD 2005c, p. 46)*

Like R&D, innovation must contain a certain degree of novelty. However, in contrast to an invention or R&D activity, an innovation is not necessarily completely new to the world. The minimum requirement for an innovation is that it must be new to the enterprise (OECD 2005c, p. 57). Thus, enterprises can also innovate on the basis of existing knowledge and technology. It is, however, essential for an innovation that the new product or process has been successfully introduced to the market (this is not necessary for an R&D activity). Compared to R&D which has clear focus on novelty in terms of *scientific discovery* and technological excellence, the term innovation is focussed on the *economic effects* of novelty.

Innovation can be further characterized by the activities it comprises (OECD 2005c, p. 91ff). These activities are either innovative by themselves, or enable the enterprise to implement innovations. Innovative activities are, in the first place, all R&D activities financed or performed by enterprises. This also includes basic research and all other components of R&D mentioned above. In addition, innovative activity also encompasses the acquisition of external knowledge, machinery, equipment and other capital goods in connection with the development and implementation of innovations. We may also regard activities in the preparation of the market introduction of an innovation as innovative activity. This includes testing and prototyping, product design, staff training, production preparations, etc.

Innovation and R&D are two overlapping terms and, to a certain degree, synonyms. R&D financed and performed by enterprises is *always* an innovative activity; in fact, the largest part of innovation expenditure in many industries consists of R&D expenditure. But not all R&D performed in a country is innovative activity, because a considerable part is done by universities which do not introduce new products or processes to the market. Some activities which fail to be recognized as R&D may be innovative activity, such as design activities, staff training activities or production preparations. In a number of service industries, these activities comprise the bulk of innovative expenditure.

The OECD admits that also enterprises have difficulties in differentiating between R&D and other innovation activities (OECD 2005c, p. 96). Given these demarcation problems, we will use the terms R&D and innovation largely as synonyms; this is no impreciseness or carelessness, but rather reflects the overlapping nature and similarities of R&D and innovation in the enterprise sector. The term R&D will be used when we refer to data that has been collected according to the criteria of the Frascati Manual.

2.5 Networks, Innovation Systems and the Embeddedness of Enterprises

Recent research on innovation highlights the importance of external sources of information and knowledge for the innovation process of enterprises. Chesbrough (2003a; 2003b) finds that many innovative enterprises have shifted to an 'open innovation' model to cope with a widening gap between the internal competencies of the firm and the problems to be mastered. They exploit ideas and knowledge not only provided by internal R&D, but also from a broad range of external sources and actors.

Enterprises therefore do not innovate in isolation, but are connected to and in exchange with other organisations at the national, regional or sectoral level. These relationships are referred to as innovation networks (Pyka and Küppers 2002; Powell and Grodal 2005; Pyka 2007). We will use the term embeddedness (Granovetter 1985) to refer to these external linkages of an enterprise with other organisations. Networks can take very different forms; special attention has been given in recent years to the relationships between enterprises and universities (Schartinger et al. 2002; Tether 2002), and technology alliances between enterprises (Hagedoorn 2002; Pyka 2002). Various authors (for example in Lundvall

1992) have also pointed out the importance of user-producer relations for innovative activity.

Economic theory has brought forward three different explanations for the existence of innovation networks (Pyka 2007, pp. 361 and 362); a production function approach in new industrial economics, an institutional approach which argues with the existence of transaction costs, and a knowledge-based approach.

The knowledge-based approach to innovation networks - which is in many aspects related to Neo-Schumpeterian economics – highlights the benefits from knowledge complementaries and synergies in innovation networks (Pyka 2007, p. 362). The decision to enter an innovation network often goes beyond a simple make-buy decision based on the marginal cost of own research vs. acquired external knowledge. This is, at first, a consequence of the characteristics of knowledge (partly tacit, context-specific and localized) which makes exchange over markets difficult or even impossible in a number of cases. In a joint R&D project, two enterprises can find common ground and develop a 'codebook' to facilitate the transfer of tacit knowledge. Networks are therefore a useful coordination mechanism for innovation diffusion in situations where make-buy decisions are not appropriate because of the non-transferability of knowledge over markets (Pyka 2007).

The function of networks in a Neo-Schumpeterian perspective, however, goes beyond co-ordination (this is also found in New Institutional economics). Networks are also means of collective problem solving between enterprises (Pyka 2007, pp. 367-370). The pooling of different competencies in joint R&D projects between enterprises can have significant advantages. There are, on the one hand, economies of scale and scope in R&D and advantages from cost-sharing. On the other hand, there are cross-fertilization effects when the knowledge bases of two enterprises are brought together and the exploitation of new combinations becomes possible.

To unveil these potentials an enterprise needs 'absorptive capacity' (Cohen and Levinthal 1989, 1990; Cantner and Pyka 1998) to understand and utilize the results of research activities of universities and other enterprises. Cohen and Levinthal (1989, p. 593) speak of a 'dual role' of R&D: "firms invest in R&D not only to pursue directly new process and product innovation, but also develop and maintain their broader capabilities to assimilate and exploit externally available information". In this perspective, the acquisition of knowledge from outside is closely linked to the internal generation of knowledge. Absorptive capacity is therefore both, a pre-requisite for and a result of participation in innovation networks. It is needed to understand and utilize external knowledge, but also grows in the course of R&D co-operation.

Empirical evidence for the importance of absorptive capacity in the exploitation of external sources of knowledge is provided by Veugelers (1997) who shows that innovation co-operation and R&D contracted out only have a significant positive effect on internal R&D if companies have a full-time staffed R&D department. Moreover, Veugelers finds that the frequency of R&D co-operation is positively associated with internal R&D expenditure. Cantner and Pyka (1998) demonstrate that building up absorptive capacity is more beneficial in technologically heterogeneous environments; the more firms differ from each other, the stronger are cross-fertilization effects.

The concept of absorptive capacity can also be applied to countries. The development literature discusses 'technology gaps' between host and home country of the MNE (Blomström et al. 2000). The technology gap, according to the United Nations, is "... the divergence between nations and communities in their abilities to access, diffuse and use scientific and technical knowledge" (UNITED NATIONS 2006, p. 3). The literature usually assumes – starting from a certain level of technological expertise – a positive relation between the size of technological gaps and spillover opportunities from by foreign-owned enterprises (Castellani and Zanfei 2003). This relationship, however, is not linear, since domestic enterprises require a certain degree of initial technological competence to utilize spillovers.

Innovation networks between organisations take various forms. A basic distinction can be made between formal innovation co-operation and informal spillovers. Formal innovation co-operation is based on contractual agreements such as joint R&D pacts, joint development agreements, or equity-based joint R&D ventures (Hagedoorn 2002, p. 478). The high degree of commitment allows the participating enterprises to utilize economies of scale and scope, reduce risks and uncertainty, and makes it easier to build up absorptive capacity for the exchange tacit knowledge (Hagedoorn and Schakenraad 1989; Caloghirou et al. 2003). Like innovation, innovation co-operation is influenced by size, sectoral affiliation, human capital or export intensity (Tether 2002; Belderbos et al. 2004).

Informal spillovers are a second source of external knowledge and information (Pyka 1997). They can be seen as the non-appropriable part of the R&D and innovation activities of enterprises or universities and arise because the results of these activities cannot be fully protected (Griliches 1992). Therefore, spillovers are usually non-pecuniary and not mediated through markets. Spillovers are bounded in space and diminish with distance between sender and receiver (Jaffe et al. 1993; Breschi and Lissoni 2001a).

Enterprises which want to utilize such localized knowledge spillovers have to be present where they occur. As a consequence, innovative activity tends to cluster locally in industries with a high level of spillovers (Audretsch and Feldman 1996). The literature on clusters and industrial agglomerations (for example Bresnahan and Gambardella 2004) have brought rich evidence for this phenomenon, some prominent examples are Silicon Valley or the Cambridge area.

The Neo-Schumpeterian literature stresses the fact that enterprises do not innovate in isolation, but are embedded in networks. Moreover, the behaviour of enterprises is also shaped by institutions – norms, rules, laws etc – that are specific for a country, region or sector. Institutions, organisations and relations between the organisations and their environment together constitute a 'system of innovation'(see Edquist 2005a for an overview of the literature). Important institutions are, for example, intellectual property rights and standards. Moreover, authors have also pointed to more general institutions such as the general attitude of the population towards science and technology, or the organisation of higher education in a country. Organisations in an innovation system are enterprises, universities, governments, the media etc. They are connected with each other through various relations such as innovation networks.

Systems of innovations therefore provide a meso or macro perspective on innovation networks. The literature mainly analyzes systems of innovation at the national level ('national systems of innovation') because the nation state is still the most important toehold for technology policy intervention (Lundvall 1992; OECD 1992; Nelson 1993; Larédo and Mustar 2001). The systems-of-innovation approach, however, has also successfully applied at the sectoral (Malerba 2002; Marsili 2002; Malerba 2005) and the regional level (Asheim and Gertler 2005).

3. Innovative Activities of Multinational Enterprises in Austria – A Summary of the Stylized Facts

This chapter sums up existing studies and other empirical evidence on the innovative activities of foreign-owned enterprises in Austria. The main focus lies on changes in the financing of innovation in Austria, including the sources of foreign funding of R&D and innovation and on the main receiving sectors. The funding perspective will be complemented by a look at foreign ownership on Austrian patent inventions.

3.1 Foreign Direct Investment in Austria

A main finding of literature on the internationalisation of innovation is that R&D and production activities of a foreign-owned subsidiary are closely related. Foreign-located innovation activities often start when the foreign-owned subsidiary grows beyond a certain scale and builds up management capacity. In this perspective, the internationalisation of innovation can be seen as a side result of foreign direct investment (FDI) and the internationalisation of production.

We will therefore start with the growth of foreign direct investment in Austria. The stock of FDI has increased considerably in the last decade and after 2000 (Figure 2). According to data collected by the Austrian National Bank, the total capital of foreign direct investment in Austria amounted to about 59 bn. Euro in 2005 (Dell'mour 2007). A striking detail is that total FDI capital increased much more rapidly than the number of employees at foreign-owned enterprises, which points to a concentration of foreign direct investment in capital-intensive sectors and considerable increases in productivity in recent years. The share of foreign-owned enterprises on sectoral employment is highest in chemical products, rubber, plastics and fuel products, electrical machinery and radio, television and communication equipment and among the manufacturers of transport equipment. In services, we find the highest shares of FDI on total capital in banking and finance and in retail trade. Foreign ownership is more frequently found in manufacturing than in service industries (Dell'mour 2007).

Figure 2: Foreign direct investment in Austria, total capital in Bn. Euro and number of employees, 1991 – 2005

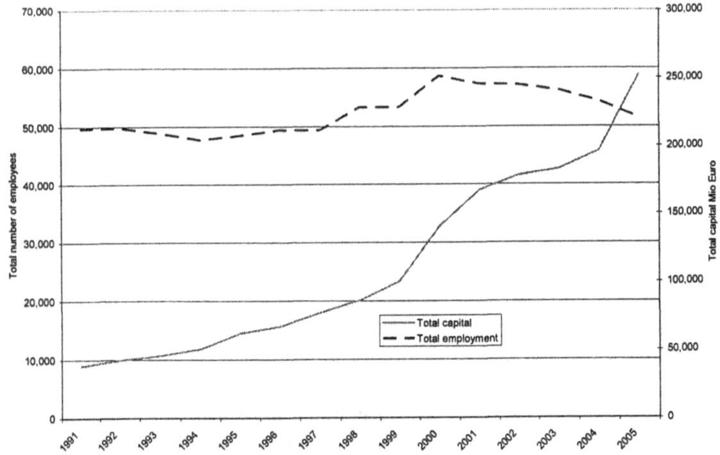

Source: Austrian National Bank (Dell'mour 2007)

The most important country of origin of FDI in Austria is Germany, followed by Switzerland and the US. The country shares have remained very stable throughout the last 15 years, with Germany accounting for about 40% of the FDI stock in Austria. Together, the Euro zone countries account for two Thirds of all FDI in Austria (Dell'mour 2007).

3.2 Changes in the Financing of R&D in Austria

The sharp increases in FDI during the last 15 years have been accompanied by drastic changes in the structure of R&D financing in Austria. Figure 3 shows the contributions of different sources to R&D financing in Mio Euro and the evolution of the GERD/GDP ratio between 1991 and 2007. Data has been delivered by the annual R&D expenditure forecast ("Globalschätzung") of Statistics Austria (2007b).

According to Statistics Austria (2007b), research and development financed by sources from abroad has surged from 60 Mio Euro (1992) to more than one bn Euro in 2007. This amounts to 15% of total R&D funding in Austria. Readers should note that this figure only includes cross-border financial transactions, and does not include R&D financed by internal funds of foreign-owned enterprises in Austria. Statistics Austria estimates the total R&D expenditures of foreign-owned subsidiaries in Austria at more than 1.6 bn. Euro in 2004 (OECD 2007b, p. 50).

Figure 3: Financing of R&D in Austria, 1992-2007

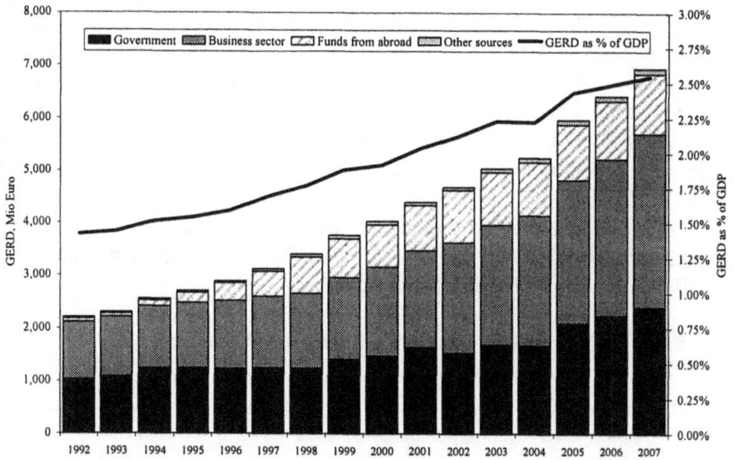

Source: Statistics Austria (2007b), Globalschätzung 2007

In the years since 2000, foreign sources increased their share by more than 250 Mio Euro. Since 2004, foreign funds grew only in absolute terms, but have declined in terms of their share on total R&D funding in Austria. This was because funding by the business sector, but also governmental funding grew faster than foreign funding. Therefore, it seems that foreign funding has reached a kind of saturation point in the Austrian Innovation System in recent years.

Additional data from Statistics Austria (2007c, table 5.07) reveal that the vast majority of foreign funding for R&D comes from multinational enterprises. In 2004, MNEs have transferred 929 Mio Euro for R&D to organisations in Austria. The contribution of the European Union to R&D in Austria, in contrast, is modest. EU funding amounts to only 87 Mio Euro in 2004.

In an international perspective, there are only two countries in the OECD and the EU, Greece and the UK, where foreign sources contribute similar shares to overall R&D spending. This special position of Austria can be clearly seen in an international comparison (Figure 4). The horizontal axis shows GERD as percentage of GDP for a particular country, while the vertical axis depicts the share of foreign funding on GERD. Moreover, the diameter of the circles depicts GERD in Million $ (2005 Purchasing Power Parities) to illustrate the absolute size of the national innovation system.

What explains Austria's exceptional performance in attracting foreign R&D funding? Obviously, a certain level of scientific excellence, measured by

GERD/GDP ratio, is necessary to attract foreign R&D. However, the countries with the highest GERD/GDP ratios – Sweden (3.89%), Finland (3.48%) or Switzerland (2,9%) – do not differ considerably in the share of foreign funding from countries with low intensities such as Italy (1.1%), Czech Republic (1.41%), Portugal (0.81%), die Slovakia (0.51%) or Poland (0,57%). Japan and Korea even have the lowest shares of foreign funding in the sample. Most countries – regardless R&D intensity – can be found in a range between five and ten percent share of foreign funding. The correlation between the share of foreign funding and R&D intensity for the countries in Figure 4 is -0.05. R&D intensity on a country level alone therefore cannot explain differences in the shares foreign funding. The absolute size of R&D expenditure is not very useful in explaining different shares of foreign funding, either.

Figure 4: GERD, share of foreign funding on total R&D expenditure and GERD/GDP ratio, 2005

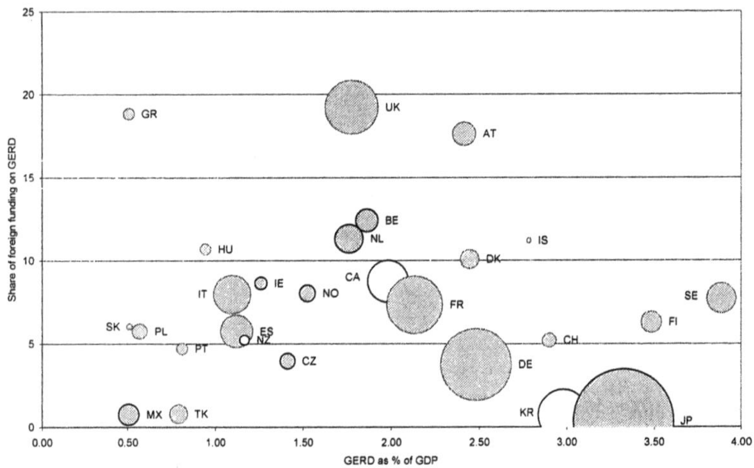

Note: CH (2004), NL (2003)

Source: OECD, Main Science and Technology Indicators 2/2007

Austria's ability to attract foreign funding therefore has to be explained by other, additional country-specific factors. Interviews with major foreign-owned R&D performers in Austria (Nones 2003; Dachs et al. 2005b) and survey evidence (Knoll 2004) have revealed that these locational advantages are, on the one hand, a large, skilled workforce, favourable corporate taxation and a generous public R&D funding and, on the other hand, Austria's geographical and cultural proximity to Germany and to Central and Eastern European Countries.

3.3 Foreign-owned Patent Inventions in Austria

Researchers have employed several approaches to measure the internationalisation of innovation. Studies have examined the *input side* of the innovation process, for example R&D financing. An alternative is to look at *innovative output*, in particular at patent data. A patent is an intellectual property right issued to protect a technological invention. By granting these rights to inventors, the patent system enhances the appropriability conditions of inventions and therefore stimulates the creation of novelty (Griliches 1990).

But the patent system is not only a legal institution. Patents are widely used a indicators of research and development activities at the level of industries and individual enterprises (Jaffe and Trajtenberg 2002). One feature makes patents very useful for studies of the internationalisation of technology in particular: since a patent protects both the owner's and the inventor's rights, it contains information on the location of the applicant (owner) and on the inventor's place of residence. By comparing these two locations, we can derive a measure for the ownership of cross-border patents[4], which can be used as an indicator for the internationalization of R&D activities (Guellec and van Pottelsberghe de la Potterie 2004). We speak of a cross-border patent when the applicant and at least one inventor reside in different countries.

Cross-border patents can take two different forms: first, patents applied in a particular country A and invented in another country B. This case illustrates the degree organisations in country A are engaged in R&D activities in country B. Second, patents invented in country A and owned by foreign applicants located in country B, which shows the degree R&D activities in country A controlled by organisations located in country B. Since we are interested in the share of the Austrian patent inventions controlled by foreign organisations, we will only deal with the second case.

An example for a cross-border patent is given in Figure 5. Here, Siemens Aktiengesellschaft, located in Munich, Germany (see line 71 in the document), applies for a patent based on an invention of Austrian inventors. The Austrian inventors (line 72) may be doing contract research for the German enterprise, or work for the Austrian subsidiary of Siemens.

[4] Cross-border patents should not be confused with the application of a patent at different patent offices. The country of residence of the applicant is NOT identical with the country where the invention is protected by a patent.

Figure 5: Example of a cross-border patent application

(19) Europäisches Patentamt
European Patent Office
Office européen des brevets

(11) **EP 1 071 034 A3**

(12) **EUROPÄISCHE PATENTANMELDUNG**

(88) Veröffentlichungstag A3:
18.09.2002 Patentblatt 2002/38

(51) Int Cl.7: **G06K 9/00**, G06K 9/62

(43) Veröffentlichungstag A2:
24.01.2001 Patentblatt 2001/04

(21) Anmeldenummer: **00113705.8**

(22) Anmeldetag: **28.06.2000**

(84) Benannte Vertragsstaaten:
AT BE CH CY DE DK ES FI FR GB GR IE IT LI LU MC NL PT SE
Benannte Erstreckungsstaaten:
AL LT LV MK RO SI

(30) Priorität: **28.06.1999 DE 19929670**

(71) Anmelder: **SIEMENS AKTIENGESELLSCHAFT**
80333 München (DE)

(72) Erfinder:
- **Egger, Robert**
8605 Kapfenberg (AT)
- **Haselsteiner, Ernst**
8010 Graz (AT)
- **Heschgl, Kurt**
A-8043 Graz (AT)
- **Windisch, Claudia**
8565 St. Johann O. H. (AT)
- **Hribernig, Gerd**
8046 Graz (AT)
- **Marius, Wolfgang**
8043 Graz/Kroisbach (AT)
- **Raunegger, Arno**
8047 Graz (AT)

(54) **Enrollment von Fingerprints**

(57) Ein Verfahren für das Enrollment von Fingerprints, bei welchem aus einer Menge von $n = N_{max}$ Fingerprints sämtliche Kombinationen von Fingerprints mit einer Anzahl z gebildet werden, wobei $z \leq N_{max}$ ist, innerhalb jeder Kombination für die darin bildbaren Paare von Fingerprints ein Match-Score-Wert m gebildet wird, alle Kombinationen, bei welchen der Match-Score-Wert aller Paare nicht zwischen einer vorgebbaren unteren und einer vorgebbaren oberen Grenze liegt, verworfen werden, für die verbleibenden Kombinationen eine Kostenfunktion als Linearkombination gewichteter Qualitätsbeiträge C_i berechnet wird, und jene Fingerprints, welche die Kostenfunktion minimieren als Satz zur Referenzdarstellung herangezogen werden.

Source: European Patent Office

We can derive an indicator of internationalisation if we sum up all cross-border patent inventions of a country and relate them to the total number of patent inventions of this country. The development of this indicator for Austria between 1989 and 2004 is shown in Figure 6. Additionally, we have included the share of foreign sources on total R&D funding in Austria in this period.

Both indicators show a similar movement; after being fairly constant in the early 1990s, they increased considerably between 1993 and 1997 and consolidate at high levels since 2000. The share of foreign-owned patent inventions was 20% in 1990, and almost doubled to 36% (2000) in only 10 years. With a share of 37% in 2004, is considerably above OECD- as well as EU-average (OECD 2005a, p. 26).The jump in foreign funding was even more pronounced.

It is striking in Figure 6 that the two graphs have nearly the same shape, but different levels. The share of foreign ownership on patents is nearly double the share on R&D financing. This can be explained by the fact that the figures on foreign funding only include trans-border financial transactions, and do not consider R&D funding that has been raised by the Austrian subsidiaries of MNEs themselves, for example from their cash-flow. Statistics Austria estimates the share of foreign-owned subsidiaries on the total R&D expenditures of the Austrian business sector to be about 45% for 2004, which is much closer to the share of foreign-owned patent inventions.

Moreover, universities and public research centers which account for a considerable share of GERD, only rarely patent. Therefore, the share of foreign-owned patent inventions may rather measure the degree of foreign control of R&D in the business sector than in the whole economy.

Figure 6: Share of patents with at least one foreign-located inventor on total Austrian patent inventions and share of foreign sources on R&D funding, 1989 - 2004

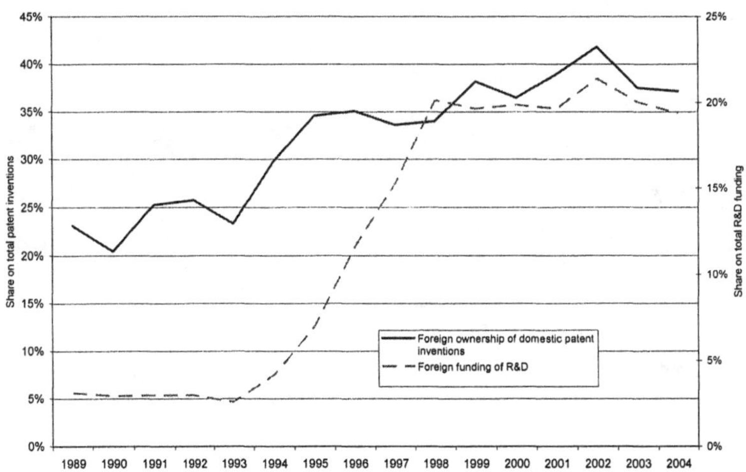

Source: Statistics Austria, European Patent Office

3.4 Where does Foreign Funding Come From?

Foreign-owned patent inventions can also tell about the countries of origin of the patent owners. Our data reveal that, similar to FDI, German and Swiss/Liechtenstein[5] parent enterprises also play a decisive role in the interna-

[5] Both countries are only counted together by FDI statistics.

tionalisation of Austrian R&D (Figure 7). These three countries lead considerable over other countries of origin in the number of owned patents. More than half of all foreign-owned Austrian patent inventions are held by a German applicant.

We see similar effects between countries that share a common language and/or history in the case of Belgium and France, the Czech Republic and Slovakia, and the US, Ireland, and the UK (Guellec and van Pottelsberghe de la Potterie 2001; see also box below). Due to the similar language, Ireland and the UK became preferred R&D locations for US multinationals in Europe. Moreover, Figure 7 clearly demonstrates the close linkage between FDI and the internationalisation of innovation. If we compare the home countries of applicants with the main home countries of FDI (see small figure), the ranking in both variables is the same.

Figure 7: Number of Austrian patent inventions with at least one foreign-located applicant according to country of origin and main home countries of FDI in Austria, 1993-2003 average

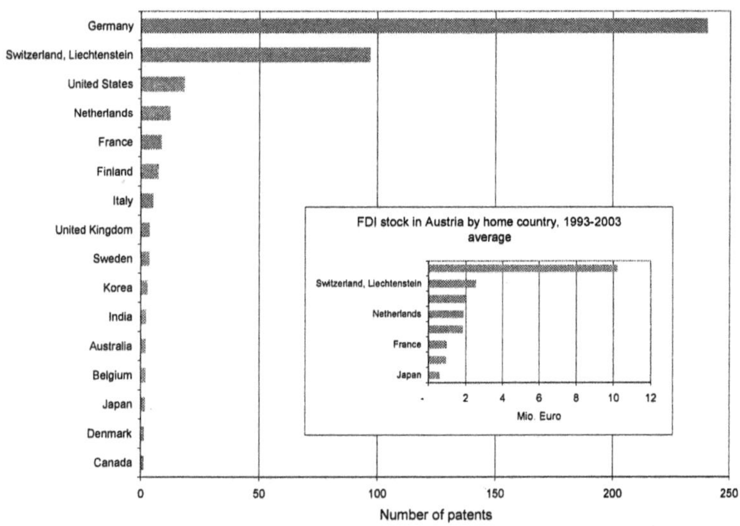

Source: European Patent Office (data compiled by the OECD), Austrian National Bank

Despite Austria's integration in the Common Market of the European Union, no other EU member state has nearly the importance of Germany or Switzerland. The largest applicant country outside the EU is the United States. Together, all Asian countries only account for the share of Finland. In the case of Austria, the internationalisation of Austrian R&D is therefore mainly an intensification of co-operation with its neighbours.

Box 1: A simple model of R&D internationalisation

Dachs and Pyka (2007) present an econometric model to investigate the determinants of cross-border patents between countries. The model reflects the basic motives and determinants of the internationalisation of corporate R&D discussed in the literature (Kuemmerle 1999b; Kumar 2001; le Bas and Sierra 2002; von Zedtwitz and Gassmann 2002; Narula and Zanfei 2005). Moreover, it follows the gravity-model approach to explain international trade flows (Leamer and Levinsohn 1995; Disdier and Head 2004) by incorporating distance between host and home country as an explanatory variable. The dependent variable is the absolute number of cross-border patent applications invented in country B (the host country) and applied for by country A (the home country) for each year from 2000 until 2004. Home countries are all EU27 countries. As independent variables, they employ total GDP and GDP per capita for all home and host countries, total R&D expenditure as percentage of GDP, and geographical distance between the countries. These variables are complemented by an index of patent right protection that reflects IPR protection, a dummy variable that indicates a common language between the two countries and another dummy that controls for EU15 membership of both countries.

Regression results indicate that the number of cross-border patents between two countries increases with relative and absolute market size of home and host country measured by total GDP and with higher levels of overall R&D intensity in both countries.

Distance between home and host country is negatively related to the number or cross-border patents which reflects the cost associated with a decentralisation of R&D. A stronger patent protection in the host country is associated with a higher number of cross-border patents, as well as a common language between two countries and a common EU15 membership. Both determinants can reduce the negative distance effect by about a Fourth. These results point to the fact that despite modern information and communication technologies have reduced the cost of exchange, geographical and cultural proximity and a common economic framework still matter for the internationalisation of R&D.

3.5 Who receives Foreign Funding in Austria?

We now turn to the receivers of foreign funding in Austria. Here, we see that foreign funding for R&D, like R&D activity itself, is very unevenly distributed amongst actors in the Austrian Innovation System. Figure 8 depicts financial relations in the Austrian Innovation System for the year 2004. Arrows illustrate financial flows between different actors including their size; total R&D expenditure of the actors can be read from the boxes. For an easier interpretation we have excluded the private non-profit sector which is very small both in terms of financing as well in R&D performance. Flows therefore do not amount to total R&D expenditure in the boxes.

Figure 8: Financial flows in the Austrian Innovation System, 2004

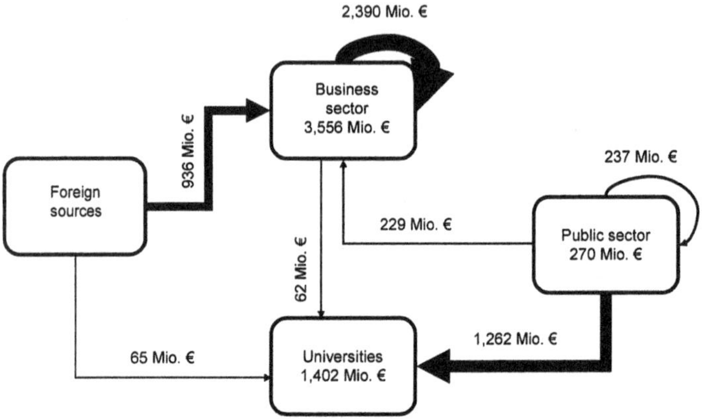

Source: Statistics Austria (2007c, table 5.07), own illustration

First, we learn from Figure 8 that foreign funding for R&D almost exclusively goes to the business sector, which absorbed 936 Mio Euro of 92% of all funds received in 2004. Foreign sources amount to 26% of total R&D expenditure of the Austrian business sector. This does not include R&D activity financed by foreign-owned enterprises with their own means. A revealing perspective on the potentials for governmental intervention gives a comparison of foreign funding and public funding of R&D in the business sector. Public funding of R&D in the business sector is only a Fourth the size (229 Mio Euro) of foreign funding and a Tenth of the money enterprises raise for R&D from own means.

R&D in the Austrian university sector, on contrary, is to the largest degree financed by public funds. Contract research by Austrian universities for enterprises abroad accounts for 19.1 Mio Euro in 2004, which is about a Third of the money Austrian universities earned from contract research for domestic enterprises. If we add another 46.1 Mio Euro of other foreign funding, mainly from the European Commission, we get a total funding of the Austrian university sector from sources abroad of about 65 Mio Euro, which is 4.6% of total university funding in Austria in 2004 (Statistik Austria 2007c, table 5.07). This share is in the range of Germany, the Netherlands or Denmark, but below the values of Ireland, Finland or the UK (OECD 2006c).

Foreign funding is even more concentrated in the business sector. According to Statistics Austria (Schiefer 2006), five industries account for 87% of foreign funding in the business sector: radio, television and communication equipment, electronic components, motor vehicles, business services and commercial R&D services. Trade is another sector with a high relative share of foreign funding, but the total amount of foreign funds in this industry is only small. There are two industries where foreign funding accounts for more than half, and four industries where it accounts for more than a Fourth of total R&D funding. Foreign funding is higher in services than in manufacturing, and we find three service industries among the sectors that depend most heavily on funds from abroad. Here, the most interesting sector is commercial R&D services. These are enterprises that do R&D on a contractual basis for clients in the business sector or public authorities. Examples are Austrian Research Centers (ARC), Joanneum Research, or the ‚*Kplus*'- und ‚K_*ind*'-centers which have been founded on public initiative to promote co-operation between universities and enterprises.

Figure 9: Funding of R&D in the Austrian business sector at the level of industries according to sources of funding, 2004

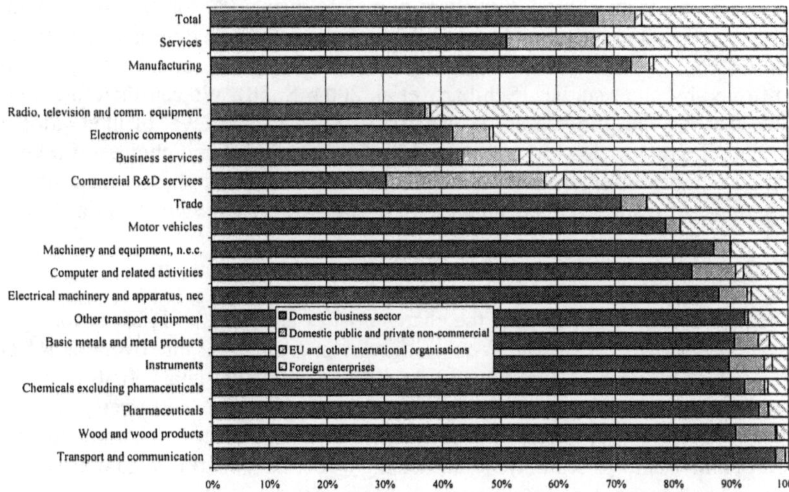

Note: Industries with a share of foreign funding of less than 1% of total R&D funding are not included.

Source: Schiefer (2006), own calculations

The high share of foreign funding in this sector demonstrates, on the one hand, that Austrian contract research organisations increasingly internationalize and work for foreign clients. On the other hand, some foreign-owned enterprises in Austria have outsourced their R&D to independent R&D organisations which are classified as providers of commercial R&D services (with only one client, though). The most prominent examples are the Institute for Molecular Pathology, a 100% subsidiary of the German pharmaceutical company Boehringer, or the Novartis Institute for BioMedical Research Vienna.

Outside the group of sectors mentioned above the role of overseas R&D funding is very limited. Its share is below one percent in a number of industries including textiles, clothing and leather, in publishing and printing, in finance, rubber and plastics products or in food and beverages. These are mostly medium-technology industries or service sectors that rely heavily on investment goods such as banking. The share of foreign funds on total R&D funding is also below average in machinery, chemicals and pharmaceuticals. In the last industry, however, we can assume that the low share is mainly a statistical artefact resulting from the outsourcing of R&D to independent organisations discussed above.

Moreover, the importance of foreign funding increases with enterprise size; the share of foreign funds on total R&D funding is 9.7% for small enterprises with less than 50 employees, and increases to 14.5% for the size class 50-249 employees. Large enterprises with more than 250 employees receive 31% of their R&D funding from abroad, this share climbs to even 42% for enterprises with more than 1,000 employees. In total, 87% of all foreign funding is absorbed by enterprises with more than 250 employees (Schiefer 2006). This finding is also confirmed by other studies (Schibany et al. 2004, S. 50). We can therefore conclude that the sharp increases, as well as the current high level of international funding of R&D in Austria are the result of the strategies and choices of a very limited number of enterprises. If some of these enterprises change their strategies, this may result in severe changes in overall R&D funding in Austria.

3.6 R&D Strategies of Foreign-owned Enterprises in Austria

A central issue of this book are the characteristics and goals of R&D of foreign-owned enterprises in Austria. We will discuss in section 4.2 that overseas R&D activities of enterprises can pursue two different principal goals: first, to adapt products and technologies to local markets in proximity to customers; second, enterprises try to get access to knowledge not available in the home country. Additionally, enterprises may be attracted by cost advantages or go abroad because of a shortage of scientific personnel at home.

What do existing studies tell about the motives of foreign-owned R&D activities in Austria? At first, we can assume that a considerable part of foreign-owned R&D activities in Austria consists of development and design to adapt products to the needs of Austrian clients. The small market size of Austria, however, can hardly justify the large inflows of funds for R&D in recent years. Indeed, two thirds of the foreign-owned enterprises in Austria regard the European and international market as the most relevant for their innovation activities (Nones

2003). This points to R&D activities that go beyond pure adaptation. We know from different studies that some foreign-owned subsidiaries in Austria enjoy a considerable degree of freedom and autonomy in their innovative activities (Schibany et al. 2004; Lueghammer and Schneider 2005). They use this autonomy for developing a distinct profile within their enterprise groups. Foreign-owned enterprises are also actively co-operating with Austrian universities (Rossak 2002, p. 66 and 70; Schibany et al. 2004), which also points to a more fundamental character of R&D activities than just adapting products. Finally, there is also rich evidence from case studies that foreign-owned subsidiaries in Austria have created radical, new-to-the-world innovations with a high economic value for the whole group. Karl-Heinz Leitner (2003) has included a number of foreign-owned enterprises in his book on radical innovation in Austria. From his case studies, there is no evidence that foreign-owned enterprises in Austria would innovate differently or create less radical innovations.

3.7 R&D Activities of Austrian Enterprises Abroad

Austria has developed into a very appealing location for R&D investments of MNEs in recent decades. But also Austrian enterprises have internationalized their R&D activities in recent years (Dachs et al. 2005b). This "active" internationalisation, however, is of considerable smaller size than the "passive" internationalisation of Austrian R&D analyzed in this book. While 40% of all Austrian patent inventions are owned by foreign residents, the corresponding share of Austrian patent applications based at least partly on foreign inventions is only 24% (OECD 2005b, p. 78f.).

The motives of Austrian enterprises to go abroad with R&D activities are mainly market-related (support of foreign production, world-wide service provision). In most cases, foreign activities are complementary to R&D activities at home. Sectors that were building up R&D activities abroad also increased their R&D activities in Austria. There are – at least in the short run – no substitution effects between foreign-located and home-located R&D (Dachs et al. 2005b).

An interesting aspect of the active internationalisation of Austrian R&D is its interrelatedness with passive R&D internationalisation. Case studies as well as patent analysis have revealed that some Austrian subsidiaries of MNEs themselves have set up subsidiaries and foreign-located R&D activities (Dachs et al. 2005b; see also chapter 9). An example is the software company Siemens PSE, a 100% subsidiary of Siemens Austria. Siemens PSE has set up a number of sub-subsidiaries in central and eastern Europe which are controlled by the Austrian subsidiary. Another example is Infineon Austria, which has recently established 100% subsidiaries in Malaysia and Bulgaria which are responsible to Vienna, not to Munich.

3.8 Chapter summary

Austria has developed into an attractive location for research, development and innovation activities of foreign-owned enterprises since the early 1990s. Foreign funds today amount to about 20% of total R&D funding in Austria. In total, foreign-owned subsidiaries control 45% of the R&D expenditures of the Austrian business sector.

With respect to R&D, Austria is now one of the most internationalized countries in the OECD. Foreign-funded R&D, however, is not equally distributed among the actors of the Austrian innovation system, but concentrated in several respects:

- Foreign funds are predominantly allocated within enterprise groups, only a third comes from contract R&D. Main source countries are Germany and Switzerland/Liechtenstein.
- Recipients of foreign funding are predominantly found in the enterprise sector in five sectors: radio, television and communication equipment, electronic components, automotive, business services and commercial R&D services.
- Outside these five sectors, foreign R&D funds are very limited in the business sector. The share of foreign funding in the university sector is below 5%.
- Large enterprises disproportionately benefit from foreign funding. More than 80% of foreign funding is received by enterprises with more than 250 employees.

Foreign funding has increased Austria's overall scientific technological performance considerably in the last 15 years. R&D and innovation strategies of foreign-owned enterprises in Austria often go beyond simple adapting. In a number of cases, Austrian subsidiaries of MNEs evolved into centers of competence within their enterprise group that are responsible for the development of specific technologies and/or products for the whole group.

4. The Linkage between Foreign Ownership and Innovation: Building Blocks from the Literature

The book relates to two questions where considerable research effort has been made in recent years: first, what determines the innovative behaviour of enterprises; second, what strategies MNEs pursue regarding the location of innovative activities. We will examine these two questions in detail in the following chapter.

4.1 The Determinants of Innovation Activities

4.1.1 Innovation and Size of the Enterprise

Discussions about the relationship between size and innovative activity go back to the times of Joseph Schumpeter. In his book "Theorie der Wirtschaftlichen Entwicklung" (1911; 1997), Schumpeter described the central role entrepreneurs and their small businesses in pushing through new "combinations". He identified their heroic endeavours as one of the principal sources of economic development, driven by the will to gain temporary monopoly power and to erode the incumbent's market position.

The rise of large industrial conglomerates in the chemical and electrical industry of Germany and the US has led Schumpeter to a reassessment of the relationship between size and innovativeness in his later work where he points out the advantages of large organisations (Schumpeter 1942). The success of these conglomerates, as he notices, is due to specialized R&D departments with trained scientific personnel and a high degree of specialisation. Innovation has been routinized in these large corporations.

Schumpeter's two views on the relationship between size and innovativeness have led the theoretical discussions on this topic ever since (Cohen and Levin 1989; Dogson and Rothwell 1994; Cohen 1995; Freeman and Soete 1997, chapter 9.3). The main argument in favour of small enterprises is their flexibility to react to new opportunities, which may be missed by large enterprises due to a lack of flexibility and administrative obstacles. Small enterprises can survive in niche markets where large enterprises are not willing to operate. They are usually run by an entrepreneur, who is personally engaged with its own money in its business and they benefit from his/her knowledge of technologies and markets. In a number of cases (technology-based start-ups), this personal knowledge is the very reason for the existence of the enterprise.

Large multidivisional and/or multinational enterprises, in contrast, usually have large internal financial means and can raise external funds to finance innovation projects more easily than entrepreneurs and small businesses (O'Sullivan 2005).

Since large companies usually run different innovation projects at different stages at one time, they can manage risk more easily through diversification and distribute the cost of failures over a larger number of projects.

Another advantage of size is specialisation and a more intense division of labour between different scientific disciplines and persons of different qualifications. In Schumpeter's words, innovation has become the business of "teams of trained specialists who turn out what is required" (Schumpeter 1942, p. 132). Moreover, there is a minimum efficient scale and decreasing fixed cost on some research projects which make them more suitable for large enterprises. Large, multidivisional enterprises have also advantages in protecting and utilizing their knowledge and in appropriating the economic returns from unforeseen innovations because they have more potential fields of application for the inherently uncertain and often unintended outcomes of research activities (Rosenberg 1990, p. 168).

The relationship between size and innovativeness has also been subject to a large number of empirical studies (see Cohen 1995 for a survey). As a main result, the propensity for an enterprise to start R&D or innovation activities as well as absolute innovative expenditure increases with size. Evidence with respect to R&D and innovation intensity, in contrast, is inconsistent. A finding from number of studies is a U-shaped connection between intensity and size which relates to the different advantages and disadvantages of small and large enterprises discussed above (Dogson and Rothwell 1994; Cohen 1995). However, some studies also report a positive or negative relationship, while others find that intensity is unaffected by size. Reasons for these diverging results are amongst others, truncated distributions of enterprise size in the samples where small enterprises are underrepresented and different measures of innovative activity (Kleinknecht 1989; Audretsch and Acs 1991).

4.1.2 Innovation and Sectoral Affiliation

A second major determinant of innovation which can already been found in Schumpeter's work is the industrial sector of the enterprise. It is one of the most robust findings in innovation studies that R&D intensity or innovativeness significantly varies between industries (recent empirical evidence can be found in OECD 2006a, Statistical Annex, Table 36). It is more difficult, however, to explain what exactly causes these sectoral differences.

A first and – from the perspective of industrial organisation – obvious candidate to cause inter-sectoral differences in innovativeness is *market concentration* (see Cohen and Levin 1989 for a survey). The possession of ex-ante market power may reduce uncertainty from competition. A high market share may also promise higher potential returns from innovation. Empirical research indeed found a positive relationship between the two variables. The explanatory power of market concentration, however, seems to be low once it is controlled for size and for other industry-level variables, and there are good reasons to assume that both variables are endogenous (Cohen 1995, p. 193).

Three other industry characteristics which have been identified to influence innovativeness and innovation intensity are *market demand, technological opportunity* and *appropriability conditions* (see Cohen 1995, p. 210 - 231 for a survey). Enterprises will engage to a higher degree in innovation activity when they expect market demand to increase in the future. A higher engagement in innovation can also be expected when technological change is fast in a sector and new technologies promise a range of applications. Finally, enterprises will innovate when they can protect their innovation from imitation, by patent law, lead time, secrecy, or product complexity.

The notion of technological opportunity points to a different strand of the literature that focuses on knowledge and learning as the main causes for industry effects on innovation. One of the most influential contributions to explain these intersectoral differences is the concept of a '*technological regime*' introduced Nelson and Winter (1982). A technological regime " ... refers to the learning and knowledge environment in which enterprises operate and defines the nature of the problems enterprises have to solve in their innovative activities." (Nelson and Winter 1982).

The concept of technological regimes influenced a number of theoretical contributions to explain the linkage between sectoral affiliation and innovation in the following years. One of these approaches is the literature on sectoral systems of innovation (Malerba and Orsenigo 1996; Malerba 2002, 2005). According to Malerba, innovation differs between sectors because sectoral innovation systems systematically differ in terms of actors and networks, the relevant knowledge base and sector-wide institutions (Malerba 2002, 2005).

Another recent approach to technological regimes is the work of Marsili (Marsili 2001; Marsili and Verspagen 2002). According to Marsili, a technological regime defines the nature of the problem firms have to solve in their innovative activities, affects the form of technological learning, shapes the incentives and constraints to particular behaviour, and influences the basic processes of variety generation and selection (Marsili 2001). She identifies five distinct technological regimes in manufacturing based on these determinants.

Theoretical contributions as well as empirical studies on intersectoral differences in innovative activities have also inspired researchers to create taxonomies and classifications of industries according to their innovative behaviour. Pavitt (1984) distinguishes between supplier-dominated, production-intensive and science-based sectors, depending on the sources of technology, requirements of users, and possibilities for appropriation. A taxonomy of industries according to their main inputs has been presented by Peneder (2002).

The best known approach to classify industrial sectors with respect to innovation and R&D is the OECD classification of sectors according to their technology intensity (Table 2). The OECD uses one indicator, aggregate expenditure on R&D as a percentage of gross output (OECD 2003b, p. 155ff), to classify manufacturing industries in five sectoral aggregates (Table 2). In the service sector, the OECD distinguishes between knowledge-intensive services and other services.

Table 2: OECD classification of industries according to R&D intensity

Classification	Industries
High-technology industries	Aircraft and spacecraft Pharmaceuticals Office, accounting and computing machinery Radio, TV and communications equipment Medical, precision and optical instruments
Medium-high-technology industries	Electrical machinery and apparatus, n.e.c. Motor vehicles, trailers and semi-trailers Chemicals excluding pharmaceuticals Railroad equipment and transport equipment, n.e.c. Machinery and equipment, n.e.c.
Medium-low-technology industries	Building and repairing of ships and boats Rubber and plastics products Coke, refined petroleum products and nuclear fuel Other non-metallic mineral products Basic metals and fabricated metal products
Low-technology industries	Manufacturing, n.e.c.; Recycling Wood, pulp, paper, paper products, printing and publishing Food products, beverages and tobacco Textiles, textile products, leather and footwear
Knowledge-intensive services	Post and telecommunications Financial intermediation Real estate, renting and business activities
Other service industries	Wholesale and retail trade; repairs Hotels and restaurants Transport and storage Community social and personal services

Source: OECD 2003

Despite some criticism for presenting a too narrow picture of innovation (Smith 2005), the OECD approach is widely known and terms such as 'high technology' or 'low technology' even found their way into everyday language. We will also use this classification to account for sector-wide differences in innovation.

4.1.3 Innovation and Human Capital

The innovation process involves problem-solving, the transformation of scientific and technical knowledge into products and processes and the matching of artefacts and practices to market needs (Pavitt 2005). All these activities involve human action; the knowledge and skills of the employees of an enterprise are therefore essential for innovative performance. We use the term human capital to refer to this knowledge and skills.

Human capital and learning is considered as central for innovation throughout the literature; an approach which in particular focuses on competencies and skills is the 'resource-based view of the firm' (Coombs 1996; Teece et al. 1997; Verona 1999). The authors stress the importance of mutual learning and the cumulative dimension of knowledge. Quality and quantity of human capital in an enterprise are therefore positively related to innovativeness. It is measured by various indicators, most often by the share of employees with tertiary education because this information is easily available in most enterprises.

A well-educated workforce is not only essential to create new knowledge, but also for learning from external sources. An enterprise needs 'absorptive capacity' (Cohen and Levinthal 1990; Cantner and Pyka 1998) to understand and utilize the results of research activities of universities and other enterprises. The quality of human capital of the enterprise is therefore decisive not only for the quality of own R&D efforts, but also for the abilities to absorb and use technology acquired by R&D co-operation, spillovers of through investment.

4.1.4 Innovation and Investment

A second major source of external knowledge beside human capital is investment in capital goods. Innovation and investment is usually considered to be positively related: innovation is not necessarily based on technology developed by the enterprise itself. New products and services can also build on knowledge embodied in machinery, transport and communication equipment and other investment goods. Different models have been developed to describe the diffusion of technology in the economy (Geroski 2000; Hall 2005).

Technology diffusion is an important source of innovation in all parts of the economy, in particular in sectors with a low level of own R&D expenditure. These sectors have been labelled as 'supplier driven' (Pavitt 1984), because they receive their technological knowledge largely embodied in investment goods. The level of investment is therefore positively related to innovativeness.

Research in recent years on technology diffusion has also focused on so called 'generic' or 'General Purpose Technologies' (Lipsey et al. 2005). The interest in these technologies is based on the fact that they find application in nearly all sectors of the economy and therefore may trigger innovation in all parts of the economy. Examples for this type of technologies are information and communication technologies; special attention has been given to innovation based on information and communication technologies in the service sectors (Hipp 2000; Miles 2005).

4.1.5 Innovation and Exports

Innovation is also closely related to exports. Following Vernon's (1966) seminal article, a number of theoretical contributions have shown that innovation is the driving force for exports in the US and other industrialized countries (see Krugman 1995 for a survey). A positive relationship between innovation and exports has also been identified by a number of empirical studies at the firm level (Greenhalgh and Taylor 1990; Bleaney and Wakelin 2002; Lachenmaier and Wößmann 2004). These studies point out the two-way causality of this relationship and the endogeneity of innovation and exports: innovative enterprises tend to exhibit a higher export intensity than non-innovators, and exporting precedes a superior innovative performance. This relationship can be explained, on the one hand, by the wish of enterprises to exploit their innovations not only at home, but also at international markets and increase the returns from their innovative activities. Exporting enterprises, on the other hand, are exposed to competitive pressure to a higher degree than enterprises that restrict their operations to the home market and therefore forced to be innovative to maintain their competitive position.

4.2 Foreign Ownership and Innovative Activity

The objective of this study is to explore whether domestically owned and foreign-owned enterprises in Austria differ in terms of innovative behaviour and embeddedness in the national innovation system. These differences may be related to factors such as size, sectoral affiliation and other determinants discussed above. Empirical evidence presented in chapter 6 confirms that foreign-owned enterprises on average are larger, employ more academic staff and are more export-oriented.

But there are two another, more generic reasons why foreign-owned and domestically owned enterprises may differ. A first one is that foreign-owned enterprises have to bear additional costs that are not borne by local enterprises when doing business in a particular country. These include the costs of maintaining co-ordination and communication over distance, but also costs to overcome institutional and social hampering factors that are discussed as the '*liability of foreignness*' in the international business literature and management literature (Zaheer 1995; Eden and Miller 2004). We will come back to this point in section 4.2.3.

A second reason why foreign-owned enterprises may have different levels of innovative efforts and output is because the strategy of their MNE group is to concentrate R&D and other innovation activities in the home country. A part of the literature argues that multinational enterprises have a tendency to concentrate the creation of firm-specific assets in the home county and exploit these specific advantages through their foreign subsidiaries. We will use the term '*competence-exploiting strategies*' to label this type of behaviour. If foreign-owned enterprises in Austria purse such a strategy, this may lead to different outcomes compared to those of domestically owned enterprises after controlling for other determinants of innovative activity discussed in the previous chapter. Innovative foreign-owned enterprises that pursue such a strategy may need less scientific personnel, perform R&D only occasionally and not permanently, and mainly co-operate with central R&D departments in the home country and other subsidiaries.

The perspective that MNEs restrict their foreign subsidiaries to the exploitation of existing technologies is not unchallenged in the literature. Various authors argue that MNEs have moved to strategies of global creation rather than exploitation of firm-specific assets. As a consequence, their innovative efforts should not differ from those of domestically owned firms, or be even higher because these enterprises concentrate innovative activities of their whole group in one particular technology. We will call this class of strategies ‚competence-creating strategies'. Their characteristics are discussed in 4.2.2.

4.2.1 Competence-Exploiting Strategies

The concept of competence-exploiting strategies originates from the 'International Product Life Cycle Model' (Vernon 1966; see Cantwell 1995; Krugman 1995 for a critical summary). Vernon proposes a specific trade and investment pattern in technologically advanced goods where initial innovation and production takes place in the US. In the course of the product life cycle, production is shifted to less advanced nations via foreign direct investment. An important hypothesis derived from this model is "that innovations are almost always located in the home country of the parent company, and usually close to the site of the corporate technological headquarters" (Cantwell 1995, p. 155).

The International Product Life Cycle Model has considerably influenced research on multinational enterprises since the 1960s. It helped to understand that multinational enterprises exist to utilize existing assets at foreign markets via their subsidiaries (Dunning 1973; Markusen 1995; Caves 1996 (1974); Markusen 2002). The concept of firm-specific assets is central to this approach: MNEs exist because they possess firm-specific intangible assets such as technological knowledge, well-known products and brands, design or management capabilities. Markusen (1995; 2002) has labelled these assets 'knowledge capital'. Dunning (1973; 1981) suggests that MNEs exploit these assets via international production and not via exports or licensing because of ownership, location and internalisation advantages associated with this mode of exploitation. In particular, these assets are intangible, fully appropriable and transferable within the enterprise. MNEs use these assets to enter foreign markets because they give them advantages over incumbent competitors. Innovative activity at the subsidiary supports the exploitation of these assets by adapting them to local needs, consumer tastes, regulation etc.

A strategy derived from this view on MNE organisation – referred to as competence-exploiting strategy throughout the study - is characterized by a concentration of long-term, strategic R&D and innovation activities at the parent enterprise in the home country. Design and engineering activities at the subsidiaries adapt firm-specific assets to the host markets in proximity to the customers and production facilities abroad. Similar strategies have been labelled, for example, asset-exploiting strategies (Dunning and Narula 1995), competence-exploiting subsidiary mandates (Cantwell and Mudambi 2005), home-base exploiting strategies (Kuemmerle 1999b), or market-driven internationalisation of R&D (von Zedtwitz and Gassmann 2002).

Competence-exploiting strategies and the centralisation of R&D at the parent company have some advantages for MNEs (von Zedtwitz and Gassmann 2002; Sanna-Randaccio and Veugelers 2003; Gersbach and Schmutzler 2006). These advantages include, for example, economies of scale and scope, more secrecy and a tighter control of core technologies. Multinational enterprises may also favour a centralisation of innovative activity because of the need for close coordination of research, development, design, production preparation and marketing activities at the initial stages of the innovation process.

Competence-exploiting strategies are also less demanding in terms of organisational structure. There is a clear hierarchy within the MNE with respect to innovation. Knowledge and information flows are mostly one-way from central innovation and R&D departments to the subsidiaries. A concentration of innovative activity in the home country is also advantageous if the home country innovation system delivers substantial spillovers to the enterprise and the technological specialisation of the enterprise strongly corresponds to the competencies of home country. Competence-exploiting strategies may also be associated with enterprises operating in demand-driven markets.

4.2.2 Competence-Creating Strategies

Empirical evidence shows that competence-exploiting strategies are dominant among the world's largest enterprises (Patel and Vega 1999; le Bas and Sierra 2002). A rising share of MNEs, however, is shifting to new ways of organizing global innovative activities. MNEs increasingly develop and improve original technology outside of their home countries instead of just utilizing the existing stock of knowledge in foreign markets. Subsidiaries develop into centres of competence within the MNE which are responsible for innovation in certain groups of products and / or technologies. This strategy have been described as strategic asset-seeking (Dunning and Narula 1995), competence-creating subsidiary mandates (Cantwell and Mudambi 2005), home-base augmenting strategies (Kuemmerle 1999b), or global R&D strategies (von Zedtwitz and Gassmann 2002).

Competence-creating strategies are driven on the one hand by technological 'supply-side' factors, such as superior local knowledge and the framework conditions for R&D and innovation in the host countries. We can find these countries in North America and Western Europe. Moreover, a number of countries, including South-East Asian countries (Korea, India and China) have shown impressive progress in science and technology in recent decades. Indicators for this catch-up are a rising number of scientists and engineers, as well as increasing numbers of patents, publications and R&D expenditure in these countries. Most of these indicators grow faster for these countries than for the OECD average (OECD 2006b, p. 41). As a result, the number of potential locations that provide the prerequisites for first-class research and development is growing.

This growing opportunity meets with the changing technology needs and strategies of enterprises. A main driver for competence-creating strategies, as Narula and Zanfei (2005) suggest, is the increasing complexity of products. Products become more and more multi-technical and incorporate a number of functionalities from different technical domains. An example is the penetration of a number of traditional products with functionality provided by ICT. As a result of complexity, enterprises have to incorporate a more diverse set of technological competences than 20 years before.

Becoming multi-technological, however, can also be regarded as a strategic move of enterprises. Research has shown that the technological competencies of large enterprises are usually rather broad and go well beyond the competences necessary to produce their core products (Patel and Pavitt 1997; Granstrand 1998). Granstrand and Sjölander (1994) speak of "multi-technology corporations" to describe the degree of diversification in the competencies of large firms. Being multi-technology has some advantages. First, it is an answer to the inherently uncertain nature of technological change. Firms, for example, find it often impossible to predict the exact cost and performance of a new product. A broad set of competences may limit the threat from this uncertainty. Moreover, firms may need a broad portfolio to avoid 'lock-ins' in certain technologies (Patel and Pavitt 1997; Pavitt 2005).

Competence-creating strategies also correspond to new views on the innovation process known as 'open innovation'. A recent contribution to this discussion is the work of Chesbrough (2003a; 2003b). Chesbrough stresses the fact that many innovative firms have shifted to an 'open innovation' model where they exploit ideas and knowledge not only provided by internal R&D, but also from a broad range of external sources and actors within and outside their innovation systems. Here, core competence is less a field defined by technologies, but lies in the process of managing the co-ordination and exploitation of external and internal knowledge sources (Christensen 2006).

A direct consequence of the new requirements from multi-technological products and 'open innovation' strategies are search and learning processes of enterprises that go beyond the borders of their parent countries and try to absorb useful knowledge wherever possible. It should be noted that absorption of knowledge does not necessarily mean own development, but also acquisition via licensing, joint development or imitation.

Another factor which affected the emergence of global sourcing and competence creating strategies were cross-border mergers and acquisitions which grew dramatically in the merger wave of the 1990s (UNCTAD 2000b). More than half of all overseas patent inventions of Japanese enterprises in the 1980s and early 1990s were due to acquisitions (Belderbos 2001).

A cross-border merger of two enterprises engaged in research and development creates a new enterprise with R&D activities dispersed over two or more countries. Does this new enterprise reorganize and concentrate strategic R&D and innovation activities in one country to cut down cost and avoid the duplication of activities, or proceed with a more decentralized organisational structure and follow a competence-creating strategy?

It is not possible to answer this question in a general way. First, it has to be noted that most mergers and acquisitions in the past decades (at least outside of ICT and pharmaceuticals) were not R&D or technology-driven (Tichy 2001). Creating a dispersed R&D organisation was therefore not a goal, but rather a by-product of acquiring market shares of reducing competitive pressure. Second, we have to consider complementarities between the knowledge bases of the acquired and the acquiring company (Cassiman et al. 2005). Mergers between partners with ex-ante complementary knowledge bases result in more active R&D performers after the merger; the opposite outcome has been observed in the case of substitutive competences. A third drawback from answering the question satisfactory is the fact that empirical evidence on the effects of cross-border mergers is scarce so far, since most studies concentrate on domestic mergers (Bertrand and Zuniga 2006).

The results from case studies, however, indicate that mergers may lead to a more globally dispersed R&D strategy. Von Zedtzwitz and Gassmann (2002) find that international R&D dispersion is often a result of non-R&D-related merger and acquisitions of parent companies. Companies which have been created by a merger show the highest degree of R&D dispersion. This is also the result of case studies on R&D internationalisation of Austrian enterprises (Dachs et al. 2005b).

Another main reason - besides the existence of valuable local knowledge - for MNEs to pursue competence-creating strategies at foreign locations is the labour market for scientists and engineers in the host countries. A shortage of skilled personnel in the home country was, for example, a main motive for Philips to take up innovative activity in Germany (Reger 2003). Labour market issues, of course, also include wage differentials between home and host country.

Competence-creating strategies are also dependent on the history of the presence of the foreign-owned enterprise in a host location. The strategic management literature describes the emergence of subsidiary mandates as a dynamic process: Birkinshaw and Hood (1998) have identified three sets of internal and external factors which determine whether a subsidiary evolves into a centre of excellence which actively contributes to the technological competences of the MNE. The first of these factors is *local environment determinism* and relates to the specific local environment the subsidiary operates in. This environment provides specific incentives, capabilities and hampering factors that shape subsidiary evolution. A second influential factor, *head-office assignment*, encompasses headquarter strategy, the assignment of tasks to the subsidiaries and allocation mechanisms for resources within the MNE. Finally, subsidiary mandates are shaped by *subsidiary choice*, the subsidiary's capability and the initiative of the managers of the subsidiary itself.

At least two of them, head-office assignment and subsidiary choice, co-evolve with dynamic, self-enforcing and self-containing feedback effects (Birkinshaw and Hood 1998); a higher degree of subsidiary choice and autonomy granted by the head office may lead to a build-up of capabilities and a more entrepreneurial behaviour at the subsidiary, which, in turn may foster of the parent enterprise-driven decentralisation strategies.

Competence-creating strategies have become more frequent during the past two decades despite the disadvantages associated with a decentralisation of innovative activity (von Zedtwitz and Gassmann 2002; Sanna-Randaccio and Veugelers 2003; Gersbach and Schmutzler 2006). Enterprises loose scale and scope economies in R&D and innovation in the home country. It becomes more difficult to keep knowledge secret when its production is geographically dispersed. Moreover, the diffusion of knowledge within the MNE becomes a more difficult task, because exchange is no longer one-way, but includes reverse knowledge transfer between subsidiaries and the parent enterprises as well as between the subsidiaries themselves.

Innovative activity at foreign locations therefore has to be associated with considerable locational advantages that compensate MNEs for the disadvantages from decentralisation. One of these advantages is access to specific knowledge at foreign locations. A number of authors report that MNE subsidiaries exhibit a high degree of embeddedness in their host country innovation systems and extensively monitor and assimilate knowledge from local sources (Birkinshaw et al. 1998; Almeida 1999; Frost 2001; Castellani and Zanfei 2002; Almeida and Phene 2004). Foreign-owned subsidiaries are described as ‚surveillance outposts 'or ‚antennas' (Florida 1997; Almeida 1999). They are located in proximity to clusters, universities or other enterprises (Cantwell and Iammarino 2000). The presence of innovative activities at the host country is a necessary precondition for accessing this knowledge due to its tacit and localized characteristics (see 2.2).

It has already been mentioned that competence-creating strategies require a higher co-ordination effort than competence-exploiting strategies. This includes two-way exchange of knowledge between parent enterprises and subsidiaries rather than a hierarchical structure. This organisational mode has been described as a network of loosely coupled organisations (Ghoshal and Bartlett 1991; Zander 1999, 2002). The subsidiary is embedded in two different networks; the internal network of relationships between various parts of the MNE, and the external network of relationships between the subsidiary and local universities and enterprises (Zanfei 2000).

Another important aspect of competence-creating mandates is entrepreneurial initiative at the subsidiary level. Subsidiary initiative is positively related with the level of technological activity at the subsidiary (Gupta and Govindarajanan 1994; Birkinshaw et al. 1998). Zanfei (2000) argues that a higher degree of independence is essential for competence-creating subsidiaries because they have to enter different external relations with enterprises and universities. Subsidiary initiative is also a driving force for the development of subsidiaries into centres of competence, beside locational advantage and parent enterprise strategy (Birkinshaw and Hood 1998).

4.2.3 Innovation and the 'Liability of Foreignness'

We have discussed in the previous sections that the ownership status of the enterprise (domestically vs. foreign-owned) can lead to differences in innovation strategy. A second possible source of performance differences are additional costs that are borne by foreign-owned, but not by domestically owned enterprises when doing business in a particular country. These costs are known as the '*costs of doing business abroad*' and/or the '*liability of foreignness*'[6] (LOF) in the international business and the strategic management literature (Zaheer 1995, 2002; Eden and Miller 2004).

The costs of doing business abroad have two principal sources. First, foreign operations (which also include exporting) incur additional *economic* costs to the MNE which arise from distance between the home and host country. Economic costs include, for example, freight, insurance, and communication costs, foreign exchange costs, or costs arising from trade barriers. It is assumed in the literature that economic costs have become less important with the ongoing integration of the world economy and the rapid development of transportation and communication techniques (Calhoun 2002; Hummels 2007).

With economic cost being fairly predictable and decreasing, discussions on the costs of doing business abroad have focussed on its social components – the liability of foreignness. LOF is a concept that draws on institutional theory. Eden and Miller (2004) argue that the main driver behind LOF is institutional distance (this term goes back to Xu and Shenkar 2002) between the home and the host country and costs arising from the LOF consist primarily of structural/relational and legitimacy costs. Eden and Miller (2004, pp. 10 and 11) decompose LOF into three hazards that incur additional costs to foreign-owned enterprises:

Unfamiliarity hazards reflect a lack of knowledge about norms, routines, habits etc. of foreign-owned enterprises compared to domestically owned enterprises. *Discrimination hazards* arise from a differential treatment – formal or informal – from governments, consumers, or the general public in the host country. Finally, *relational hazards* relate to internal and external organisation costs, such as agency cost arising from difficulties of managing and supervising employees from a distance, or additional cost of negotiating, monitoring and settling external relationships and building up trust with domestic organisations.

---

6 Eden and Miller (2004) show that the terms ,costs of doing business abroad' and ,liability of foreignness' have originally been used as synonyms by the main authors in this field. Today, the term 'liability of foreignness' reflects the social costs of doing business abroad, while ,costs of doing business abroad' include both, economic and social costs.

The literature usually assumes that the liability of foreignness decreases with time when, for example, operations at the subsidiary are run by local personnel. The LOF is therefore far less relevant for long-established subsidiaries, as well as for acquisitions (Zaheer and Mosakowski 1997). This is also the case in many Austrian subsidiaries, since many of them have a long history of presence in the country.

There are, however, some costs that may be persistent, because of institutional differences between the host and home country which reproduce itself in MNE-wide routines. We cannot expect that foreign-owned enterprises will completely follow different norms, values and habits in the host country, even if the management of the subsidiary knows them. The subsidiary is also embedded in the norms, values and habits of the MNE, which, in turn, are shaped by the home country. Potential differences in these institutions are:

a) The 'time horizon' of agents (Lundvall 1998; Drejer 2000): the Anglo-Saxon systems are characterised by a shorter time horizon in corporate governance than the Japanese and German systems, which are known for working with a quite long time horizon in investment decisions.

b) The role of 'trust' and the way that 'authority' is expressed: the German and Japanese systems are perceived as being more trust-oriented in business matters than the Anglo-Saxon systems. Moreover, Lundvall (1998, p. 409 f) argues that a mixture of trust and authority is necessary in order for learning to take place efficiently in master-apprentice relations. The learning capabilities of Asian countries in certain areas are suggested to be rooted in the special kinds of authority relations in these countries.

c) Differences in the legal systems, accounting standards and codes of corporate governance between the home and host country (Buckley 2000, p 297). A common distinction is made between the market-based system of corporate governance found in Great Britain and the US and the bank-based system of Japan, Germany and other European countries (Dimsdale and Prevezer 1994). German and European corporate governance is usually characterized by concentrated ownership of listed companies. Moreover, German and European enterprises are associated with a strategy to maximize the stakeholder value, whereas the Anglo-Saxon system is thought to follow a shareholder value maximizing approach. The Anglo-Saxon system is also characterized by a strong minority protection and dispersed ownership.

d) Cultural differences between the home and host country. If two countries are close in cultural aspects, enterprises which want to serve both markets usually have only little need for product adaptations. Dekimpe et al. (2000) for example, suggest that the diffusion of innovation from one country to another is easier between similar countries in terms of culture, social and economic factors than between economies isolated from each other. Successful business practices from the MNE home country may also be a success in the host country. Geographical and cultural proximity between parent enterprise and subsidiary may also help to minimize monitoring cost and overcome agency problems.

A LOF also helps to get access to localized knowledge in the host country, because it helps to overcome communication barriers and problems associated with the articulation of tacit knowledge (see 2.2). Zaher and Mosakowski see costs from the liability of foreignness mainly arise "from the foreign firm not being sufficiently embedded in the information networks in the country of location" (Zaheer and Mosakowski 1997, p. 445). Empirical support for this claim comes from data on co-patenting (Guellec and van Pottelsberghe de la Potterie 2001) shows that geographical proximity and a common border language significantly explain mutual patenting activities at the national level. Similar neighbourhood effects have been identified by Ebersberger and Lööf (2005) for the Nordic countries.

Neighbourhood effects – FDI in Austria mainly originates from Germany and Switzerland – and the long presence of many foreign-owned enterprises in Austria should keep additional costs from the LOF low in Austria. However, the liability of foreignness could make a difference in innovation behaviour between enterprises from Germany and Switzerland on the one hand and enterprises originating form other countries on the other hand, since the latter will face more severe communication barriers and problems associated with the transfer of tacit knowledge. We will therefore interpret the LOF as a reason for differences *within* the population of foreign-owned enterprises.

4.2.4 Effects of Multinationality and Group Membership

Another aspect of performance differences between foreign-owned and domestically owned enterprises are effects that emerge from being part of an enterprise group versus being an unaffiliated enterprise. A number of studies (e. g. Doms and Jensen 1998; Frenz and Ietto-Gillies 2007) on the effects of foreign ownership report that differences shrink or even disappear if foreign-owned enterprises are compared only to domestically owned multinationals. An explanation for this observation is the fact that some advantages of foreign-owned enterprises result from group membership, and are therefore also shared by domestic multinationals. One of these advantages is the existence of internal networks of information and knowledge exchange in the MNE. Other advantages include enhanced opportunities for risk-sharing, because MNEs are less vulnerable to external shocks in one country than enterprises that operate only on one location. (Globerman et al. 1994; Caves 1996). Multinationality may also include a higher chance to commercialize innovations, because products that fail to meet consumer tastes in one country may be successful in another market. Frenz and Ietto-Gillies (2007) find that multinationality is positively related to innovativeness. Moreover, innovativeness increases with the degree of multinationality.

4.3 Operationalisation of the Research Questions

In chapter 1 we have stated the two basic questions of this study:

- Are there systematic differences in innovative activities between foreign-owned and domestically owned enterprises in Austria?
- If differences exist, are they related to foreign ownership?

Based on our discussion of the literature we can now reformulate and operationalize these research questions. The innovative behaviour of enterprises is determined by a number of factors, including enterprise size, sectoral affiliation, levels of investment, the stock of human capital, or export intensity. Once we control for these factors, we should be able to see the effects of foreign and domestic ownership on the innovative behaviour and embeddedness of enterprises.

Here, however, we are faced with two plausible lines of argument, each of which receives ample support in the empirical literature. Are the current strategies of MNE subsidiaries in Austria characterised by competence-creating, competence-exploiting, or both? More fundamentally, which line of argument helps us making sense of what we are able to observe in Austria? The main line of investigation of this study is therefore a test between two alternative assumptions about the strategic orientation of foreign-owned subsidiaries in Austria regarding innovation. The remainder of this study sets out to explore this question empirically.

If *competence-exploiting strategies* prevail, the role of subsidiaries basically boils down to a support of production and marketing by adapting technologies created at home country to the conditions of the host market.

We can therefore expect that foreign-owned subsidiaries that pursue such a strategy exhibit a lower level of permanent R&D activity and a lower level of innovative input than domestically owned enterprises because firm-specific assets are mainly created by the parent enterprise. The fact that innovations are based on existing technologies does not necessarily affect innovativeness and innovative output as such; however, we can expect that competence-exploiting behaviour results in a lower share of products new to the market compared to domestically owned enterprises because the main tasks of the subsidiaries are redesign, product customization and adjustments.

Competence-exploiting strategies of foreign-owned subsidiaries also affect embeddedness in the host country innovation system. We expect that subsidiaries exhibit a higher appreciation of MNE-internal information sources and a lower propensity to enter into co-operation with domestic partners compared to domestically owned enterprises since the main task of the subsidiary is to exploit existing assets. Superior knowledge is available from internal sources of the MNE and there is no need to acquire it by means of external co-operation, which may cause involuntary spillovers and the danger that knowledge 'leaks out'. Cultural distance and other effects related to the liability of foreignness (see 4.2.3) may further reduce the propensity to co-operate.

We come to different conclusions when we assume a *competence-creating behaviour* of subsidiaries. Here, there is no reason to assume that foreign-owned enterprises spend less on innovative input compared to domestically owned enterprises or are less frequently engaged in permanent R&D activity. In contrast, they should not differ in these parameters from domestically owned enterprises, because they are part of the same innovation system and take advantage of the same locational factors as their domestically owned counterparts. Some of them even exhibit a higher innovative intensity because they are centres of competence for certain technologies within their MNE.

In contrast to competence-exploiting strategies we do not expect a lower innovative output in terms of products that are new to the market compared to domestically owned enterprises. In fact, foreign-owned subsidiaries could even exhibit a superior innovative performance when they successfully combine own research efforts and existing firm-specific assets.

A competence-creating strategy of subsidiaries also leads to a different co-operative behaviour. If the strategy of the subsidiary is to enhance the stock of expertise of the MNE and tap into local knowledge, we can expect that foreign-owned enterprises more frequently enter into co-operation with domestic partners than in the case a competence-exploiting strategy is in place.

To sum up, we test two alternative assumptions about the strategic orientation of foreign-owned subsidiaries in Austria regarding innovation:

A0: Foreign-owned subsidiaries in Austria predominantly pursue competence-exploiting strategies.

A1: Foreign-owned subsidiaries in Austria predominantly pursue competence-creating strategies.

If A0 is correct, we expect to find the following pattern:

- Foreign-owned enterprises exhibit a lower level of R&D personnel and a lower level of innovative input compared to domestically owned enterprises because firm-specific assets are mainly created by the parent enterprise.
- Foreign-owned enterprises exhibit a lower share of products new to the market compared to domestically owned enterprises because the main tasks of MNE subsidiaries are redesign, product customization and adjustments.
- Foreign-owned enterprises exhibit a higher appreciation of information from inside the MNE compared to domestically owned enterprises because the subsidiaries mainly draw on these internal sources.
- Foreign-owned enterprises exhibit a lower propensity to enter into co-operation with domestic partners compared to domestically owned enterprises because superior knowledge and assets is available from internal sources of the MNE.

If A1 is correct, there is no reason why foreign-owned enterprises should exhibit a different innovative performance than domestically-owned enterprises since they are exposed to the same incentives and restraints from the business environment and the host country innovation system like domestically owned enterprises are.

Moreover, we expect to find effects related to the liability of foreignness. A similar language and the geographical and cultural proximity between Austria and its three German-speaking neighbouring countries, Germany, Switzerland, and Liechtenstein, should manifest in a superior performance of subsidiaries of German and Swiss/Liechtenstein MNEs compared to subsidiaries from other countries. We assume that these enterprises also find it easier to access local knowledge in Austria and therefore exhibit a higher propensity to co-operate with Austrian partners compared to other foreign-owned enterprises. The effects from the liability of foreignness, however, may be very small, because a number of foreign-owned enterprises have been established for a long time in Austria.

A third prediction relates to the effects of group membership. Performance differences between foreign-owned enterprises and domestically owned group enterprises should be smaller than between foreign-owned enterprises and domestically owned non-group enterprises, because advantages of group membership are shared by both, foreign-owned and domestically owned group enterprises.

5. Data

5.1 The Community Innovation Survey (CIS)

The empirical analysis in the following chapters draws on the results from the third wave of the Community Innovation Survey (CIS 3). CIS 3 is a survey based on a common questionnaire administered by Eurostat and national statistical offices in all EU member states, Iceland and Norway. It aims at assessing various aspects of the innovative behaviour and performance of enterprises (Statistik Austria 2002; EUROSTAT 2004). The results cover the period 1998-2000.

The methodology of CIS is based on the work of various working groups of the OECD as well as national activities. The aim of these activities was to broaden the understanding of innovation by including not only research and development, but also other innovative efforts (Salazar and Holbrook 2004, p. 255 and 256). The results of these activities have been published in 1992 in the Oslo Manual (latest edition: OECD 2005c).

The Oslo Manual-type of innovation survey has found wide spread in a number of countries including the European Union, Canada, the US, and Latin America. The merits of this type of innovation can best be seen in Europe (Smith 2005, p. 165 ff): The three rounds of CIS provided robust empirical evidence on the level of innovative behaviour and delivered a rich dataset for analytical studies. The CIS results point to some persistent variety in innovative behaviour between countries, sectors and over time which also gave reason for policy intervention. Moreover, CIS has also shed light on the innovative activities of service industries for the first time.

Despite (and maybe also because of) these merits, CIS has also been criticised in recent years for some shortcomings (Tether 2001; Salazar and Holbrook 2004):

A first concern about CIS is that the questionnaire still focuses on technological innovation and disregards other, *non-technological* forms of innovation such as marketing or organisational innovation. As a consequence, some argue that the CIS underestimates innovation in services, but also in traditional (so-called low-technology) sectors. This concern is part of a broader debate on how to measure innovation in services: can we take the concept of innovation surveys in manufacturing and apply it to services? Some authors (for example Djellal and Gallouj 1999) argue that we need different measures because innovation is different in many parts of the service sector: the distinction between product and process innovation, for example, is not applicable for many service firms. Moreover, it is difficult to judge if the customerisation of a service is already an innovation. The current approach of CIS towards service industries is to use one unified questionnaire and exchange the term 'product' for 'service' in the case of service industries. However, with the latest edition of the Oslo Manual, attempts were made to broaden the concept of innovation and also include management, organisational and marketing innovation (Bloch 2007a).

A second concern is that CIS places too little attention on innovation networks and on a *systemic view* on innovation. Although CIS includes questions on external information sources and co-operation partners, we don't know about the frequency of these contacts, their intensity, and about their impact on innovative performance. A similar concern is that the CIS questionnaire is not capable of dealing with R&D outsourcing, internationalisation issues and other distributed models of innovation. An extension of CIS to include questions that track relationships among firms and organisations to enable the use of mapping and social network analysis would be highly appreciated by some authors (Salazar and Holbrook 2004).

Salazar and Holbrook (2004, p. 262) also discuss the problem of the *respondent*. They argue that the mix of financial and non-financial data requested by the questionnaire cannot be answered by one person alone. Hence, the answers may be biased in one or the other direction, or they can become contradictory if the questionnaire has been answered by several persons. There may also be a gender-related bias since female employment is concentrated in the service sector in many countries.

All these concerns about CIS are relevant and should be kept in mind. However, CIS is one of the very few data sources available to tackle the questions of this study. We will therefore employ enterprise-level CIS data for Austria provided by Statistics Austria for a descriptive analysis in chapter 6 and for a multivariate analysis in chapter 7. Chapter 8 will use a sample of CIS data from other European countries to put the results for Austria in an international perspective.

The CIS questionnaire identifies foreign ownership with two questions. First, enterprises are asked if they are part of an enterprise group. If the answer is Yes, the questionnaire asks where the parent enterprise of the group is located (EUROSTAT 2004, p. 290).

The Austrian CIS sample consists in total of 1,304 enterprises, 618 enterprises which belong to a group of enterprises and 676 which do not. 396 of the group enterprises are Austrian-owned, another 121 are owned by a German, a Swiss or a Liechtenstein based parent enterprise, 54 are Anglo-Saxon owned, another 47 enterprises originate from other parts of Europe, and 10 are from outside Europe, but are not Anglo-Saxon owned.

Table 3: Sample size and composition

Ownership	Number of observations	
Austrian-owned, but not group member		676
Part of a group:	618	
... Austrian		396
... German-Liechtenstein-Swiss	121	
... Anglo-Saxon *	54	
... European **	47	
... Others	10	
All Foreign-owned:		232
Total		**1,304**

Note: * includes CA, IE, UK, US, ZA; ** includes BE, FI, FR, IT, LU, NL, NO, PT, SE, SI

Source: Community Innovation Survey 3 Austria

5.2 Independent Variables

5.2.1 Ownership Variables

We recoded the information on the ownership status and the home country of the parent enterprise in a number of dummy variables. There are two dummies associated to domestically owned enterprises, and five dummies that identify foreign-owned enterprises. The two dummies identifying domestically owned enterprises are DOM_UNI, related to domestically owned enterprises which are not part of an enterprise group, and DOM_GROUP, which identifies domestically owned enterprises which are part of an enterprise group. We will refer to the two categories of enterprises as domestically owned group enterprises and domestically owned non-group enterprises.

Dummies that describe the foreign-owned enterprises are partly overlapping; *FOROWN* is the general category that includes all foreign-owned enterprise regardless of the home country of the parent enterprise; *GLS* denotes all enterprises with a parent enterprise in Germany, Liechtenstein or Switzerland, the German speaking neighbouring countries of Austria; *AS* identifies Anglo-Saxon owned enterprises; *EURO* includes all European-owned enterprises except GLS and AS enterprises; *OTHERS* is a category that includes all foreign-owned enterprises except those with a parent located in Germany, Liechtenstein or Switzerland.

Table 4: Variables describing the ownership status

Variable	Description
DOM_UNI	Domestically owned enterprise not part of an enterprise group
DOM_GROUP	Domestically owned enterprise part of an enterprise group
FOROWN	Foreign-owned enterprise
GLS	Foreign-owned enterprises with parent enterprise in Germany, Liechtenstein or Switzerland
AS	Foreign-owned enterprises with parent enterprise in Canada, Ireland, the UK, the US or South Africa
EURO	Foreign-owned enterprises with parent enterprise in an European country other than GLS or AS
OTHERS	Foreign-owned enterprises with parent enterprise in a country other than GLS

Source: Community Innovation Survey 3 Austria

This setup may be confusing at first, but allows to study the influence of ownership on innovation in great detail. For example, we are able to distinguish between effects due to group membership vis-à-vis foreign ownership. Moreover, we are able to study effects from the liability of foreignness - whether there is an advantage of enterprises from neighbouring countries with a common language over enterprises from other countries. Unfortunately, it is not possible to distinguish between domestic uninational and domestic multinational enterprise groups to examine the effects of multinationality.

5.2.2 Other Independent Variables

Independent variables other than the foreign ownership dummies employed in the analysis can be grouped in various classes.

A first class of these variables describes enterprise characteristics. Here, size is measured by the logarithmic number of employees (*LNEMP*). The data set also holds information about the number of university and 'Fachhochschule' graduates. We used this information to calculate the share of employees with tertiary education for each enterprise (*TERTSHR*). Embodied technology transfer to the enterprise is measured by the logarithmic amount of investment in capital goods per employee (*LNINVEST*). Additionally, we also include the share computer hardware has on overall investment (*INVCO*) of the enterprise to account for the importance of information and communication technologies for innovation. *EST* indicates that the enterprise has been established during the period the questionnaire refers to, which, by definition, increases the probability of innovation. *RD* indicates that the enterprise is engaged in permanent opposed to occasional or no R&D activity. The dummy *FUND* shows if the enterprise has received public funding for its innovation projects.

A second set of variables describes the target markets and market growth expectations of the enterprise. *EXSHR* measures export intensity of the enterprise. It is measured by exports as a percentage of turnover. *GROWTH* captures demand growth expectations and has a value of one if the enterprise expects growth in its main market.

We also use a set of five sectoral dummies which follows the classification of sectors according to technology intensity proposed by the OECD (see section 4). High-technology and medium-high technology sectors have been merged into one category because of the low number of high-technology enterprises in the Austrian sample. *SELT* is the reference case in the regressions. Moreover, some of the dependent variables described in the next section also serve as independent variables in some regressions. These variables are *LNIPC, CO,* and *RDENG.*

Table 5: Other independent variables

Category	Variable	Description
Enterprise characteristics	LNEMP	Number of employees, logarithm
	TERTSHR	Share of employees with tertiary education
	LNINVEST	Investment per employee in Euro, logarithm
	INVCO	Investment in computer hardware as a percentage of total investment
	EST	Enterprise has been established between 1998 and 2000
	RD	The enterprises is engaged in permanent R&D activity
	FUND	Enterprise received public financial support for innovation
	EXSHR	Exports as a percentage of turnover
	GROWTH	Growth expectations for the main market of the enterprise
Sectoral classification	SEMHT	High technology and medium-high technology sector according to OECD
	SEMLT	Medium-low technology sector according to OECD
	SELT	Low technology sector according to OECD
	SEKIS	Knowledge-intensive business services according to OECD
	SEOS	Other service sectors

Source: Community Innovation Survey 3 Austria

5.3 Dependent Variables

The choice between innovation activity indicators is a 'non-trivial' one, as Kleinknecht et al. (2002) pointed out. Therefore, we do not restrict the analysis of ownership effects on innovative behaviour to a single indicator; rather, we analyse the influence of foreign ownership on a broad spectrum of indicators ranging from innovation input indicators to innovation output indicators and indicators which deal with information sources and co-operative behaviour (Table 6).

5.3.1 Innovative Behaviour

The most basic aspect of innovative behaviour is whether the enterprise has introduced an innovation or not. The dummy variable *INNOV* takes the value of one for all enterprises which introduced technologically new or significantly improved products or processes to the enterprise, regardless of the success, and zero otherwise. The commitment towards research and development of the enterprise is captured by the dummy variable *RDENG*. *RDENG* takes a value of one if the enterprise has been engaged in R&D activities between 1998 and 2000 and zero otherwise.

The financial means devoted to innovation projects are measured by logarithm of total innovation expenditure per capita (*IPC*). Additionally, we include a measure for the intensity of research and development efforts (*RDYRS*), which indicates the share of R&D personnel in the workforce of the enterprise. If foreign-owned enterprises restrict themselves to the adaptation of products and processes we should find significant lower values in theses two variables, which, of course, could be associated with a similar or even higher innovativeness measured by *INNOV*.

Innovation output is measured by two variables: the dummy variable *INMAR* takes a value of one if the enterprise has launched a product innovation that is new to the market. The questionnaire does not indicate if this innovation is new to the Austrian or the international market. Another indicator of innovative output is *TURNIN* which measures the share of sales generated by new and significantly modified products on the overall turnover of the enterprise in 2000.

Table 6: Dependent variables

Category	Variable	Description
Selection equation	INNOV	Decision of the enterprise to carry out any innovation project
Innovative behaviour	LNIPC	Innovative expenditure per employee, logarithm
	RDYRS	R&D personnel intensity; R&D personnel per employee
	INMAR	Product innovation that is new to the market
	TURNIN	Share of turnover generated by new and significantly modified products
Embeddedness	SORINT	Information sources within the enterprise and the own group
	SOREXT	External information sources
	CO	Innovation co-operation
	CODOM	Domestic innovation co-operation
	COINT	International innovation co-operation

Source: Community Innovation Survey 3, Statistics Austria

5.3.2 Embeddedness in the Austrian Innovation System

Embeddedness refers to the degree enterprises draw on information and knowledge from their business environment and the surrounding innovation system. The CIS includes two indicators of embeddedness: the first one is the degree the enterprise utilized various information sources; the second one is innovation co-operation.

Information relevant for innovation can diffuse through various channels into the enterprise such as demonstration effects, imitation and reversed engineering, or loose supplier-customer-relationships. Compared to other channels of knowledge and information transfer, such as co-operative agreements, these information sources are far less formal, less intense, do not imply reciprocity, and may therefore be closer to the idea of spillovers as known in the international business literature (see Blomström and Kokko 1998, p. 3).

The CIS questionnaire covers nine different information sources which have been aggregated into two dummy variables, *SORINT* which covers all internal sources (within the own enterprise and within the group) and *SOREXT*, which covers all external sources, such as competitors, specialized literature, universities etc. The variables takes a value of one if the enterprise regards any internal or external source as important or very important.

A second indicator for embeddedness is the degree enterprises enter into innovation co-operations. Innovation co-operations are formal agreements on a contractual basis which include not only knowledge exchange but also allow sharing the risks of innovation projects or exploiting scale advantages to R&D. In contrast to information sources, co-operative arrangements involve an exchange in both directions and mutual learning.

In the CIS questionnaire, enterprises are asked if they entered any innovation co-operation and, if yes, about the type of partner(s). Possible partners include other enterprises within the MNE group, competitors, clients, suppliers, consultants, commercial R&D laboratories, public research centers and higher education organisations including universities. We also know the location of the partner from the questionnaire, but have no information about the frequency of co-operation or if it was a single event or a continuing relationship.

The results on innovation co-operation from the questionnaire have been condensed to three variables; *CO*, which indicates if the enterprise has co-operated at all, domestic co-operation (*CODOM*), and international co-operation (*COINT*).

6. Descriptive Analysis of Austrian CIS Data

The empirical analysis proceeds in three steps. We will first show some basic characteristics of the population and examine major differences between foreign-owned and domestically owned enterprises with descriptive statistics (chapter 6). In a second step, we examine how foreign ownership determines innovative behaviour vis-à-vis other variables in a multivariate regression analysis (chapter 7). Finally, we will rerun selected parts of the descriptive and multivariate analysis with a CIS sample covering firm-level observations from 15 European countries (chapter 8) to see if the Austrian results can be generalized for other countries.

6.1 Enterprise Characteristics

We begin with a comparison of enterprise characteristics between foreign-owned and domestically owned enterprises in a number of variables. Table 7 shows the mean values for employment, turnover, export share and the propensity to innovate for different groups of enterprises. The last two rows depict the difference between all foreign-owned and all domestically owned enterprises in the sample and present the results of a t-test on the null hypothesis of equal means between the foreign-owned and domestically owned enterprises. T-tests of the differences between all groups are provided in the Annex.

The differences between foreign-owned and domestically owned enterprises in Table 7 are large and mostly statistically significant (see also Table 28). Foreign-owned enterprises - on average - employ more personnel than domestically owned enterprises, have a higher turnover, exhibit a higher propensity to export and a employ more people with tertiary education.

Besides differences *between* the two groups of foreign-owned and domestically owned enterprises, we also find a considerable degree of heterogeneity *within* the two groups. Domestically owned non-group enterprises are significantly smaller than both foreign-owned and domestically owned group enterprises, employ significantly fewer personnel with tertiary education and show a lower propensity to export. Moreover, there is also a gap between enterprises belonging to a German, Liechtenstein or Swiss group and foreign-owned enterprises with a parent enterprise in another country. Enterprises in the latter group are smaller on average in terms of employment. GLS enterprises are also superior to domestically owned group enterprises in the number of employees and turnover. Together, both groups of foreign-owned enterprises have a higher turnover from exports than domestically owned enterprises.

Table 7: Ownership status and enterprise characteristics; all enterprises, means

Ownership status	Employment, persons	Turnover, 1,000 Euro	Share of exports on turnover	Tertiary employment as % of total employment
Domestically owned non-group	62	10,812	13%	4.8%
Domestically owned group	306	91,842	21%	6.3%
Foreign-owned without GLS	177	62,636	31%	9.3%
GLS	326	85,987	32%	7.5%
Diff. Foreign-Domestic and Sig.	+102	+34,117	+19% pts.	+2.6% pts.
Significance	**	***	***	**

Note: * significant at 10%; ** significant at 5%; *** significant at 1%, % pts are percentage points.

Source: Community Innovation Survey 3, Statistics Austria

Further major differences between foreign-owned and domestically owned enterprises can be found in their sectoral affiliation. Foreign-owned enterprises, in particular GLS enterprises, are more often present in high-technology or medium-high technology sectors (Table 8). Domestically owned enterprises, in turn, are overrepresented in low-technology and medium-low technology sectors and in the case of domestically owned group enterprises in knowledge-intensive service industries such as banking, consulting, or business services. Differences between GLS enterprises and enterprises from other countries are not significant.

As discussed in section 4, innovation is very much sector-specific; we can therefore assume that differences in sectoral affiliation between foreign-owned and domestically owned enterprises also affect variables related to innovation. The last row of Table 8 shows that this is in fact the case. The propensity to innovate declines steadily with the technology intensity; enterprises in low-technology industries show an average propensity of only 46% compared to 80% in high technology and medium high technology industries. As a consequence, different sectoral affiliations will affect innovativeness and may explain gaps between foreign- and domestically owned enterprises. We will therefore control for sectoral affiliation in the multivariate analysis.

Table 8: Sectoral affiliation according to OECD classification, all enterprises, means

Ownership status	High and medium high technology	Medium low technology	Low technology	Knowledge intensive services	Other services
Domestically owned non-group	6%	10%	23%	5%	56%
Domestically owned group	10%	11%	9%	44%	26%
Foreign-owned without GLS	15%	6%	12%	11%	57%
GLS	22%	8%	7%	11%	52%
Diff. Foreign-Domestic	+11.4%pts.	-2.9% pts.	-9% pts.	-8.7% pts.	+9.4% pts.
Significance	***	-	***	**	***
Share of innovators	80%	54%	46%	61%	25%

Note: * significant at 10%; ** significant at 5%; *** significant at 1%, % pts are percentage points.

Source: Community Innovation Survey 3, Statistics Austria

6.2 Innovative Behaviour

We find further differences between foreign-owned and domestically owned enterprises in basic indicators describing the innovative behaviour of the enterprises (Table 9). The numbers (except the first column) now include only innovative enterprises. Differences between all foreign-owned and all domestically owned enterprises including their statistical significance are again given in the last two rows of the table. The differences between all four groups and their statistical significance are reported in the Annex (Table 28).

We first look at the propensity to innovate. In total, the average foreign-owned enterprise has a higher probability to be innovative than the average domestically owned enterprise, as can be seen from the last two rows in the first column of Table 9. The chance to find an innovative enterprise among domestically owned group enterprises is more than two times higher than among domestically owned non-group enterprises. The share of innovators is also significantly higher among GLS enterprises and other foreign-owned enterprises compared to domestically owned non-group enterprises.

Average innovative expenditure in absolute terms is highest for GLS enterprises, followed by domestically owned groups and other foreign-owned enterprises. The higher innovative expenditure is also persistent if we look at median values (which are not reported in the table). It is therefore not caused by only a few enterprises with superior expenditure but rather reflects differences through the whole enterprise population.

Interesting results reveal if we relate innovative expenditure to turnover or the number of employees (last two columns of Table 9). First, we see that domestically owned non-group enterprises have higher relative innovative expenditure than domestically owned group enterprises. Since non-group enterprises are considerably smaller, this may be a result of the U-shaped relationship between size and innovative activity (Dogson and Rothwell 1994) and point to some specific advantages of small firms discussed in section 4.

Second, we see that the gap between GLS enterprises and other groups in the sample diminishes once we look at intensities and not absolute values. The gap is not statistically significant anymore in most cases (Table 28). Foreign-owned enterprises show an advantage over domestically owned enterprises in innovative expenditure per employee, but a disadvantage if we measure innovative expenditure as a percentage of turnover. This demonstrates the need to relate on more than one indicator in comparisons of innovative performance between the two groups.

Table 9: Indicators of innovative behaviour and performance, only innovators, means

Ownership status	Propensity to innovate	Innovative expenditure, 1,000 Euro	Innovative expenditure as % of turnover	Innovative expenditure per employee, Euro
Domestically owned non-group	29%	696	14.3%	7,164
Domestically owned group	63%	2,583	9.3%	6,328
Foreign-owned without GLS	44%	2,026	9.4%	5,851
GLS	51%	4,896	10.3%	8,769
Diff. Foreign-Domestic	+6% pts	+1,878	- 1.6% pts	+ 1,000
Significance	*	**	-	-

Note: * significant at 10%; ** significant at 5%; *** significant at 1%, % pts are percentage points.

The first column is based on all enterprises, the preceding column include only innovative enterprises.

Source: Community Innovation Survey 3, Statistics Austria

Foreign-owned enterprises also exhibit a superior performance in other innovation-related variables (Table 10), in particular if they are affiliated to a German, Lichtenstein or Swiss enterprise group. GLS enterprises employ on average more R&D personnel in absolute and relative terms than any other group. They have also a higher propensity to introduce products and processes new to the market compared to all other groups. Foreign-owned group enterprises with parent enterprises in other countries are also superior to domestically owned enterprises (esp. if they are no group members), but do not match the performance of GLS-owned enterprises.

Another important result from Table 9 and Table 10 is that foreign-owned enterprises are in many variables more similar to domestically owned group enterprises than to domestically owned non-group enterprises. This reflects advantages from group membership discussed in 4.2.4 which are shared by all enterprises affiliated to a group regardless of the parent country.

Table 10: Indicators of innovative behaviour and performance (2), only innovators, means

Ownership status	Number of R&D personnel	R&D personnel as % of total employment	Propensity to introduce products new to the market	Share of turnover from new products
Domestically owned non-group	9	7.8%	39.4%	29.7%
Domestically owned group	23	5.8%	44.5%	22.6%
Foreign-owned without GLS	24	5.3%	58.8%	29.6%
GLS	46	8.1%	65.2%	29.0%
Diff. Foreign-Domestic	+20.7	+0.7% pts.	+19.9% pts.	+3.8% pts.
Sig.	**	-	**	-

Note: * significant at 10%; ** significant at 5%; *** significant at 1%, % pts are percentage points.

Source: Community Innovation Survey 3, Statistics Austria

6.3 Composite Innovation Indicators

Indicators such as R&D personnel or the share of turnover from new products have been criticised by a number of authors in recent years as being too simple to reproduce the complex nature of innovation. As a consequence, different composite indicators combining the indicators presented above have been proposed that grasp various dimensions of innovation behaviour and strategy in one variable. An example is the work of Arundel and Hollanders (2005) who distinguish between *strategic innovators, intermittent innovators*, *technology modifiers* and *technology adaptors*. The categories are identified via a combination of the variables *degree market novelty*, *permanent R&D activity*, *in-house R&D*, *main market* and *co-operation*. Strategic innovators for example, the type of firm most likely to yield significant innovations of economy-wide importance, is defined as a firms that have developed innovation at least partly in-house, perform R&D on a continuous basis, have introduced at least one product that is new to their market, and are active in national or international markets.

The taxonomy of Arundel and Hollanders is an excellent tool to analyze inter-industry and inter-country differences in innovation behaviour, but requires a high data quality and the absence of missing values due to the large number of variables used. A simpler set of composite indicators has been proposed by

Carter Bloch (2007b). We will use this taxonomy in this chapter. Besides simplicity, a second advantage is that Bloch focuses on novelty as the main distinguishing criteria between various patterns of innovative activity. This approach corresponds which the dichotomy of competence-creating and competence-exploiting strategies of enterprises presented in the previous chapter.

Bloch (2007b) places a greater emphasis on output measures, particularly whether product innovations are new to the market or new to the firm only. The 'market' comprises the firm's own competitive environment. Hence, a product innovation new to the market of an enterprise that operates on international markets may be considered of a higher value than a market novelty from an enterprise that operates on the domestic market. Carter Bloch (2007b, p. 2) proposes the following four composite indicators:

1. New to market, international market

2. New to market, domestic OR new to firm, international

3. New to firm, domestic (and in house)

4. New to firm, domestic, adopted

The combination of international market focus and the introduction of market novelties which characterizes the first indicator can be interpreted as the most extensive mandate a foreign-owned subsidiary can receive from the parent enterprise: world-wide responsibility for the development of market novelties in a particular product group. It is equivalent to the notion of *competence-creating* innovation strategies presented in the previous chapters. Subsidiaries which pursue such a strategy can be regarded as centres of competence within their enterprise groups, because they were the first (including other subsidiaries) to introduce a new product or process to the international market.

The second indicator includes enterprises that introduced market novelties and are focussed on the national market or focus on international markets and introduced innovations new to the firm. We may also assume that enterprises which exhibit such behaviour play a significant part in the innovative strategies of their groups that goes beyond product adaptation. This can include a regional or world-wide mandate.

Competence-exploiting behaviour, in contrast, is mainly found in the last two categories of Bloch's taxonomy which include innovators that developed innovations to the national, regional or local market or adapted existing products and processes for the national market.

We apply the composite indicators to our dataset in Table 11. Foreign-owned enterprises focus to a higher degree on innovations new to international markets than domestically owned enterprises. In particular, about a third of all GLS-owned innovating enterprises relate to this category. The difference in the share of enterprises that have introduced innovations new to international markets between foreign-owned and domestically owned enterprises is highly significant. A higher share of foreign-owned enterprises can also be found in the second category that identifies innovations new to the domestic market, or innovations new to the firm introduced at international markets. Both results are a strong indication that foreign-owned enterprises predominantly pursue competence-creating strategies in Austria.

On contrary, the last two indicators show significantly higher means for domestically owned enterprises, in particular domestically owned non-group enterprises. Innovations new to the firm and focussed on domestic markets are the dominant mode of innovation in this group. This result is a clear rejection of the assumption that foreign-owned enterprises in Austria would predominantly pursue competence-exploiting innovation strategies.

Table 11: Composite indicators of innovative behaviour and performance, only innovators, means

Ownership status	New to market, international market	New to market, domestic OR new to firm, international	New to firm, domestic (and in house)	New to firm, domestic, adopted
Domestically owned non-group	15%	30%	40%	15%
Domestically owned group	23%	31%	33%	12%
Foreign-owned without GLS	29%	37%	27%	8%
GLS	35%	40%	21%	3%
Diff. Foreign-Domestic	+12.9 pts.	+ 7.8 pts.	- 12.7 pts.	- 8.0 pts.
Sig.	***	-	**	**

Note: * significant at 10%; ** significant at 5%; *** significant at 1%, % pts are percentage points.

Source: Community Innovation Survey 3, Statistics Austria

6.4 Embeddedness in the Austrian Innovation System

Finally, we take a look at the embeddedness of foreign-owned enterprises compared to their domestically owned counterparts. As discussed above, innovation co-operations are formal agreements on a contractual basis which go well beyond a simple exchange of information in terms of formalisation, durability and the commitment of the relationship. One may suspect an advantage for domestically owned enterprises and a stronger embeddedness in their home country's innovation system when it comes to innovation co-operation. Foreign-owned enterprises are embedded internal MNE innovation networks and may not need to rely on co-operation in their host countries.

But this is not the case, as can be seen in Table 12. Foreign-owned enterprises show a higher propensity for innovation co-operation than their domestically owned counterparts. Foreign-owned enterprises are only slightly less active in domestic innovation co-operation, and this lower propensity to co-operate with domestic partners is compensated by a higher willingness to enter international co-operation. Readers should note that the numbers in the last three columns of the table show shares of a particular type of co-operation as percentage of all co-operating (not innovating) enterprises.

Table 12: Indicators of co-operative behaviour, means

Ownership status	Propensity for innovation co-operation	Propensity for domestic innovation co-operation	Propensity for international innovation co-operation	Propensity for co-operation with domestic science+
Domestically owned non-group	16.8%	84.8%	51.2%	27.2%
Domestically owned group	29.3%	84.9%	61.6%	57.5%
Foreign-owned without GLS	24.5%	50.0%	75.0%	33.3%
GLS	33.9%	84.7%	61.9%	57.1%
Diff. Foreign-Domestic	+5.9% pts	- 0.8 %pts	+3.7% pts	+6.5% pts
Sig.	-	-	-	-

Note: * significant at 10%; ** significant at 5%; *** significant at 1%, % pts are percentage points.

The first column includes all innovators, the three last rows only co-operating enterprises. The numbers in the last three columns of the table show shares of a particular type of co-operation as percentage of all *co-operating* (not innovating) enterprises. +Domestic science base includes domestic universities, private and public R&D centres.

Source: Community Innovation Survey 3, Statistics Austria

Again, major differences exist within the two groups of foreign-owned and domestically owned enterprises. GLS and domestically owned group enterprises constantly exhibit a higher propensity to co-operate than domestically owned non-group enterprises and enterprises from another country than Germany, Switzerland or Liechtenstein. GLS enterprises behave like domestically owned group enterprises in many aspects.

A particularly interesting result is revealed in the last column of Table 12 which relates to differences in the propensity to co-operate with the domestic science base – universities, private and public research organisations. Science-industry co-operation is seen by many researchers as crucial for well-functioning innovation systems. Descriptive statistics reveals that both groups of foreign-owned enterprises do better (but not statistically significant) than domestically owned non-group enterprises in this type of innovation co-operation. This indicates that these enterprises are well-integrated into the Austrian national system of innovation. In particular, the share of GLS-owned enterprises which enter co-operations with academia exceeds that share of domestically owned non-group enterprises by far and is similar to Austrian group enterprises.

Based on the descriptive statistics, we find that foreign-owned enterprises, on average, are more often innovative, spend more on their innovative activities, employ more researchers and are more often engaged in co-operative arrangements than the average domestically owned enterprise. Firms with a strategic focus on market novelties for international markets are clearly overrepresented in the group of foreign-owned enterprises. On contrary, firms that do incremental innovations and adaptations to local markets are underrepresented in the group of foreign-owned enterprises compared to domestically owned firms.

These results are clearly in favour of the assumption that foreign-owned enterprises pursue competence-creating strategies in Austria. They do not only rely on existing knowledge, but create new one through R&D and other innovation activities. It is, however, too early to conclude that foreign-owned enterprises are superior in innovative activities *due to their ownership status*. The previous tables have shown that differences exist not only in inputs and performance, but also in size, the propensity to export, sectoral affiliation etc. We know from the discussion in chapter 4 that these and other factors have a major influence on the innovative behaviour of enterprises. In order to discriminate between ownership and other factors likely to influence the propensity to innovate, such as size, sectoral affiliation, investment or human capital, we will employ multivariate regression analysis in the following chapter.

7. Multivariate Analysis of Austrian CIS Data

7.1 Econometric Approach

The econometric analysis employs a two equation sample selection model to test the assumptions stated above. This model is a standard tool in various evaluation studies, for example in the evaluation of labour market programmes. We will therefore focus on the rationale and the pre-conditions for the application of the model and give only brief technical explanations. A detailed description can be found in many econometric textbooks (for example, Wooldridge 2002, p. 616ff, or Kennedy 2003, p. 281ff).

This type of model is appropriate because data is truncated due to the questionnaire design; we observe some variables such as size, export intensity or sectoral affiliation for *all* enterprises. A number of other variables such as innovative expenditure, however, can only be observed for *innovative* enterprises. Thus, the availability of most dependent variables – and therefore the composition of the sample - depends on whether or not the enterprises have introduced an innovation. The group of enterprises for which we have data on innovative behaviour constitute a non-random, self-selected sub-sample of the whole population. Self-selection is not a problem if we just want to draw conclusions about the sub-sample. It may be, however, a source for biased results if we want to examine facts about the whole population.

Self-selection is created by an unmeasured variable (we may it call "innovative capacity" in our case) which affects the dependent variable in two ways. First, it creates a non-random sample. Second, the unmeasured variable affects the dependent variable. It is likely that non-innovative enterprises would also exhibit a below-average innovation performance, because they are lacking innovative capacity, like the resources, incentives or other preconditions for successful innovation.

Thus we may overestimate some determinants of innovation if we only consider innovators. Ordinary Least Squares regression based on this truncated population would yield biased results on the determinants of innovative behaviour including foreign ownership. Linear regression that does not take into account sample selection may overestimate the influence of these common explanatory variables, because the decision to start innovative activity may be influenced by the same variables which also determine innovative performance (e.g. innovation expenditure).

The set-up of the empirical analysis corrects for this fact. We employ a Heckman selection model (Heckman 1976; Crepon et al. 1998). The main idea of this type of models is to add a second equation (selection equation), which determines whether an enterprise is included in the sample or not. Simply speaking, we then include the probability that an enterprise is included in the sample as an additional right-hand variable in the function equation which examines the association between the variable of interest and a number of independent variables.

This idea is described in equations (1) and (2). Such a model adds to the regression model of interest:

$$y = x\beta + u \qquad (1)$$

a selection equation that relates the selection criteria (s) to a set of exogenous explanatory variables z:

$$s = z\gamma + v \qquad (2)$$

where s is one if the enterprise was selected and hence we observe y, and zero otherwise. X and z are sets of exogenous explanatory variables, β and γ are their coefficients, u and v the error terms of the two regressions.

The expected value of y conditional that s = 1, equals $x\beta$ plus an error term including the inverse Mills ratio at $z\gamma$:

$$E(y|z,s=1) = x\beta + \rho\lambda(z\gamma) \qquad (3)$$

The coefficient γ is estimated by a probit regression, x is estimated by a linear regression if the dependent variable is continuous and a probit regression if it has a binary outcome. A full specification of equations (1) and (2) is given in 7.2 The Heckman model will be estimated with the statistical software package STATA (function heckman and heckprob). STATA computes selection and function equation simultaneously by maximum likelihood estimation.

The findings of chapter 6 suggest that there exist differences not only between foreign-owned and domestically owned enterprises, but also within the two groups. For example, we found that domestically owned enterprises are more similar to foreign-owned enterprises in size and export intensity than to domestically non-group enterprises. There are also large differences between GLS-owned and Anglo-Saxon owned enterprises in some variables. Therefore, a more differentiated approach to identify the effects of foreign ownership than just to compare all foreign-owned with all domestically owned enterprises is needed.

We will compare four different cases (see also Table 13):

- All domestically enterprises vs. all foreign-owned owned enterprises.
- Domestically owned group enterprises vs. domestically owned non-group enterprises vs. all foreign-owned enterprises.
- Domestically owned group enterprises vs. domestically owned non-group enterprises vs. GLS-owned enterprises vs. Anglo-Saxon owned enterprises vs. enterprises from other European countries.
- Domestically owned group enterprises vs. domestically owned non-group enterprises vs. GLS-owned enterprises vs. all other foreign-owned enterprises.

Domestically owned group enterprises serve in all but the first case as the reference category.

Table 13: Grouping of ownership dummy variables

Case	1	2	3	4
All domestically owned enterprises	R			
Domestically owned group enterprises (DOM_GROUP)		R	R	R
Domestically owned non-group enterprises (DOM_UNI)		x	x	x
All foreign-owned enterprises with a parent enterprise from an European country other than Germany, Switzerland, Liechtenstein or Anglo-Saxon countries (EURO)			x	
All foreign-owned enterprises with a parent enterprise from an Anglo-Saxon country (AS)			x	
All foreign-owned enterprises with a parent enterprise from Germany, Switzerland or Liechtenstein (GLS)			x	x
All foreign-owned enterprises except Anglo-Saxon or GLS -owned (OTHERS)				x
All foreign-owned enterprises (FOROWN)	x	x		

Note: R: Reference category

Econometric studies that use a large number of dummy variables – such as our econometric setup - may face the problem of perfect or near perfect multicollinearity of independent variables when two or more dummies are approximately linear with each other (see Wooldridge 2002 or other textbooks). Multicollinearity can also occur in regressions that use data sets where some dummy variables are one or null or one for most observations. In this case, the dummy is highly similar to the intercept term of the regression. Multicollinearity causes large standard errors of the estimated coefficients, since small changes in the independent variables may lead to large variations in the coefficients.

Econometric textbooks provide advise how to deal with multicollinearity. First, multicollinearity can be detected in advance by a careful examination of the theoretical and empirical literature for possible relationships between the independent variables. For example, we know from previous studies that foreign ownership tends to be positively correlated with size. This relationship, however, is weak, as can be seen in correlation matrix of the independent variables in Table 27. There are no other independent variables which are highly correlated. We can therefore assume that there are no sources of multicollinearity in our data.

7.2 Empirical Model

Based on the discussions of the factors that influence innovative activity in 4.1, we now formulate the two equations of the empirical model. To examine the effects of ownership on innovative activity, we first estimate the following model of the propensity to innovative which also serves as the selection equation:

$$INNOV_{i} = \alpha_{k} + \beta_{1k}FOROWN + \beta_{2k}LNEMP + \beta_{3k}GROWTH + \beta_{4k}TERTSHR + \beta_{5k}EXSHR + \beta_{6k}LNINVEST + \beta_{7k}INVCO + \beta_{8k}EST + \beta_{9k}SEMHT + \beta_{10k}SEMLT + \beta_{11k}SEKIS + \beta_{12k}SEOS$$

Detailed descriptions of the independent variables are given in 5.2. The propensity to innovate is associated to the log firm size, growth expectations of the enterprise, the share of employees with tertiary education, export intensity, the log of investment, the share of ICT investment on total investment, whether or not the enterprises has been established during the observation period and the sectoral dummies of technology intensity according to the OECD.

The second equation of the Heckman model relates various measures of innovative input, output, and co-operative behaviour to the right-hand variables. For innovation intensity LNIPC, it is specified as follows:

$$LNIPC_{i} = \alpha_{k} + \beta_{1k}FOROWN + \beta_{2k}LNEMP + \beta_{3k}GROWTH + \beta_{4k}EST + \beta_{5k}RD + \beta_{6k}FUND + \beta_{7k}EXSHR + \beta_{8k}LNINVEST + \beta_{9k}INVCO + \beta_{10k}SEMHT + \beta_{11k}SEMLT + \beta_{12k}SEKIS + \beta_{13k}SEOS$$

We use a similar specification with minor adjustments for all dependent variables except co-operation.

7.3 Regression Results

7.3.1 Innovative Behaviour

Propensity to Innovate

We first estimate the selection equation for the Heckit model with the propensity to innovate as the dependent variable. This selection equation – as explained in the previous section – is needed to account for the effect that some data is only available for innovative enterprises. Moreover, the outcomes of this estimation are also an interesting result itself, because it tells about the linkage between innovativeness and foreign ownership.

Results from the regression analysis are reported in Table 29 for all four combinations of ownership dummies described above. The regression analysis does not confirm the results of the descriptive analysis of Table 9 that foreign-owned enterprises in general are more innovative than domestically owned enterprises (Table 29, case 1). Rather, foreign-owned enterprises are more innovative because they differ in a number of other independent variables: they are larger, have a higher growth expectation in their target markets, have a higher share of exports on turnover, invest more, and operate more frequently in high-technology sectors.

Another result from the descriptive analysis is confirmed by multivariate analysis. There is indeed a significant difference between domestically owned group and domestically owned non-group enterprises that cannot be explained by other right-hand variables such as size, sector or export intensity. The results from Table 29 indicate that group membership indeed has a positive influence on innovativeness (case 2).

More heterogeneity appears when we split up the sample into various subgroups of foreign-owned enterprises (Table 29, cases 3 and 4) Subsidiaries with a parent enterprise from a non-GLS country have a significantly lower propensity to innovate than domestically owned group enterprises. This is not the case for GLS-owned enterprises. The result confirms the finding of Table 9 and is a strong indication for effects from the liability of foreignness.

The further analysis employs the Heckit approach presented in section 7.1.

Innovative Input

Once foreign-owned enterprises decide to engage in innovation activities, innovative input measured by the level of innovation expenditure per capita (*lnIPC;* Table 30) or R&D personnel intensity (*RDYRS;* Table 31) is significantly positively related with export intensity, the existence of permanent R&D activities at the enterprise, the availability of public funding, sectoral affiliation and investment intensity. Moreover, innovative input is significantly negatively affected by the size of the enterprise. This is an unusual result, but in line with theory that predict different advantages of both small and large enterprises in innovation and previous findings which found a U-shaped relationship between the two variables.

In contrast to the findings from the descriptive analysis, in the multivariate analysis the relationship between innovative input and ownership is statistically insignificant. There is no indication that the innovation effort of foreign-owned enterprises is lower and therefore no support for the assumption that foreign-owned enterprises pursue competence-exploiting strategies. The only exception is R&D personnel intensity, which is significantly higher if an enterprise is under German, Swiss or Liechtenstein ownership compared to the average domestically owned group enterprise after controlling for right-hand variables.

Innovative Output

Foreign ownership does not significantly affect innovative output, either. We neither see an influence on the probability to generate market novelties (*INMAR*, Table 32*)*, nor on the economic significance of innovation, measured by the shares of new products on turnover (*TURNIN*, Table 33). The probability to generate market novelties (*INMAR*) is significantly higher for larger enterprises and enterprises in growing markets. Moreover, we see a positive relationship between permanent R&D activities and the ability to create market novelties.

In the case of the economic significance of innovation, the regression results only indicate a positive relationship between innovative expenditure per capita (*lnIPC*) and *TURNIN* in all four cases at the usual significance levels. The fact that only one out of 13 right-hand variables is significant at the 5% error level can be interpreted as an indication of the inherently uncertain nature of innovative activity and the fact that innovative output is randomly distributed between enterprises of various sizes and sectors (Marsili and Salter 2005). The probability to generate market novelties is positively associated with enterprise size, growth expectations and permanent R&D activities. In contrast to *TURNIN*, *INMAR* is not related to the level of innovative expenditure.

To sum up, the results show that foreign ownership is not associated with a higher or lower innovative input or output once we control for right-hand variables. The assumption that foreign-owned enterprises pursue competence-exploiting strategies therefore has to be rejected with respect to both, innovative input and output. In contrast, the non-significance of foreign ownership dummies indicates the presence of competence-creating strategies.

7.3.2 Embeddedness

Information Sources

One of the advantages of being a subsidiary of a multinational enterprise compared to an unaffiliated enterprise is the availability of internal firm-specific assets and access to the knowledge and information of the enterprise group. The regression results show that internal information sources are indeed significantly more appreciated by foreign-owned than by domestically owned group enterprises. In contrast to other regressions, the results of Table 34 only include foreign-owned enterprises and domestically owned group enterprises because domestically owned non-group enterprises - by definition - cannot draw on information sources from within their enterprise group. The results of the Wald chi^2 statistics[7] indicate a probability higher than 10% that at all coefficients equal zero. Therefore, the results presented above have a higher conclusiveness than the one on information sources.

Despite a higher valuation for internal information sources, foreign ownership has no adverse effect on the usage of information from external sources which also includes the science system (Table 35). Therefore, we conclude that internal sources are not regarded as a substitute for external information sources, as could be expected in the case of asset-exploiting behaviour. We therefore conclude that foreign-owned enterprises in Austria rely on external information sources additional to their internal sources.

Co-operation

Differences between foreign-owned and domestically owned enterprises with respect to co-operation behaviour may result from richer internal knowledge sources and a stronger embeddedness of MNE subsidiaries in MNE intra-firm networks. In the case of competence-exploiting behaviour, we expect to find that foreign ownership is associated with a lower propensity to co-operate with domestic organisations of the home country.

Table 36 shows that co-operative behaviour is positively associated with permanent R&D activities, export orientation and the level of investment. Moreover, we see that enterprises in the service sector exhibit a higher propensity to co-operate compared to enterprises in low-technology sectors. The results, however, give no indication that foreign ownership negatively affects the propensity to co-operate in general. We see that only Anglo-Saxon ownership negatively

---

7 The Wald chi^2 statistics tests joint significance and is equivalent to the F-Test in the linear regression.

affects co-operation (Table 36, case 4). This finding is discussed in more detail below.

Following Cassiman and Veugelers (2002), we have added an additional right-hand variable that measures the importance of incoming spillovers by the perceived importance of external sources of information to the enterprise. CIS asks for a judgement on the importance of various external sources of information (suppliers, customers, competitors ...). We use factor analysis to reduce these judgements to one variable which is the score of a one-factor solution of the factor analysis. This one-factor solution is the only solution with an eigenvalue larger than 1. This variable (sorext) is statistically significant and positively related to the propensity to enter co-operation.

In the regressions of Table 37 and Table 38, we distinguish between domestic and international co-operation. Here, we do not have the same statistical confidence in the result like in the previous ones since the results are based on a considerably lower number of cases; only one out of five innovative enterprises co-operates in the sample. The Wald chi^2 test of the hypothesis that all coefficients are zero cannot be rejected only in three of the eight cases of Table 37 and Table 38 at usual significance levels.

The results of Table 37 are surprising, likewise; we expected to find a negative influence on the willingness to co-operate with domestic organisations due to the richness of MNE-internal knowledge sources in the case of competence-exploiting strategies. Foreign ownership, however, shows no effect compared to domestic group enterprises whereas being a domestically owned non-group enterprise significantly decreases (case 3). Again, the only exception is the group of Anglo-Saxon owned enterprises. Enterprises of this group have entered no domestic co-operation.

The comparable degree of domestic co-operation shows that foreign-owned subsidiaries are strongly embedded in the Austrian national innovation system, even stronger than domestically owned non-group members. This finding fits with the results on information sources, which showed that knowledge and information from external sources is not a substitute, but absorbed in *addition* to internal resources.

Even more surprising is the case of international co-operation (Table 38). It is neither positively nor negatively affected by foreign ownership, an important result given that the co-operation variables in our analysis only reflect *external*, not internal international co-operation. The results indicate that foreign-owned enterprises enjoy a relatively high level of independence in their innovative activities; otherwise, co-operations with partners outside of Austria would have been formed by the subsidiaries in the country of the partner or by the central

R&D department of the parent enterprise itself. We have, however, also to consider in this case that the Wald chi^2 test does not indicate that all coefficients are different from null at the usual confidence levels.

With respect to the two assumptions stated above, we find only little support for the statement that foreign-owned enterprises in Austria pursue competence-exploiting strategies. We do not observe that foreign ownership negatively affects the likelihood of an enterprise to enter into national or international co-operative arrangements. This observation points to a high degree of embeddedness into the Austrian innovation system. GLS-owned enterprises and enterprises owned by MNEs from other European countries (excl. Anglo-Saxon countries) do not significantly differ from domestically owned group enterprises in their likelihood to co-operate with national and international partners. Only the Anglo-Saxon owned enterprises seem to be different; there is no collaboration activity with Austrian partners of what ever type.

We therefore have to reject the assumption that foreign-owned enterprises pursue competence-exploiting strategies with respect to innovative behaviour and embeddedness.

7.3.3 Effects from the Liability of Foreignness

We argued that the liability of foreignness (LOF) and cultural proximity in particular matters for innovation and embeddedness. We assumed that GLS-owned enterprises exhibit a superior performance over enterprises from other countries because they are closest to domestically owned enterprises as well as possible external co-operation partners in terms of language and culture. The descriptive analysis of chapter 6 indeed pointed to a superior performance of GLS-owned enterprises compared to Anglo-Saxon and European-owned enterprises.

The multivariate analysis only partly confirms this result. Table 14 gives compares all dependent variables for the significance of the home country dummies. In five out of ten variables, there is no significant influence of these dummies.

Table 14: Effects from the liability of foreignness: summary of regression results

Variable	Effect from the LOF	Reference Case
INNOV	-EURO ** -AS *	DOM_GROUP
LNIPC	...	DOM_GROUP
RDYRS	+GLS *	DOM_GROUP
INMAR	...	DOM_GROUP
TURNIN	...	DOM_GROUP
SORINT	+EURO ***	DOM_GROUP
SOREXT	...	DOM_GROUP
CO	-AS *** -Others *	DOM_GROUP
CODOM	-AS (No domestic co-operation) -Others**	DOM_GROUP
COINT	...	DOM_GROUP

Note: * significant at 10%; ** significant at 5%; *** significant at 1%, % pts are percentage points.

- (+) indicates a negative effect of foreign ownership. LOF: Liability of Foreignness.

Source: Community Innovation Survey 3, Statistics Austria

Contrary to the descriptive analysis, the results of the multivariate analysis do not indicate that GLS ownership is associated to a superior performance compared to domestically owned group enterprises. On contrary, there is only a significantly positive influence of GLS ownership on the average number of R&D personnel.

In three of the ten variables, Anglo-Saxon and / or European ownership negatively influences innovative performance and embeddedness. Anglo-Saxon enterprises exhibit a significantly lower propensity to undertake R&D activities and to enter into domestic co-operations, but there is no general pattern that this group would perform worse in all variables. We draw the conclusion from these findings that Anglo-Saxon owned enterprises in Austria follow competence-exploiting strategies to a higher extent than enterprises from other countries.

7.4 Summary and Conclusions from the Empirical Analysis

The empirical analysis has revealed the following results:

Based on the descriptive statistics, we find that foreign-owned enterprises - on average - are more innovative, spend more on their innovative activities, employ more researchers and co-operate more often than the average domestically owned enterprise. The gap between foreign-owned and domestically owned enterprises widens if we compare domestically owned enterprises with enterprises originating from Austria's neighbouring countries Germany, Liechtenstein or Switzerland. Moreover, there is also a gap between domestically owned group enterprises and domestically owned non-group enterprises. This shows the heterogeneity within the broad categories of foreign-owned or domestically owned enterprises and demonstrates the need for an analysis that distinguishes different sub-groups within these categories.

Multivariate analysis suggests that the impact of foreign ownership on innovative behaviour is neutral. Once foreign-owned enterprises decide to innovate, the impact of foreign ownership on the outcome variable is mostly not statistically significant. We neither find a superior innovative output, nor a lower innovative input between the two groups. Moreover, foreign ownership is not associated with a lower degree of embeddedness in the domestic innovation system in general. Many differences between the two groups found in descriptive statistics can therefore be explained by size, sectoral affiliation, export intensity, or investment levels rather than by foreign ownership.

The results from both, descriptive and multivariate analysis are clearly in favour of the assumption that foreign-owned enterprises pursue competence-creating strategies in Austria. We can reject the assumption that foreign-owned enterprises in Austria would predominantly follow competence-exploiting strategies. Austrian subsidiaries of multinational enterprises actively create new knowledge through innovation and R&D activities, instead of exploiting existing knowledge, and play an active role in enhancing the stock of knowledge and technologies available in their enterprise group.

The results with respect to the liability of foreignness are mixed. As expected, there is virtually no difference between GLS-owned and domestically owned enterprises. Anglo-Saxon and European-owned enterprises, in contrast, show a significantly inferior performance in some variables, but there is no general pattern that one group would perform worse in all variables. We draw the conclusion that Anglo-Saxon owned enterprises pursue competence-exploiting strategies to a higher extent than enterprises from other countries.

Foreign ownership can therefore not be regarded as an important determinant of innovative behaviour and embeddedness of enterprises. Innovativeness and the creation of new products is rather related to other factors, such as size of the enterprise, its technological capabilities, incentives from the market, or appropriability conditions and technological opportunity reflected by its sectoral affiliation.

8. An International Perspective on Foreign Ownership and Innovation

The final chapter of the empirical analysis puts the Austrian results in an international perspective. We will first review existing studies on foreign ownership and innovation from a number of countries. In a second step, we will rerun the analysis of the previous chapters with a sample of CIS data containing nearly 50,000 observations from 15 countries. We will then compare the international results with the results from Austria to see if there are any similarities between countries regarding foreign ownership and innovation.

8.1 Previous Results on Foreign Ownership and Innovation

The availability of CIS data for a number of European countries brought about a growing number of studies on innovative behaviour of foreign-owned enterprises in recent years. The most comprehensive work on the effects of foreign ownership in recent years has been done for the Nordic countries (Ebersberger and Lööf 2004, 2005; Ebersberger et al. 2005). Ebersberger and Lööf (2005) use CIS data for Denmark, Iceland, Finland, Norway and Sweden and a model specification that is only slightly different from the one employed in this study.

In a descriptive analysis, Ebersberger and Lööf (2005) illustrate that foreign-owned enterprises have a higher innovative performance in all five Nordic countries. Moreover, the data shows larger differences in innovative behaviour between enterprises *from different countries* than between foreign-owned and domestically owned enterprises *of one country*. This indicates a strong influence of national innovation systems and the existence of incentives and framework conditions that influence both, foreign-owned and domestically owned enterprises.

The multivariate analysis of Ebersberger and Lööf (2005) reveals that foreign-owned exhibit a similar innovative input and a higher innovative output than domestically owned enterprises in most cases. The embeddedness of foreign-owned enterprises in intra-firm networks is higher than in the case of domestically owned enterprises[8]. A different result is found for the embeddedness of foreign-owned enterprises in the domestic innovation system. Foreign-owned enterprises show no difference to domestically owned enterprises. The only exception is Sweden, where Anglo-Saxon owned enterprises exhibit a higher (and not a lower, like in the case of Austria) propensity to co-operate with domestic universities.

Balcet and Evangelista (2005) examine the innovative strategies of foreign-owned enterprises in Italy with CIS2 data. As a main result, they find that for-

[8] Eberberger and Lööf (2005) only include group enterprises in their analysis

eign-owned subsidiaries show a higher propensity to innovate, rely more on R&D activities and tend to cooperate less with other enterprises and organisations than domestically owned enterprises. They conclude that: "the greater innovativeness of foreign subsidiaries depends on a double composition effect: their concentration in science-based and scale-intensive industries and their larger size" (Balcet and Evangelista 2005, p. 86).

The results of Balcet and Evangelista are partly confirmed by a second study with Italian CIS data (Castellani and Zanfei 2004). Castellani and Zanfei find that foreign-owned enterprises outperform domestically owned non-group enterprises, but show a weaker performance than enterprises affiliated to an Italian multinational enterprise. These Italian multinationals also have a higher propensity to co-operate with domestic partners than foreign-owned enterprises.

The effect of multinationality on innovation is also demonstrated in a paper from the UK (Frenz and Ietto-Gillies 2007). Frenz and Ietto-Gillies show that enterprises that are part of a multinational group are more innovative than uninational enterprises in a number of input, performance and output indicators. This effect increases with a rising level of multinationality, measured by the number of countries where the enterprise group is active. A significant difference between enterprises affiliated to UK-owned and non-UK multinational groups could not be found. Griffith et al (2004), however, come to different conclusions in a descriptive analysis of the R&D activities of foreign-owned enterprises in the UK. R&D intensity of foreign-owned enterprises is higher than the R&D intensity of British-owned domestic enterprises, but lower than that of British-owned domestic multinationals.

Evidence on the innovative performance of foreign-owned enterprises also exists for the Netherlands (Sadowski and van Beers 2002; van Beers et al. 2004; Sadowski and Sadowski-Rasters 2006). Sadowski and Sadowski-Rasters find that foreign ownership is positively correlated with the propensity of enterprises to innovate. This relationship is highly significant. The propensity to introduce 'real innovations' (= products and processes new to the market), in contrast, is unaffected or negatively affected by foreign ownership. Another study from the Netherlands reports that the propensity to co-operate with domestic public science and technology institutions is negatively correlated to foreign ownership (van Beers et al. 2004).

Finally, two studies besides the one at hand, have examined performance differences between foreign-owned and domestically owned enterprises in Austria. Schibany et al (2004) find considerable higher levels of R&D and innovation intensity for foreign-owned enterprises in a descriptive analysis of CIS data. Their results are similar to our descriptive analysis in chapter 6. In contrast, Falk and Falk (2006) find that foreign-owned enterprises perform worse than their domestically owned counterparts. Falk and Falk – similar to this study - also use data from the Third round of CIS for Austria; however they restrict their analysis to one indicator, innovative expenditure as a fraction of turnover, and exclude all enterprises not affiliated to an enterprise group.

The brief review of previous research on the effects of foreign ownership shows some common results across countries – even though the methodology of the studies differs considerably:

First, no study except one provides evidence that foreign-owned enterprises perform worse than their domestically owned counterparts. Second, most studies find a superior performance between foreign-owned and domestically owned enterprises in descriptive statistics. Third, this effect is due to differences in size, export intensity, sectoral affiliation and other enterprise characteristics and not foreign ownership; differences mostly disappear after controlling for these enterprises characteristics. Forth, a superior performance of foreign-owned enterprises is only found when foreign-owned enterprises are compared with domestically owned non-group enterprises and enterprises which solely operate in their parent country.

A limitation on a number of these studies is that a majority of them concentrate on only a few innovation input and output variables and none of them includes a variable measuring embeddedness. Therefore, one of the purposes of this section is to compile additional empirical evidence by analyzing of CIS data from 15 countries.

8.2 Sample

Empirical investigations of innovative behaviour including different countries has been made possible by EUROSTAT's publication of a dataset with firm-level micro data from the CIS (referred to as EUROCIS in this document) for scientific purposes in autumn 2006. The EUROCIS dataset includes nearly 50,000 observations from 13 EU member countries[9], Norway and Iceland. Table 39 reports for each country total GDP, GDP per capita and gross domestic expenditure as percentage of GDP. The countries vary considerably in terms of market size, measured in total GDP and GDP per capita, as well as in their technological and scientific capabilities, as can be seen from GERD/GDP ratios. Belgium is most similar to Austria in the three indicators.

To guarantee confidentiality and to prevent the identification of an individual enterprise, EUROSTAT has employed various procedures to keep names of en-

[9] Belgium, Bulgaria, Czech Republic, Estonia, Germany, Greece, Hungary, Latvia, Lithuania, Portugal, Romania Spain, Slovakia.

terprises anonymous within the data (EUROSTAT 2006). All geographical information except the country of residence of the firm has been deleted. Furthermore, EUROSTAT employed the following procedure to micro-aggregate the metric variables. First, for each country and each metric variable, the observations were sorted by variable value in descending order and then assigned to groups of three observations. Then, for each of the group weighted means were calculated and each individual value replaced with the weighted mean of the group.

The country sub-samples vary considerably with respect to size, sectoral affiliation, export shares and the shares of foreign-owned enterprises (Table 40). A large number of observations come from Bulgaria and Romania, the newest EU member states, and only a relatively small sample – compared to economic significance within the EU – from Germany. To correct for these differences, EUROSTAT provides weights for each observation. We decided not to use these weights for two reasons: first, weights may help to receive representative absolute data, but are tricky in regressions - since you have to correct weights for each missing value; and second, by using country dummy variables we correct for country effects anyway.

The analysis of chapter 6 and 7 has shown that it is not sufficient to distinguish between foreign-owned and domestically owned enterprises to understand the effects of foreign ownership on innovation. Generally, foreign-owned enterprises are more similar to enterprises belonging to a domestic enterprise group than to unaffiliated domestically owned enterprises. Moreover, there is also a considerable degree of heterogeneity within the foreign-owned enterprise population. Enterprises affiliated to a German/Swiss/Liechtenstein-owned group perform better in the descriptive analysis than enterprises affiliated to a parent enterprise located in another country. In the international comparison these differences have also to be taken into consideration.

There is also a considerable variation in the data between countries with respect to group and non-group enterprises, as well as between foreign-owned enterprises of different home countries, as seen in Figure 10. Countries have been sorted according to the share of foreign-owned enterprises in the sample. From the left, the figure shows Bulgaria with 1.8%, to the right we see Belgium with 31.2%. The share of enterprises belonging to a domestically owned enterprise group is highest in the countries with the highest GDP per capita – Norway, Germany and Belgium. These countries are also the ones with the lowest shares of non-affiliated enterprises. In this respect, they are the countries most similar to Austria in the sample.

Figure 10: Ownership status of enterprises in the EUROCIS Database and in Austria

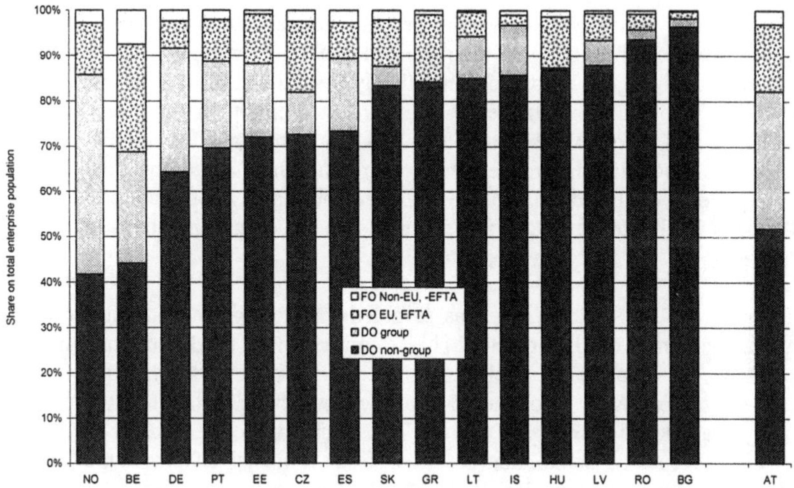

Note: FO: Foreign-owned, DO: Domestically owned

Source: Community Innovation Survey 3, Statistics Austria and EUROSTAT database

8.3 Descriptive Analysis of EUROCIS Data

We start with the propensity to introduce product and/or process innovations. Chapter 5.2 has shown that the average foreign-owned enterprise in Austria has a higher probability to be innovative than the average domestically owned enterprise. This is also the case in all countries in our sample, as can be seen from Table 41 in the annex. The difference between the two groups is highly significant (1% error level) in all countries with the exception of Hungary and Iceland. Iceland is the country where the gap between the two groups is smallest.

Another important result of Table 41 is that differences in innovativeness are on average larger between *countries* than between *foreign-owned and domestically owned enterprises of one country*. The standard deviation of the propensity to innovate is about 43% of the mean between countries, while the standard deviation of the differences between domestically owned and foreign-owned enterprises is only 29% of the mean. In other words, the level of innovativeness of both, foreign-owned and domestically owned enterprises, is determined by country-wide factors to a considerable degree. This points to the importance of national innovation systems, including institutions, market demand and relations to other actors for the level of innovative activity of both foreign-owned and domestically owned enterprises.

8.3.1 Innovation Input and Output

The analysis below will only consider innovative enterprises. The following tables provide information on the means of different variables of innovative behaviour for foreign-owned and domestically owned enterprises for the 15 countries as a whole and the differences in means including their significance. Moreover, we will report the comparable values for Austria and the number of countries with a positive difference between foreign-owned and domestically owned enterprises. For the purpose of this chapter, the tables are structured similar to the ones in chapter 6, but do not distinguish between group and non-group enterprises.

The analysis of Austrian data has revealed that foreign-owned enterprises on average are more R&D intensive. This is confirmed for the 15 countries of comparison. The number of R&D personnel is significantly higher for foreign-owned enterprises in 12 of the 15 countries and lower in three countries, Germany, Latvia and Hungary (Table 9). The result for Germany can be explained by the existence of a small number of large R&D intensive German multinationals, which employ a very large R&D staff; if we look at median values instead of means, the average foreign-owned enterprise in Germany employs seven persons in R&D, while the average domestically owned enterprises employs three researchers.

Innovative expenditure as a percentage of turnover, in contrast to R&D personnel, is significantly *lower* for foreign-owned enterprises. There is, however, a considerable heterogeneity in this indicator between countries; innovative expenditure is higher for foreign-owned enterprises in eight and lower in seven countries. In Germany, mean values for foreign-owned and domestically owned enterprises are similar down to the second digit. A lower innovative expenditure can also be observed in Austria.

A closer inspection of the data reveals that the higher average number of R&D personnel results from the fact that foreign-owned enterprises on average spend more on research and development, but less on other innovative activities such as the acquisition of external technology, design or preparation for market introduction. An explanation for the difference in this behaviour is the sectoral composition of the sample - where domestically owned enterprises are overrepresented in low-technology and services sectors which are less R&D intensive - but invest more in other innovation-related activities.

Table 15: Indicators of innovative behaviour and performance for 15 countries and Austria, only innovators, means

Ownership status	Number of R&D personnel	Innovative expenditure as % of turnover	Propensity to introduce products new to the market	Share of turnover from new products
Domestically owned enterprises	21.4	11.7%	44.6%	26.5%
Foreign-owned enterprises	19.5	9.7%	49.7%	25.3%
Diff. Foreign-Domestic, 15 countries	- 1.9	- 2% pts.	+5.1% pts.	- 1.2% pts.
Significance	-	***	***	**
Diff. Foreign-Domestic, Austria	+20.7	- 1.6% pts.	+19.9% pts.	+ 3.8% pts.
Significance	**	-	**	-
Number of countries with positive differences	3/15	7/15	14/15	10/15

Note: * significant at 10%; ** significant at 5%; *** significant at 1%, % pts are percentage points.

Source: Community Innovation Survey 3, Statistics Austria and EUROSTAT database

With respect to innovative output, foreign-owned enterprises exhibit a higher propensity to introduce market novelties, but their innovative activity results in a lower share of new products and processes on turnover (Table 9, last two columns). Both results are significant for the whole sample of enterprises from 15 countries. The result on the probability of market novelties is also very homogenous at the level of individual countries with 14 out of 15 countries showing a positive difference between foreign-owned and domestically owned enterprises. Here, the advantages of multinational enterprises, in particular the ability to transfer technology, management skills or successful products between countries, clearly show up. The result also mirrors sectoral composition of the group of foreign-owned enterprises where the share of high-technology enterprises is higher. This group, in turn, introduces market novelties more frequently.

The results on new products in turnover, in contrast to market novelties, are much less uniform. The value is higher for foreign-owned enterprises in ten of the comparison countries (despite a lower value in total), but we find significant differences in any direction only in four of the 15 countries. Theory would suggest that these differences are largest in medium- and low-income countries where intangible assets possessed by foreign-owned enterprises can give MNE affiliates a huge advantage over incumbent domestic enterprises. The two countries with the lowest GDP per capita – Bulgaria and Romania – indeed exhibit the largest difference, while Belgium and Germany reveal relatively small gaps in turnover from innovations. It is, however, difficult generalize this result and to find some form of regularity on how the differences between foreign-owned and domestically owned enterprises relate to country characteristics for all countries. Positive or negative differences can be found in high-income as well as low-income countries as well as in countries with a high and low share of foreign-owned enterprises or R&D intensities.

The analysis of composite indicators describing the innovative strategy of enterprises in chapter 6 revealed that a higher share of foreign-owned enterprises in Austria - compared to domestically owned enterprises - follow a strategy targeted at introducing market novelties, combined with a focus on international markets. We find a similar result for the 15 countries at the aggregate as well as at the level of individual countries. The dominant strategy in both, foreign-owned and domestically owned enterprises, focuses at innovations new to domestic markets or innovations new to firm with an orientation towards international markets. There are, however, significantly more enterprises in the population of foreign-owned enterprises (22.6% vs. 13.6%), which have introduced market novelties and have an international market focus than in the group of domestically owned enterprises. The international comparison, therefore, confirms the result of the descriptive analysis of Austrian CIS data. This finding does not refute the assumption that foreign-owned enterprises would mainly focus on adapting existing technologies for local markets; however, it demonstrates that this strategy is less frequently found among foreign-owned than among domestically owned enterprises.

Table 16: Composite indicators of innovative behaviour and performance for 15 countries and Austria, only innovators, means

Ownership status	New to market, international market	New to market, domestic OR new to firm, international	New to firm, domestic (and in house)	New to firm, domestic, adopted
Domestically owned enterprises	13.6%	42.9%	34.7%	8.8%
Foreign-owned enterprises	22.6%	47.7%	24.3%	5.4%
Diff. Foreign-Domestic, 15 countries	+9.1% pts.	+4.7% pts.	-10.4% pts.	- 3.4% pts.
Significance	***	***	***	***
Diff. Foreign-Domestic, Austria	+12.9% pts.	+7.8% pts.	-12.7 pts.	- 8.0% pts.
Significance	***	-	***	-
Number of countries with positive differences	14/15	11/15	0/15	0/15

Note: * significant at 10%; ** significant at 5%; *** significant at 1%, % pts are percentage points.

Source: Community Innovation Survey 3, Statistics Austria and EUROSTAT database

8.3.2 Embeddedness in the Host Country Innovation System

We now turn to innovation co-operation. Foreign-owned subsidiaries are embedded in MNE-internal innovation networks as well as in external relations in the host country. The literature assumes that a main goal of the presence of MNEs in a host country is to absorb local knowledge.

Both assumptions imply a high level of co-operative activity. Column two in Table 17 reveals that foreign-owned enterprises indeed are more prone to enter into innovation co-operation when compared to their domestically owned counterparts. The gap between the two groups is large – more than 13% points – and is a factor that can be observed in all comparison countries under study – even when the propensity for co-operation considerably varies between them.

Table 17: Indicators of co-operative behaviour for 15 countries and Austria, means

Ownership status	Propensity for innovation co-operation	Propensity for domestic external co-operation	Propensity for co-operation with domestic science⁺
Domestically owned enterprises	28.7%	80.1%	50.9%
Foreign-owned enterprises	42.0%	68.0%	43.6%
Diff. Foreign-Domestic, 15 countries	+13.3% pts.	-12.1% pts.	-7.3% pts.
Significance	***	***	***
Diff. Foreign-Domestic, Austria	+5.9% pts.	-0.8% pts.	+6.5% pts.
Significance	-	-	-
Number of countries with positive differences	14/14	3/14	3/14

Note: * significant at 10%; ** significant at 5%; *** significant at 1%, % pts are percentage points.

The first column includes all innovators, the numbers in the last two columns of the table show shares of a particular type of co-operation as percentage of all *co-operating* (not innovating) enterprises. ⁺Domestic science base includes domestic universities, private and public R&D centres. Information on Greece is missing.

Source: Community Innovation Survey 3, Statistics Austria and EUROSTAT database.

We will now differentiate between co-operation with various partners. The figures in the two columns to the right in Table 17 only consider enterprises active in co-operations. If we solely look at co-operation agreements with *domestic partners*, the average foreign-owned co-operative enterprise has a significantly lower propensity to enter into these agreements than the average domestically owned enterprise. This gap between foreign-owned and domestically owned enterprises in domestic external co-operation is largest in countries that have high GERD/GDP ratios, such as Germany, Iceland and Belgium, and lowest in countries with a low R&D intensity, Bulgaria and Romania. One explanation of this pattern is the fact that the potential for spillovers is higher in countries with a strong science base. This hypothesis also fits with the results for Austria, where we can observe only a very small gap of -0.8 % points.

The gap between the two groups is smaller for co-operation with the *domestic science base* (universities, governmental and private research centres) than for total external domestic co-operation. This reflects the fact that foreign-owned enterprises are more often found in technology-intensive sectors, which, in turn, exhibit a higher propensity to co-operate with universities and public labs.

Readers should note that the last three columns in Table 17 denote the shares of a particular type of co-operation as percentage of *all co-operating*, and not of *all innovative enterprises*. If we relate the figures to the total number of innovative enterprises, all types of co-operation are more frequently found among foreign-owned than among domestically owned enterprises, since the overall propensity to co-operate of the latter group is higher.

The largest differences in co-operative behaviour can be observed in international co-operation. Here, we now see positive, instead of negative differences. International co-operation is the dominant form of co-operation for foreign-owned enterprises and the reason for a higher overall propensity to co-operate for this group. In the sample, 80% of all co-operating enterprises have international co-operations, compared to only 47% among domestically owned enterprises.

A positive difference between foreign-owned and domestically owned enterprises can be observed in each country, including Austria. The gaps are largest in Romania, Iceland, Hungary and Norway, and smallest in Belgium, Lithuania and Latvia. This list of countries already indicates that the gap is not related to the size of the host country or its scientific strength. We see only small gap for Austria, too.

Table 18: Indicators of co-operative behaviour for 15 countries and Austria, means

Ownership status	Propensity for international innovation co-operation	Propensity for co-operation with international science+
Domestically owned enterprises	47.8%	16.3%
Foreign-owned enterprises	80.1%	22.2%
Diff. Foreign-Domestic, 15 countries	+32.3% pts.	+5.8% pts.
Significance	***	***
Diff. Foreign-Domestic, Austria	+3.7% pts.	+3.5% pts.
Significance	-	-
Number of countries with positive differences	14/14	10/14

Note: * significant at 10%; ** significant at 5%; *** significant at 1%, % pts are percentage points.

The first column includes all innovators, the numbers in the last three columns of the table show shares of a particular type of co-operation as percentage of all *co-operating* (not innovating) enterprises. +Domestic science base includes domestic universities, private and public R&D centres.

Source: Community Innovation Survey 3, Statistics Austria and EUROSTAT database

This high level of international co-operation refers to one of the largest gains a host country can win from the presence of foreign-owned enterprises; they can act as bridges in international knowledge transfer between the host country and foreign universities and enterprises, presumably located in the home countries of their parent enterprises. This knowledge further diffuses in the host country through various channels as described in section 10.1. The last column of Table 18 demonstrates that this bridging function is not only fulfilled with respect to internal international co-operation, but also in co-operation with foreign universities. Foreign-owned enterprises co-operate significantly more with universities and research centers outside the host country than domestically owned enterprises.

8.3.3 Differences within the Groups of Foreign-owned and Domestically Owned Enterprises

The analysis of Austrian data has revealed large differences within the groups of foreign-owned and domestically owned enterprises - which help to understand how different types of ownership can result in performance differences. We have demonstrated that, in several ways, domestically owned enterprises affiliated to an enterprise group behave much more similar to foreign-owned enterprises than to domestically owned non-group enterprises.

This can also be observed for the EUROCIS data. Table 19 distinguishes between domestically owned non-group enterprises, domestically owned group enterprises, foreign-owned enterprises with parent enterprises in an EU or EFTA country, and foreign-owned enterprises from outside Europe.

Table 19: Indicators of innovative behaviour for 15 countries according to ownership status, means

Indicator	DO non-group	DO group	FO EU, EFTA	FO non- EU, EFTA
Propensity to innovate	27.3%	56.6%	52.4%	62.6%
Number of R&D personnel (persons)	20.6	24.0	17.9	25.4
Innovative expenditure as % of turnover	12.3%	9.8%	9.4%	11.0%
Propensity to introduce products new to the market	44.6%	44.7%	48.7%	53.4%
Share of turnover from new products	27.5%	23.3%	24.9%	27.1%
Strategy towards new-to-market innovations at internat. markets	12.6%	16.8%	20.4%	31.2%

Note: * significant at 10%; ** significant at 5%; *** significant at 1%, % pts are percentage points.

The first row includes all enterprises, the numbers in the following rows of the table relate only to innovative enterprises.

Source: EUROSTAT, Community Innovation Survey 3 database

Domestically owned non-group enterprises show a considerably lower propensity to innovate than any other group and are to a lesser degree oriented towards product novelties at international markets. Once they decide to innovate, however, innovative expenditure as well as turnover generated by innovations is higher than in any other group. This can also observed in the Austrian data.

Like in the Austrian case, we see that domestically owned group enterprises are more similar to foreign-owned enterprises than to domestically owned group enterprises in almost every indicator. Moreover, there are also differences between foreign-owned enterprises with respect to their country of origin. Affiliates from outside Europe show a higher propensity to innovate, employ more R&D personnel, bring more innovations to the market and are more oriented towards international markets. Similar differences between GLS-owned and Anglo-Saxon owned enterprises in Austria have been explained by geographical distance and the liability of foreignness. However, these factors do provide an appropriate explanation in this case - since they should lead to a higher, but not to a lower performance of European enterprises when compared to non-European enterprises. We will further investigate this finding below.

Domestically owned non-group enterprises also co-operate less often than the three other groups. Non-group enterprises are considerably smaller than the other three types of enterprises, and co-operation requires a minimum of financial resources, absorptive capacity and/or managerial capacities which non-group enterprises may have difficulties to fulfil. Once non-group enterprises clear this threshold and enter co-operative agreements, differences between the four groups get smaller. Domestically owned non-group enterprises, for example, are more often co-operating with partners from the market (suppliers, customers, competitors) than foreign-owned enterprises. However, they cannot match with the propensity for international co-operation exhibited by the other three groups.

Table 20: Indicators of co-operative behaviour for 15 countries according to ownership status, means

Indicator	DO non-group	DO group	FO EU, EFTA	FO non-EU, EFTA
Propensity for innovation co-operation	24.3%	43.0%	41.1%	45.4%
Propensity for co-operation with domestic science	46.5%	59.6%	40.5%	56.1%
Propensity for co-operation with domestic market	58.3%	61.8%	50.9%	46.1%
Propensity for international co-operation	45.1%	53.8%	79.4%	82.5%
Propensity for co-operation with international science	13.8%	22.3%	21.1%	28.1%

Note: * significant at 10%; ** significant at 5%; *** significant at 1%, % pts are percentage points.

The first row includes all innovative enterprises, the numbers in the following rows of the table relate only to enterprises active in innovation co-operation.

Source: EUROSTAT, Community Innovation Survey 3 database

To sum up, the descriptive analysis of the EUROCIS dataset with respect to differences in innovative behaviour between foreign-owned and domestically owned enterprises reveals uniform patterns of enterprise behaviour for all countries in most variables. The most heterogeneous results can be found in innovative expenditure intensity and in the share of new products on turnover. In some indicators, such as domestic external co-operation, heterogeneity between different countries in the sample can clearly be attributed to country characteristics such as scientific capabilities and economic size which make co-operation more attractive. Differences among countries in other indicators, such as the share of turnover from new products, seem to be uncorrelated with country characteristics.

The Austrian CIS and the EUROCIS data show similar signs in ten and different signs in three of the 13 variables. Different signs can be found in the number of R&D personnel, the share of turnover from new products, and the propensity to co-operate with the domestic scientific organisations. Foreign-owned enterprises exhibit a worse performance in these indicators when compared to their domestically owned counterparts in the EUROCIS countries, but a better performance in Austria. This may be explained, on the one hand, by some peculiarities of the Austrian Innovation System, such as the low level of innovation co-operation -

which makes it easy to outperform domestically owned enterprises. On the other hand, we know that differences in performance exist within the group of foreign-owned enterprises and German/Swiss/Liechtenstein-owned enterprises perform better in the descriptive analysis than Anglo-Saxon-owned enterprises. Multivariate analysis revealed that this is mostly due to structural differences and not cultural proximity. Nevertheless, the fact that German/Swiss /Liechtenstein are performing so well may explain why the whole group of foreign-owned enterprises performs better in Austria than in the comparison countries.

8.4 Multivariate Analysis of EUROCIS Data

The multivariate analysis of Austrian CIS data in chapter 7 has revealed that differences in innovative performance between domestically owned and foreign-owned enterprises are due to enterprises characteristics (size, sector ...) than to the ownership status. We will now rerun some of the regressions of chapter 7 using the EUROCIS dataset to see if this result is an exception or valid for other countries as well.

8.4.1 Variables Included in the Analysis

The econometric analysis uses the same two-equation sample selection model as employed in chapter 7. Due to differences in the available variables, we will adjust the right-hand variables. We use the log of turnover instead of the log of employment as a measure of enterprise size. This implies that we cannot include the share of employees with tertiary education on total employment in the regression. Instead, we use the log of the number of employees with tertiary education. Moreover, information on growth expectations and on investment in ICT is not available.

We account for the influence of country characteristics in two ways: first, by including country dummies in the list of right-hand variables of the selection equation; and second, by including the share of *GERD on GDP* and *total GDP* as right-hand variables in the function equation. Both entities have been identified as major determinants of foreign-located R&D of enterprises (see chapter 4 for a discussion).

Total GDP (*LNGDP*) proxies total market size of the country. It is measured at current prices and in Mio USD Purchasing Power Parities (PPP). GDP data has been delivered by the April 2007 edition of IMF's World Economic Outlook Database[10].

---

[10] http://www.imf.org/external/ns/cs.aspx?id=28

The share of GERD on GDP (*RDINTENSITY*) is a general measure for the scientific and technological capabilities of a country. Data on total R&D intensity has been taken from the 2007/1 edition of OECD's Main Science and Technology Indicators (OECD 2007a) and from the online database of the UNESCO Institute for Statistics[11].

Table 21: Independent variables in the EUROCIS-data

Category	Variable	Description
Enterprise characteristics	LNETURN	Turnover in 2000, Euro, logarithm
	LNEMPHI	Number of employees with tertiary education, logarithm
	LNINVEST	Investment per employee in Euro, logarithm
	EST	Enterprise has been established between 1998 and 2000
	RD	The enterprises is engaged in permanent R&D activity
	FUND	Enterprise received public financial support for innovation
	EXSHR	Exports as a percentage of turnover
	SIGMAR	The main market of the enterprise is the international market
Sectoral classification	SEMHT	High technology and medium-high technology sector according to OECD
	SEMLT	Medium-low technology sector according to OECD
	SELT	Low technology sector according to OECD
	SEKIS	Knowledge-intensive business services according to OECD
	SEOS	Other service sectors
Country characteristics	RDINTENSITY	Gross domestic expenditure as a fraction of GDP, Average 1998-2000
	LNGDP	Total GDP, Average 1998-2000, logarithm

Source: Community Innovation Survey 3 EUROSTAT

It was impossible to strictly replicate the various classes of foreign-owned enterprises used in the analysis of Austrian CIS data with the EUROCIS data. We therefore employ three different set-ups to model foreign ownership in the regressions (Table 22): In the first case, we only distinguish between foreign-owned and domestically owned enterprises. The second version of the model includes domestically owned group enterprises as the reference category, domestically owned non-group enterprises and foreign-owned enterprises. In a third case, we distinguish between domestically owned non-group and group enterprises (the reference category), on the one hand, and foreign-owned enterprises from the EU and from non-EU countries on the other hand.

[11] http://www.uis.unesco.org

Table 22: Ownership dummy variables in regressions with EUROCIS data

Case	1	2	3
All domestically owned enterprises	R		
Domestically owned group enterprises (DOM_GROUP)		R	R
Domestically owned non-group enterprises (DOM_UNI)		x	x
All foreign-owned enterprises with a parent enterprise located in an EU or EFTA country (EU)			x
All foreign-owned enterprises with a parent enterprise located outside the EU or EFTA (non_EU)			x
All foreign-owned enterprises (FOROWN)	x	x	

Note: R: reference category

We will calculate all three cases for the EUROCIS data, and, as a comparison, case 1 and 2 for the Austrian data. A further differentiation of foreign-owned enterprises for Austria is useless, since the sample is quite small and we cannot reproduce the classification used in the analysis of Austrian data with the EUROCIS sample.

8.4.2 Innovative Behaviour

We first estimate a probit model with the propensity to innovate as the left-hand variable for the 15 countries of the EUROCIS database and for Austria. Due to restrictions by Statistics Austria we are not allowed to merge the Austrian and the EUROCIS data and estimate one single model.

Propensity to Innovate (Selection equation)

We first estimate a regression with the propensity to innovate as left-hand variable. This regression will serve as the selection equation for the Heckman probit estimates of innovative input, output and embeddedness.

The results show that foreign ownership is negatively associated with innovativeness compared to domestically owned group enterprises in both the Austrian and the EUROCIS model (Table 42). The effect is larger for Austria than for the EUROCIS countries. We also find that domestically owned non-group enterprises are less innovative than domestically owned group enterprises. Similar signs between the two models can be found in most other right-hand variables, including enterprise size, employment of academics, investment, and in the sectoral dummies for high- and medium-high tech, other services and utilities. Country effects have been calculated with Bulgaria - the country with the lowest share of innovators - as the reference category.

Innovative Input

We first analyze innovative input measured by innovation expenditure as a percentage of turnover (Table 43). Both, the EUROCIS and the results for Austria show no significant relationship between foreign-ownership and innovative input in the three specifications used in Table 43. Domestically owned non-group enterprises, however, perform worse compared to domestically owned group enterprises in the EUROCIS data (case 2 and 3). This is in line with the literature which assumes that some advantages of group membership are shared by domestically owned and foreign-owned enterprises.

Performance differences revealed in the descriptive analysis are therefore better explained by enterprise characteristics and not by ownership. One of these characteristics is size. The estimation of the determinants of innovation expenditure intensity reveals that input increases, and not decreases with size, like in the results for Austria. It is not the aim of this study to further investigate this finding, since extensive literature exists on the relationship between size and innovativeness. However, we want to point out that this is not because of a U-shaped relationship between the two variables. We included turnover and turnover squared in an alternative version of the model not reported here; both variables were insignificant.

An unexpected result is the negative and highly significant relationship between permanent R&D activity and innovation input intensity. Here, we have to consider that R&D expenditure only accounts for about half of total innovation expenditure, which also includes the cost for the acquisition of technology, machinery, the cost of design and costs associated with market introduction of new products. The sectoral dummies, in contrast, show the expected signs. A higher degree of innovation input intensity is also associated with rising levels of R&D intensity in the host country – which is also predicted by the literature.

Innovative Output

We measure innovative output with two indicators: first, by examining whether or not the enterprise has introduced a market novelty; and second, with the share of new or considerably modified products on turnover.

The EUROCIS results show a characteristic pattern we already know from the analysis of the Austrian CIS data: There is a significant advantage for foreign-owned enterprises indicated by a positive coefficient when we compare foreign-owned and domestically owned enterprises (case 1). When we split the group of domestically owned enterprises into group and non-group enterprises (case 2 and 3), this difference only remains with respect to non-group enterprises. Foreign ownership is therefore positively related with the introduction of market novelties - only if we compare foreign-owned enterprises to domestically owned non-group enterprises.

The coefficients of the other variables show the expected signs. Market novelties are positively related to the number of persons with academic training, investment, received funding, R&D activity, and innovative expenditure intensity. The level of R&D intensity at the country level has no influence; however, we see that the probability of a market novelty increases with market size, measured by total GDP of the host country. We can also see sectoral effects in the results; high-tech, medium-high-tech and medium-low tech have a higher propensity to introduce market novelties than enterprises from low-tech sectors, while service enterprises have a lower propensity.

The results for the share of turnover from new products are quite similar to those for market novelties, with the exception that Austrian domestically owned non-group enterprises show a positive, and not a negative sign compared to domestically owned group enterprises. This coefficient, however, is only significant at the 10% level. Turnover from new products, in contrast, is associated with significantly higher export shares, a larger number of academic personnel, and rising innovative expenditure. It is more frequently found in high- and medium-high-tech and knowledge-intensive sectors.

8.4.3 Embeddedness

Results from the Austrian CIS data have shown that only Anglo-Saxon enterprises have a considerably lower propensity to enter innovation co-operation with domestic partners. There was no significant effect of foreign ownership if *all* domestically owned enterprises were compared with *all* foreign-owned enterprises. It was, however, difficult to get proper estimation results because only a small number of enterprises co-operate in Austria.

The results with the EUROCIS data reveal a more differentiated picture than the Austrian data. Co-operation with domestic partners external to the enterprise group is neither positively nor negatively associated with foreign ownership if we compare both groups (Table 46, case 1). This is, however, due to the aggregation, as we see in the second and third column. There is a significantly negative effect of foreign ownership compared to domestically owned group enterprises. This effect is smaller than the effect from being a domestically owned non-group enterprise. Both foreign-owned groups differ only slightly in this effect. The Austrian results show a similar significant effect from ownership only at the 10% level; this may result from the fact that we cannot identify Anglo-Saxon enterprises in the EUROCIS sample. Another explanation is that differences in co-operation between foreign-owned and domestically owned enterprises shrink with rising scientific and technological capabilities of the host country. The descriptive analysis has shown that the gap between foreign-owned and domestically owned enterprises is smallest in Belgium, Germany, and Austria.

All other right-hand variables show the expected signs. Host country R&D intensity is positively related, while total market size is negatively related to domestic external co-operation. As an interpretation, we assume that the propensity to co-operate increases with potential spillovers, but decreases with the size of the country and therefore the number of potential co-operation partners.

We get similar results with respect to co-operation with scientific organisations in the host country (Table 47). A negative effect of foreign ownership is due to two reasons: first, the differences between foreign-owned enterprises and domestically owned group enterprises – which happen to perform better than any other group; and second, to the negative performance of EU enterprises when compared to non-EU enterprises. The effect of the former is significantly negative, while the effect of the latter is not significant. Together as a single group, both perform worse than domestically owned group enterprises as well as compared to all domestically owned enterprises. A negative effect is also present in the Austrian data. Here, we know from the analysis in chapter 7, that these differences are mainly due to Anglo-Saxon enterprises.

Finally, we estimate the propensity for international co-operation for Austria as well as the 15 countries of comparison. Descriptive statistics have already revealed that Austria is very different in respect to international co-operation. There is a huge margin for foreign-owned enterprises in this indicator for the 15 EUROCIS countries. The number of foreign-owned enterprises engaged in international co-operation is nearly two times the number of their domestically owned counterparts. A similar margin cannot be observed in Austria.

The regressions confirm this result: Foreign-owned enterprises are associated with significantly higher propensity to enter international co-operation in the EUROCIS data, but not in the Austrian data. The EUROCIS results indicate that foreign-owned enterprises even have an advantage compared to domestically owned group enterprises – but not in Austria. It seems that one of the biggest advantages from the presence of foreign-owned enterprises – linking domestic organisations to international knowledge, does not unfold in the case of Austria – since foreign-owned enterprises in Austria do not co-operate across borders. This may be the result of an overall lower propensity to co-operate in Austria (Schiefer 2007), which also hampers international co-operation. One may also assume that they do not need to co-operate because they are satisfied with external knowledge available in Austria. A plausible answer as to why Austrian enterprises do not co-operate may be found in future research. Recent approaches to identify reasons for the low co-operation propensity of Austrian enterprise by means of a comparative analysis of Austrian and Finnish CIS data has been inconclusive so far (Dachs et al. 2008b).

8.4.4 Summary of the Effects of Foreign Ownership

The analysis of the effects of foreign ownership with respect to innovation with EUROCIS data revealed a number of similarities, but also differences between Austria and the countries of comparison. In general, the effect of foreign ownership is larger in co-operation behaviour than in innovation input and output. This can be explained by the rich internal sources of information and knowledge available to MNE subsidiaries, which reduce the need for external co-operation. Performance differences between foreign-owned and domestically owned enterprises are related rather to enterprise characteristics such as size, sector, absorptive capacity or the propensity to do R&D than the ownership status. Foreign ownership makes a (significant) difference in a number of cases. The coefficients of the ownership variables, however, are considerably smaller than those for R&D activity or sectoral affiliation - which indicates that other variables accounting for enterprise characteristics are more decisive.

Moreover, we have learned that foreign ownership as such is a less useful category to analyse the effects of ownership. One has to differentiate between various groups of foreign ownership, and, even more important, make a choice about the comparison group. In a number of variables, differences between foreign-owned and domestically owned group enterprises are smaller than between domestically owned group and non-group enterprises. This can be clearly seen from the summary of the findings given in Table 23.

The table lists the coefficients of dummies identifying foreign-owned and domestically owned non-group enterprises. Domestically owned group enterprises are the reference case. We see that the coefficients of foreign-owned enterprises are all smaller than those of domestically owned non-group enterprises and insignificant in three of the six dependent variables. In some cases, the analysis found significant effects from ownership *only* when domestically owned enterprises are split up into two groups.

We could not identify effects from the liability of foreignness except in one case: foreign-owned enterprises from outside of Europe have a higher propensity to enter into co-operation with domestic science than foreign-owned enterprises from European countries. This is counter-intuitive, since we expect that non-European enterprises would suffer more from the liability of foreignness than European enterprises. It may, however, indicate that non-European foreign-owned enterprises are more often pursuing competence-creating strategies.

Table 23: Summary of the effects of group membership and foreign ownership from the analysis of EUROCIS and Austrian data

	15 countries		Austria	
	DO non-group enterprises	FO enterprises	DO non-group enterprises	FO enterprises
Innovation expenditure intensity	-0.164***	-0.043	-0.120	-0.037
Market novelties	-0.193***	0.015	-0.353**	-0.098
Turnover from innovations	-0.036***	-0.001	0.093*	0.072
Domestic external co-operation	-0.375***	-0.236***	-0.275	-0.335*
Domestic science co-operation	-0.305***	-0.252***	-0.595**	-0.395*
International co-operation	-0.383***	0.262***	-0.218	0.015

Note: * significant at 10%; ** significant at 5%; *** significant at 1%, % pts are percentage points.

Reference category: domestically owned group enterprises. DO: domestically owned, FO: foreign-owned.

Source: Community Innovation Survey 3 EUROSTAT and Statistics Austria

Austrian and international results show similar signs in most ownership indicators. The Austrian results, however, are not significant in a number of cases. Differences between foreign-owned and domestically owned enterprises in Austria are therefore smaller than in other countries - even if we correct for enterprise characteristics. This conclusion is supported by three findings:

First, descriptive analysis has already shown that the gaps between foreign-owned and domestically owned enterprises are smaller in Austria than in the countries compared.

Second, the results for Austria show that other enterprise characteristics than ownership are highly significant and more powerful in explaining performance differences.

Third, results from case studies and interviews indicate that foreign-owned enterprises in Austria indeed pursue competence-creating strategies to a considerable degree. We can therefore conclude that the different results between Austria and the group of comparison countries point to distinct characteristics of the innovation system and differences in enterprise strategies rather than to an incomparability of the data.

Results similar to our findings can be found in other studies – especially in studies dealing with the small open economies of the Nordic countries. Therefore, it is appropriate to conclude that our results are not an exception, but part of a common story across countries. The Product Life Cycle Model and subsequent theories found in the international business literature may therefore, as suggested by Cantwell (1995), be better suited to explain the behaviour of MNE originating from the US, than from European economies with a high degree of internationalisation and long-lasting relationships to neighbouring countries and other European countries alike.

9. The Emergence of Subsidiary Mandates: A Case Study on Foreign-Owned Enterprises in Austria

9.1 Introduction

Econometric analysis is a powerful tool to examine regularities between dependent and independent variables for a large number of entities, but it cannot exemplify the individual strategies of enterprises. Therefore, we now complement and further illustrate the findings from the previous chapters with a case study on the R&D and innovation strategies of selected foreign-owned enterprises in Austria. Previous work that dealt with this topic (Nones 2003; Schibany et al. 2004; Lueghammer and Schneider 2005) concluded that a considerable number of these enterprises have a high level of independence and do not just exploit existing knowledge, but pursue strategies to enhance the knowledge base of the group. The empirical analysis in the previous chapters has also revealed that foreign-owned enterprises in Austria do not differ from their domestically owned counterparts in most indicators of innovative performance. Therefore, we may speak of the presence of competence-creating strategies in the case of foreign-owned enterprises in Austria.

Such a strategy differs considerably from approaches where R&D is concentrated in the home country and foreign-owned subsidiaries mainly exploit existing technologies. Here, we think of multinational enterprises as a network of loosely coupled organisations (Ghoshal and Bartlett 1991) rather than a hierarchical structure. Entrepreneurial initiative at the subsidiary level has more room to unfold than in a centralized organisation. It also requires a more complex organisational strategy of the MNE and poses different managerial challenges to the enterprise (Gupta and Govindarajanan 1994; Criscuolo and Narula 2005).

The strategic management literature has identified three sets of internal and external factors which influence whether or not an subsidiary evolves into a centre of excellence which actively contributes to the technological competences of the MNE (Birkinshaw and Hood 1998). The first of these factors is *local environment determinism* and relates to the specific local environment the subsidiary operates in. This environment provides specific incentives, capabilities and hampering factors that shape subsidiary evolution. A second influential factor, *head-office assignment*, encompasses headquarter strategy, the assignment of tasks to the subsidiaries and allocation mechanisms for resources within the MNE. Finally, subsidiary mandates are shaped by *subsidiary choice*, the subsidiary's capability and the initiative of the managers of the subsidiary itself.

At least two of them, head-office assignment and subsidiary choice, co-evolve with dynamic, self-enforcing and self-containing feedback effects (Birkinshaw and Hood 1998); a higher degree of subsidiary choice and autonomy granted by the head office may lead to a build-up of capabilities and a more entrepreneurial behaviour at the subsidiary, which, in turn, may foster of the parent enterprise-driven decentralisation strategies.

We will now employ this framework to analyze the mandates of seven foreign-owned enterprises in Austria in an exploratory case study. We have seen in the previous chapters that foreign-owned enterprises in Austria do not differ from domestically owned enterprises in their innovative behaviour once we control for size, sectoral affiliation, investment and other factors. This has led us to the conclusion that foreign-owned enterprises in Austria rather pursue competence-creating than competence-exploiting strategies. The purpose of this chapter is to examine and illustrate these strategies in more detail.

The analysis of this chapter is based on interviews and published material such as annual reports and newspaper articles to get a comprehensive picture of the role of the Austrian subsidiaries within their enterprise groups. The interviews followed a semi-structured questionnaire. Interview partners were the R&D managers or representatives of the general management of the enterprises.

We will start the analysis with a short description of the sample and a quantitative assessment of the contribution of the subsidiaries to total R&D output of their groups. Following the framework, we will then examine the opinions of the enterprises on locational advantages and disadvantages in Austria, head office assignment of mandates in R&D, and subsidiary initiative. This includes the division of labour and responsibilities for research, development and innovation within the enterprise group. Other important issues are the independence of the subsidiary and their mandates in particular technologies or products.

9.2 Case Study Sample

The sample consists of seven enterprises. It includes two enterprises from the information and communication technologies sector and four enterprises from the chemical and pharmaceutical industry. We have chosen these sectors because they rank amongst the most internationalized industries (Barba Navaretti and Venables 2004). Moreover, we have included one enterprise from the pulp and paper industry, a sector where Austria has traditional strengths.

A second criterion was the significance of R&D activities. Each of these enterprises ranks amongst the most important performers of R&D in Austria. Five of them are among the 50 largest applicants of Austrian patent inventions[12] at the European Patent Office between 2000 and 2005. Two of the enterprises included

[12] Patent documents name one or more applicants (often enterprises) and one or more inventors of a patent, including their place of residence. Austrian patent inventions refer to all patents invented by Austrian residents.

here rank first and second in this list. Together, the seven enterprise groups own 10% of all patents based on Austrian inventions, and 40% of all foreign-owned patents based on Austrian inventions of this period.

Three enterprises are affiliated to a German, another three to an Anglo-Saxon and one is affiliated to a Nordic parent enterprise. All enterprises have a long history with one dating far as back as the nineteenth century. With one exception, they all have been present in Austria for at least ten years. Three enterprises have been founded as Austrian-owned enterprises and were acquired by a foreign parent enterprise in the second half of the 1990s; the other four enterprises were established as Greenfield investments.

All enterprises in the sample have more than 250 employees and are considered large when compared to the average enterprise size in the Austrian manufacturing sector, which is 22 (Statistik Austria 2005).

9.3 Patent Output of the Subsidiaries

Before we start with the interview results, it is useful to complement the subjective views of our interview partners with a quantitative measure. We use the number of inventions from different countries applied for a patent by the group to measure the importance of R&D activity in Austria vis-à-vis the home country and other locations.

The analysis considers all patent applications published by the European Patent Office between January 2000 and December 2005. Patent applications have been allocated to different groups according to the list of subsidiaries included in the consolidated accounts published in the annual reports of the companies. We use information of the location of the inventor, who is mentioned with his or her full name and address in the patent document, to identify the share of patent activity originating from Austria.

The quantitative results confirm that their enterprises hold a considerable share on the group's overall R&D activities. In total, patent applications based on Austrian inventions (and therefore on the activities of the Austrian subsidiary) have a share of more than ten percent in three cases, and a share above one percent in two out of the seven cases. The Austrian subsidiary has a share below 1% in only one case. We have excluded one multinational enterprise from this comparison because of a very low total number of patent applications. As an example, the results for three of the seven enterprises are given in the table below. Due to confidentiality, we will not present results for all enterprises of our sample.

Table 24: Shares of different inventor countries on the total patent applications of Baxter, Infineon and Siemens to the European Patent Office, 2000 – 2005

Siemens (world total: 11,348)		Baxter (world total: 305)		Infineon (world total: 3,160)	
Inventor Country	Share	Inventor Country	Share	Inventor Country	Share
DE	80%	US	67%	DE	77%
US	8%	**AT**	**12%**	US	11%
AT	**3%**	GB	8%	**AT**	**6%**
IT	2%	BE	8%	FR	1%
CH	2%	DE	3%	SE	1%
FR	1%	CH	1%	SG	1%
CA	1%	FR	1%	IL	1%

Note: Countries below 1% are not reported, rows therefore may not sum up to 100%

Source: European Patent Office

A share between one and ten percent on all patent applications of the enterprise group may not sound too impressive. However, it is a lot if we consider that most multinational groups still concentrate R&D in the home country. In a ranking of the R&D locations according to the total number of patent inventions, Austria is the most important R&D location outside of the home country of the parent enterprise in one case, ranks second in four cases and seventh in one case. In three out of the seven cases, Austria is the most important European R&D location outside the home country and only excelled by the US subsidiary and the home country in terms of patent inventions in a global comparison.

Therefore, the enterprises included in this case study are indeed major contributors to the technological capabilities of their enterprise groups and play an important role in the global organisation of their R&D activities. They are competence-creating and actively contribute to the technological capabilities of their enterprise groups, and do not just exploit existing technologies.

9.4 Perception of Locational Advantage in Austria

According to Birkinshaw and Hood (1998), a first influential factor on subsidiary evolution is the local environment. It provides specific incentives, capabilities and hampering factors that shape subsidiary evolution. With respect to science and technology, these determinants include the availability of scientists and engineers; the quality of academic research and university education; localized knowledge in clusters and other agglomerations; important clients that trigger technological specialisation of the subsidiary; the existence of knowledge spillovers or funding opportunities for research and innovation.

The interviewees regard Austria's geographical proximity to Germany on the one hand and to the new member states of the EU on the other hand as a primary locational advantage. Despite modern communication technologies and air travel, the interviewees still regard it as an important advantage to have a short travelling distance to the head office of their enterprise group. The geographical proximity to the new member states helped to attract some head office functions like regional mandates.

All enterprises in the sample regard the quality of Austrian universities as a major locational advantage of the country. Research activities and the academic education at Austrian universities are highly valued by the interviewees.

A second locational advantage of Austria is the availability of skilled personnel and the cost of labour in Austria. Austria has a well-educated labour force in many scientific and technical disciplines. Labour productivity of R&D personnel is higher than in a number of other European countries and it even surpasses Germany. The majority of enterprise representatives, in particular the representatives of subsidiaries with a German parent enterprise, are convinced that this advantage was decisive in building up R&D capacities in Austria.

A point of critique raised by the interviewees is a lack of flexibility they observe among Austrian employees. Another advantage is the high quality of life in Austria, which makes it easier to recruit foreign specialists despite wage differences.

Conflicting views have been expressed about the public administration and the political environment. The interviewees stress the advantages of political stability, a favourable corporate taxation and lower administrative burdens in Austria. Some aspects of the Austrian promotional system are regarded as less favourable. The interviewees acknowledge the continuous efforts to increase public funds for R&D and innovation made by federal and provincial governments in recent years. However, they are concerned about the high number of individual schemes and the resulting lack of transparency and scattered resources which, in the opinion of the interviewees, should be more focused on specific areas.

9.5 Local Embeddedness of the Subsidiary

An important result of the empirical analysis of the previous chapters is the fact that foreign ownership is not associated with a lower intensity to co-operate with local partners in the host country (except in the case of Anglo-Saxon enterprises). Foreign-owned enterprises benefit from local knowledge available in enterprises, universities and clusters, and external relationships with these partners may constitute a considerable, although hardly quantifiable influence on subsidiary development.

A strong embeddedness in the Austrian innovation system is also a characteristic of the enterprises of this case study. Most enterprises in the sample actively co-operate with domestic enterprises and universities in various innovation and R&D projects. All seven enterprises maintain various joint activities with Austrian universities. Co-operation encloses all stages of the innovation process from basic to applied research and product development. In terms of commitment and extent, the activities range from financing graduate level work and contract research to joint R&D projects in the European Framework programmes and joint research organisations.

The interviewees point out three advantages of their relations with Austrian universities for their enterprises. First, despite modern communication technologies, a number of interviewees find it easier to build up a long-standing relationship and co-operation with a partner in the same location. Second, all enterprises stress the high quality of research done at Austrian universities. Third, co-operation with domestic universities is not only regarded as a source of new knowledge, but also as a means for recruitment.

Besides co-operation with academia, five of the seven enterprises are also engaged in joint R&D activities with Austrian enterprises. A pivotal role in these joint activities have the 'Kplus' and 'K_ind' programmes, promotional measures provided by the funding agency FFG to promote co-operation between enterprises and universities.

Two enterprises in the sample are *not* co-operating with Austrian enterprises. The reasons can be found in the specialisation of the Austrian subsidiary. The interviewees feel, on the one hand, that there is no sufficient expertise in the Austrian enterprise sector that would justify joint projects. On the other hand, they complain that potential partners in Austria are too small and provide too little capacity for their needs.

9.6 Headquarter Assignment and Internal Co-ordination

A second decisive factor for subsidiary evolution is the assignment of tasks by the head office and the mechanisms in place to allocate resources within the MNE. We have demonstrated with patent data that all enterprises of this case study actively create new knowledge and technologies not only for the Austrian market, but for the whole enterprise group and therefore are endowed with such a competence-creating mandate. Results of other studies based on interviews and other material confirm this finding (Nones 2003; Schibany et al. 2004; Lueghammer and Schneider 2005).

There are, however, differences in the scope of this mandate and the independence the enterprises enjoy within their group. These differences are related to the co-ordination mechanisms in place within the MNE to maximise the benefits arising from different locations, while minimizing the cost arising from parallel developments and communication failure.

One way to deal with these co-ordination problems are explicit mandates for a certain product group granted by the central R&D department of the group. Four of the seven enterprises in the sample hold such product mandates. They are responsible for all R&D activities (in one case excluding basic research) of their group in one or more well-defined areas. There are different models in place, how research agendas are fixed, and which activities are financed; in most cases, however, financial decision are made at the head office while agendas are formulated jointly between central R&D and the subsidiary management. This type of organisation is common in the pharmaceutical industry, where the knowledge bases for certain products and processes are highly distinct, cumulative and specialized (Marsili 2001, p. 167).

Another form of co-ordination which could be observed among the enterprises of the sample does not employ explicit long-term mandates but is project based. The allocation mechanism is more competitive; R&D labs at the subsidiaries receive internal orders on a project basis from the product divisions of the MNE. The R&D labs compete to a certain degree for these internal orders and have to report to the product division, not to the central R&D department. We find this organisational form in three of the seven enterprises, two of them from the information and communication technologies industry.

Finally, we have one enterprise in the sample which does not fit into the two co-ordination modes presented above because it is actually co-ordinating all R&D activities of its group. It used to be domestically owned and has been acquired by a foreign-owned group. After acquisition, the new Austrian subsidiary was one of only two locations with R&D activities in its group and became the corporate head office for R&D.

9.7 Subsidiary Initiative

A third determinant of subsidiary evolution is the initiative and entrepreneurial spirit of the subsidiary itself. Product mandates and headquarter functions can concede considerable autonomy to the subsidiaries. It is up to the management of the subsidiaries to put this autonomy into entrepreneurial initiative. What may sound obvious is far from being a common behaviour of subsidiaries; international comparisons show that subsidiary initiative is absent in a large number of cases (Birkinshaw et al. 1998).

All interview partners confirm that their enterprises indeed took these chances and developed a considerable level of initiative in recent years. It is, however, difficult to assess these issues on grounds of the subjective judgements of the management. Our interview partners presented two sorts of evidence to underpin their statements:

A first indication of subsidiary initiative is the growth of R&D personnel at the subsidiary. All enterprises could increase the scale of their R&D activities and the number of R&D personnel employed. Although we cannot prove this claim with individual enterprise data, we know from aggregate data on patenting and R&D expenditure that foreign-owned enterprises in Austria considerably enlarged their activities (chapter 3).

The interviews also allow an insight on the performance of enterprises after a foreign takeover. Three enterprises in the sample have been acquired by foreign-owned MNEs in the second half of the 1990s. Almost ten years later, we observe an increase in the number of research personnel in two, and a constant number of research personnel in one enterprise. The R&D manager of one enterprise mentioned that there was a reduction in R&D personnel due to an adjustment of the competences of each location within the MNE. These job losses, however, have been compensated in the following years by an increased demand for the R&D services of the Austrian subsidiary. The interviewees acknowledge that this favourable development after takeover cannot be explained by their entrepreneurial initiative alone - since the expertise of the subsidiary was an important reason for the takeover in two cases. There were considerable complementarities between the acquiring MNE and the acquired enterprise. However, the interview partners are convinced that the development after ownership change would not have been so successful without a lack of entrepreneurial spirit in their enterprises.

A second indicator of subsidiary initiative, besides scale, is whether or not the enterprise could gain mandates and headquarter functions or lost competences in recent years. There is no enterprise in the sample that lost competences in R&D to other subsidiaries of the group in the last ten years (or after acquisition). Four out of the seven enterprises could increase their competences. One enterprise has enlarged its activities from applied to basic R&D. Another subsidiary became the regional co-ordinator for all R&D activities of its group in Middle and Eastern Europe and one enterprise is co-ordinating the R&D activities of the group in a specific product segment.

Two enterprises even have set up their own R&D subsidiaries in Eastern Europe and Asia. These enterprises are formally owned by the Austrian subsidiary and report to them and not to the group's headquarter. Infineon Austria (see below) is one of the enterprises where we can observe such a 'second-tier internationalisation'. The literature does not know very much about this type of internationalisation so far, but we can assume that 'second-tier' internationalisation will only occur in sectors where internationalisation is most advanced and subsidiary mandates are most extensive. The most obvious candidates are information and communication technologies and pharmaceuticals. From a network perspective (Criscuolo and Narula 2005), second-tier internationalisation means a lower overall degree for the parent enterprise and multi-hub structures instead of communication that all passes a single hub. This makes communication easier in a specific part of the network, but at the cost of a loss of communication between these sub-networks.

Box 2: Head-office assignment and subsidiary choice: the case of Infineon Technologies Austria AG

An illustration of subsidiary development is the evolution of Infineon Austria AG (abbr: Infineon Austria). Infineon Technologies Austria AG is a 100% subsidiary of Infineon Technologies Holding BV (NL) and has its main location in Villach, Carinthia. Infineon Austria currently employs about 2,600 employees and is one of the largest enterprises in the field of Information and Communication Technology in Austria. The enterprise is also one of the major R&D performers in the country with over 800 employees working in research and development and a total R&D expenditure of 20% of turnover (Infineon Austria AG 2006).

The parent enterprise of Infineon Austria, Infineon Technologies, has been founded in 1999 when the semiconductor activities of Siemens were concentrated in a separate enterprise. The Infineon Group is organized in three business groups: Communications (COM), Memory Products (MP), and the Automotive, Industrial and Multimarket (AIM) business group. As a result of fundamental organisation changes in recent years, the three business groups of Infineon enjoy a high degree of autonomy in their fields and operate as "companies within the company" (Infineon Technologies AG 2006, p. 40). Infineon has moved decision making processes and the responsibility for production and R&D activities to the three business groups. They can now independently confer production and R&D mandates to local subsidiaries. There is a certain level of internal competition for these mandates.

Infineon Austria considerably benefited from this organisational structure and the high degree of autonomy for the subsidiaries. The enterprise could gain important production and R&D mandates in the Automotive, Industrial and Multimarket field. In 1997, Villach became a Centre of Competence and main location for power electronics in AIM. Sales headquarter functions for Austria, the new EU member states and South Eastern Europe were transferred to Villach in 1999. In 2003, Villach became the group-wide headquarter of the AIM group. Furthermore, central IT responsibilities for the development of software and the worldwide management of the Infineon IT infrastructure have been shifted to Austria as well.

As a group-wide headquarter for the Automotive & Industrial business group, Infineon Austria is not only a recipient of production mandates, but is also actively pushing internationalisation. Infineon Austria is currently setting up two subsidiaries abroad, a new production site in Kulin, Malaysia and a development centre in Bucharest, Romania. Kulin has started operations in March 2006 will employ about 1,700 employees in its final stage. The Bucharest development centre established itself in December 2005 has about 50 employees. Both enterprises are subsidiaries of Infineon Austria and accountable to the Villach headquarter.

The motives for Infineon Austria to expand their operations abroad were manifold. The first motive was based on its need to keep pace with the growing demand in the automotive sector and to increase production and development capacity. Moreover, Infineon Austria is also attracted by the lower wages in Malaysia and Romania. These advantages outweigh disadvantages such as different business practices, etc..

As the two new sites are an expansion of Infineon's capacities, there is no relocation of production or R&D from Austria to Romania or Malaysia in the short run. However, in the future, the interviewee sees a new division of labour between old and new plants. Austria will focus on R&D, while Malaysia will be more engaged in production activities. The Romanian activities are small and will support development at the Austrian subsidiary.

Source: Dachs (2008)

9.8 Concluding Remarks

We have analyzed R&D mandates and the three underlying factors of subsidiary evolution identified by Birkinshaw and Hood (1998) - local environment, head office assignment and subsidiary choice – for seven foreign-owned enterprises in Austria. All enterprises have broad mandates for R&D in certain product segments or technologies, and quantitative patent analysis suggests that they are important contributors to the technological capabilities of their enterprise groups.

It turned out that all three drivers of subsidiary development identified by Birkinshaw and Hood (1998) are present and influential:

The *local environment* in Austria provided the necessary human resources to build up R&D capacity, in some cases at lower cost than in the parent country.

Foreign-owned enterprises benefit from local knowledge at Austrian universities and enterprises. The interviewees see in the Austrian R&D promotion system a major locational advantage.

All head-offices have mechanisms in place to *assign different forms of responsibility* to the subsidiaries. This may be a mandate for a certain product segment, a competitive project-based mechanism or the co-ordination of responsibilities for certain regions and/or product segments.

The enterprises included in the case study took advantage of these internal mechanisms and developed a considerable level of *entrepreneurship and subsidiary initiative*. They enlarged their mandates and increased capacity at their locations.

The interviews clearly demonstrated the interrelatedness and self-enforcing nature of the relationship between head office assignment, subsidiary initiative and, to a lesser extent, the local environment. The trend towards a less centralized organisational structure and network relationships between parent enterprise and subsidiaries gave the subsidiaries room to develop more independence and initiative. They could develop this initiative because the Austrian innovation system provided favourable framework conditions to build up R&D capacity. These enhanced capacities, in turn, were an important argument of the subsidiary management in favour of more organisational decentralisation and larger subsidiary mandates.

10. Policies to Benefit from the Internationalisation of Innovation

The final chapter moves the focus from the enterprise level to the countries level. We ask what countries can actually do to maximise the benefits from the internationalisation of innovation.

To answer this question, we first discuss the relevant literature on the effects of the internationalisation of innovative activities on countries and develop a comprehensive list of the opportunities and challenges for host countries identified in the literature.

In a second step, we examine the international policy framework for the internationalisation of innovation. National policies in this field are embedded in transnational regulations such as the EU legislation concerning state aids and R&D funding, or international trade agreements and regulations established under the World Trade Organisation (WTO). These regulations considerably shape the range of policy measures countries can employ to influence the process of internationalisation.

The final section of this chapter discusses what countries can actually do to maximise the benefits from the internationalisation of MNE innovative activities. Here, the results from literature review and the survey of existing policy measures are joined with the findings from the empirical analysis of the study.

10.1 Opportunities and Challenges from the Internationalisation of Innovation

Prior to the formulation of a policy for the internationalisation of innovation, it is important to be aware of the challenges and opportunities this development poses to countries. There is a considerable amount of literature on the economic benefits and costs from foreign direct investment and the internationalisation of production for countries (see Lipsey 2002; Barba Navaretti 2004 for recent surveys). The basic line of argumentation is the well-known idea of comparative advantage in foreign trade: countries benefit from internationalisation via an increased international division of labour according to different factor endowments of the countries. Moreover, the literature distinguishes between effects from the presence of innovative foreign-owned enterprises in a country (*host country effects)* and the effects for an economy when domestically owned enterprises locate innovative activities abroad (*home country effects)*. Since this study focuses on the effects of internationalisation for the home country, we will only deal with home country effects.

A considerable smaller part of the literature is dealing with benefits and challenges of the internationalisation of innovative activity (Archibugi and Iammarino 1999; Meyer-Krahmer and Reger 1999; UNCTAD 2005, chapter 6; Veugelers 2005). The main effects for countries that host foreign-owned enterprises identified in the literature are summarized in Table 25.

Table 25: Opportunities and challenges from the internationalisation of innovation

Opportunities	Challenges
• Innovative expenditure and capacity increases • Knowledge and information flows to the host economy • Demand for skilled personnel • Structural change and agglomeration effects	• Loss of control over domestic innovative capacity and commercialisation • Separation of R&D and Production • Less strategic research, less radical innovations, more adapting • Less interaction of foreign-owned firms with local organisations

Source: Adapted from UNCTAD (2005, p. 180), Archibugi and Iammarino (1999), Meyer-Krahmer and Reger (1999), Veugelers (2005).

10.1.1 Potential Opportunities for the Host Country

Aggregate Innovation Expenditure

Increases in aggregate R&D and innovation expenditure are probably the most visible effects from the presence of R&D units of multinational enterprises in a country. R&D investments of MNE subsidiaries can increase a country's overall level of research, development and innovation activities substantially and in a short time. But also established foreign-owned subsidiaries can contribute disproportionately to a country's growth of gross domestic expenditure on R&D (GERD) because they do not depend solely on their own internal sources for R&D funding, but can also access financial means from the parent enterprise. Moreover, foreign-owned enterprises predominantly operate in technology-intensive sectors which, on average, spend more on R&D than other industries.

We have shown in chapter 3 that Austria has seized these opportunities from internationalisation. Foreign funding of R&D activities has increased faster than any other funding source during the last 15 years. If we deduct the share of foreign funding, total R&D intensity in Austria would be around 0.4 percentage points lower (2007: 2.15% vs. 2.54%). These figures even underestimate the impact of MNEs on aggregate national spending because they only include cross-border payments and do not account for R&D expenditure financed by the subsidiaries themselves.

R&D financing from foreign sources has therefore considerably helped to increase overall R&D intensity in Austria. A similar effect of foreign funding can also be observed in Canada, Iceland or the UK (Lonmo and Anderson 2003).

Knowledge and Information Flows

A second important, but less visible benefit for host countries, are knowledge and information flows from foreign-owned enterprises to organisations in the host country. This also includes, to a large part, spillovers (see Blomström and Kokko 1998; Keller 2004 for a review). According to Blomström and Kokko (2003), spillovers are the strongest argument as to why countries should try to attract inward investment. Other authors, however, are more sceptical. Reinhilde Veugelers, for example, finds that, "it is fair to conclude that the results on positive spillovers on host economies are not strong and robust" (Veugelers 2005, p 37). Görg and Strobl (2001), on the other hand, indicate that the number of studies that identify positive spillovers roughly equals the number that identify no effects or even negative consequences from the presence of foreign-owned enterprises.

Here, readers should notice that the concept of spillovers found in the international business literature and in the FDI literature is different in some respect from the concept of knowledge flows in the innovation literature which are also frequently labelled as spillovers. Both concepts put emphasis on different aspects and, one has to add, without paying too much attention to the other field.

In the innovation literature, knowledge spillovers refer to the fact that innovativeness and productivity growth of enterprises and sectors is not only related to their own R&D, but also to R&D efforts and knowledge creation in other industries (Griliches 1992, 1995). Here, the term spillovers stresses the importance of exchange for the innovation process, particularly in the innovation systems literature (Edquist 1997, 2005a). It refers - to a lesser extent - to the non-compensation criterion, which is essential for the international business and FDI literature and the general definition of spillovers in economics. In some cases, spillovers may also include knowledge transfers that are partly compensated for, such as contract research or joint research projects.

Spillovers in the context of the international business literature, in contrast, do not exclusively focus on the transfer of information or knowledge, but also include other effects the receiver does not compensate for (Blomström and Kokko 1998; Görg and Strobl 2001). One example is a lower price level in a certain market due to increased competition after market entry of a foreign enterprise. The concept 'spillovers', as used in the context of this study, will follow the innovation literature and include all transfers of knowledge and information between economic agents.

It has been mentioned above that a number of authors are sceptical about the importance of spillovers for the host country because positive effects do not show up in a considerable number of empirical investigations. A reason for this vagueness of the results, besides measurement and estimation issues (Görg and Strobl 2001), is the fact that spillovers from MNE subsidiaries to the local economy do not occur automatically. Veugelers (2005) discusses three preconditions for their occurrence:

First, foreign-owned subsidiaries have to possess knowledge valuable to domestic enterprises. This knowledge can be created by the subsidiary itself, or, by the parent enterprise or another subsidiary of the MNE. In the latter case, foreign owned subsidiaries could be seen as 'bridges' that allow access to knowledge-bases of other countries where the MNE is active. One can assume that such a situation is more likely in the case of competence-creating subsidiaries.

A second precondition is the willingness of the sender to allow spillovers. This is most likely when enterprises sell their knowledge or actively enter into exchange and co-operation with their business environment. MNEs, however, may also try to restrict knowledge spillovers and hold their knowledge secret from other enterprises in the host country.

A third precondition is sufficient absorptive capacity of receiving organizations. We have discussed absorptive capacity in chapter 2.5. The ability to absorb knowledge is largely dependent on previous levels of knowledge stocks, knowledge creation and knowledge diversity at the enterprise. Internal R&D activities improve the capabilities of enterprises to de-codify the "spilled" knowledge (Kathuria 2002).

When these three preconditions are met, knowledge can diffuse to the local innovation system. This knowledge diffusion takes two different channels:

A first important channel for knowledge transfer between foreign-owned enterprises and the domestic economy is the labour market (Görg and Strobl 2005). Employees of foreign-owned enterprises acquire skills – by formal in-house training, but also by gaining experience by learning-by-doing –and continue to use these skills in other enterprises after they have left the MNE. Given the tacit nature of knowledge transfers, it is feasible that this channel is the main diffusion mechanism in many countries. The performance of this transmission channel, however, very much depends on country- and industry-specific conditions, as demonstrated by Giarattana et al (2004) for the software industry in India, Israel and Ireland.

Disembodied flows of knowledge and information are a second important type of knowledge transfer from foreign-owned enterprises to the host economy. They can take various forms, ranging from informal exchange ('demonstration effects' in the international business literature) and reverse engineering to formal co-operation in research projects between foreign-owned enterprises and domestic organisations. Another distinction is between horizontal spillovers, occurring between enterprises of the same sector, and vertical spillovers, which result from customer-supplier relationships. The importance of vertical spillovers stressed by the FDI literature (Javorcik 2004) has an equivalent in the discussions of user-producer interaction in the innovation literature (for example Lundvall 1988).

Despite the large interest in the topic, empirical evidence on disembodied flows of knowledge and information between foreign-owned and domestically owned enterprises is scarce. A considerable body of literature has studied the determinants of formal R&D co-operation in recent years (Cassiman and Veugelers 2002; Schartinger et al. 2002); only some have also included foreign ownership as a right-hand variable. Tether (2002), for example, finds that foreign ownership of UK enterprises results in a higher probability to enter into a co-operative arrangement with suppliers and customers compared to domestically owned enterprises.

Direct evidence on less formal channels such as demonstration effects is scarce, too. Empirical studies on spillovers in the international business and FDI literature usually correlate productivity of domestically owned firms and the extent of foreign presence in their sector (for example Keller and Yeaple 2003) or in supplier- or customer-sectors (Javorcik 2004). This is a set-up too broad to distinguish between various types of spillovers and spillovers from other sources than foreign-owned enterprises.

Case studies which differentiate between various types, in contrast, may provide results that are hardly to be generalized. Moreover, there are some studies using patent citations to examine knowledge flows *from* the host economy *to* foreign-owned enterprises (Frost 2001; Castellani and Zanfei 2002; Almeida and Phene 2004), but, to our knowledge, no exercise that would investigate knowledge flows in the opposite direction.

To our knowledge, there are no studies for Austria that would directly measure knowledge flows between foreign-owned and domestically owned enterprises or other domestic organisations, either. We can, however, conclude from various sources that these flows are present and considerable. Different studies show that foreign-owned enterprises frequently enter into co-operative arrangements with Austrian universities and domestically owned enterprises, which is an important pre-condition for knowledge flows (Rossak 2002, p. 66 and 70; Schibany et al. 2004). Foreign-owned enterprises also participate in Austrian funding schemes to promote R&D co-operation, such as K-ind, K-plus and their successor, COMET[13]. Moreover, the empirical analysis of this study has delivered

13 http://www.ffg.at/content.php?cid=340

additional evidence for the embeddedness of foreign-owned enterprises in the Austrian innovation system. We can therefore assume that Austria benefits from spillovers from foreign-owned enterprises and domestic organisations.

Demand for Skilled Personnel

The presence of foreign-owned enterprises may also have positive effects on the host country labour markets for R&D personnel and other highly skilled personnel. In fact, labour market shortages at home are a major reason for the internationalisation of R&D, as Reger (2003) examines in a case study on Philips' internationalisation in the 1970s and 1980s. Foreign-owned enterprises are attractive employers for scientists and engineers; on average, they pay higher wages and employ more skilled personnel than domestically owned enterprises (Driffield and Taylor 2000; Lipsey 2002). Since foreign-owned enterprises more frequently operate in high- and medium-high technology areas, they may also have a higher demand for certain skills than the average domestically owned enterprise.

The labour market effects of additional demand for skilled personnel from a new Greenfield investment or an extension of existing subsidiary operations will depend on the wage elasticity of labour supply in various skill groups and on the availability of alternative employment opportunities for scientists, engineers and technicians. There may be a positive effect in the short run if R&D and technical personnel is unemployed. New career opportunities from foreign investment have even led to a "reverse brain drain" in some developing countries (UNCTAD 2005, p. 185). However, the entry of multinational enterprise may also lead to a crowding out and increased competition with local enterprises for R&D personnel in the short run - since MNE subsidiaries may offer higher wages and more attractive career opportunities. Moreover, empirical evidence shows that the entrance of foreign-owned firms increases wage inequality between different skill groups (Driffield and Taylor 2000).

In the long run, skill intensity may increase throughout the whole economy due to structural change triggered by foreign direct investment, and, in turn, foster efforts in education, which further increase the attractiveness of the country for foreign investment. An illustration of these effects is case of Ireland (Barry 2004).

Foreign-owned enterprises are also important employers for R&D personnel in Austria. According to Statistics Austria (Statistik Austria 2007a), foreign-owned enterprises in Austria employ a total R&D staff of 10,820 persons (full-time equivalent), or roughly every third employee in corporate R&D in Austria in 2004. Due to a higher share of foreign-owned enterprises in high-technology sectors, the share of foreign-owned enterprises on R&D personnel is higher than their share on total employment (11%). Statistics Austria also provides some results for selected industries. Here, the share is highest in radio, television and communication equipment (NACE 32), where nine out of ten researchers work for foreign-owned enterprises, followed by the pharmaceutical industry with a foreign share of 71%. In general, the share of researchers in foreign-owned enterprises is higher in manufacturing than in services.

Structural Change and Agglomeration Effects

Another effect associated with the presence of foreign enterprises is a faster structural change towards a more R&D intensive industrial structure. Structural change, in turn, promotes economic growth by shifting resources to more high value-added activities ("structural bonus hypothesis" - see Timmer and Szirmai 2000; Peneder 2003).

Foreign direct investment affects industrial structure in two ways: First, directly, because MNE subsidiaries more frequently operate in high-technology sectors. Foreign investment may lead to higher sectoral growth and, in turn, to a higher overall growth rate. The effect is more pronounced in the case of Greenfield investment than in the case of an acquisition; however, foreign direct investment in existing enterprises can also raise overall growth when the new owners increase the firm's productivity.

A second effect from FDI on structural change is more indirect: foreign-owned enterprises may increase aggregate demand for high-quality intermediary goods and/or impose higher requirements for product quality. Both are incentives to domestic suppliers to upgrade their production processes and therefore favour the growth of technology-intensive suppliers in the country. This effect is very similar to the concept of "vertical spillovers" in the FDI literature (Javorcik 2004). The most prominent example for the effects of FDI on local suppliers is Ireland (Barry 2004; Barry and van Egeraat 2005).

This positive indirect effect from the presence of foreign-owned subsidiaries on structural change may be – at least partly – counterbalanced by another indirect effect, which is known as the "competition effect" of foreign direct investment (Blomström and Kokko 1998; Aitken and Harrison 1999). Multinational enterprises – as new entrants - challenge incumbent enterprises and raise the degree of competition in the host country. This may, on the one hand, bring prices down and force domestically owned enterprises to become more productive and move into higher value-added activities. The competition effect, on the other hand, could also have negative effects on aggregate growth in the host country when domestically owned enterprises have to leave the market due to fierce competition.

Effects from the presence of multinationals on economic structure may be more pronounced at the regional and local level than at the national level (Young et al. 1994; Bellandi 2001; Pavlínek 2004 for Central and Eastern Europe). This is, at first, a result of size. An investment of a certain size simply constitutes a larger share on overall economic activity and the technological capabilities in a city or a region than in the whole country.

Second, the structural effects of FDI may be stronger in some regions because technology-intensive activity tends to be geographically concentrated, and this concentration becomes stronger over time (Asheim and Gertler 2005). This can be explained by two, partly complement arguments (Breschi and Lissoni 2001b); the existence of agglomeration economies, such as specialized labour markets and the tacit characteristics of knowledge discussed above. As a result, foreign-owned subsidiaries in clusters are more embedded into their local environment, more autonomous, but also more internationally-oriented than foreign-owned subsidiaries in other industry sectors (Birkinshaw and Hood 2000; Lorenzen and Mahnke 2002).

To our knowledge, no study has investigated the structural and agglomerative effects of foreign-owned enterprises in Austria. There is, however, rich evidence that foreign-owned subsidiaries also constitute major players in some of Austria's industrial clusters. Examples are the Styrian and Upper Austria Automotive Cluster (Magna Steyr, Magna Powertrain, BMW, Infineon). We can clearly see the concentration effects of foreign-funded R&D - which predominantly is found in the Vienna and Graz region and Upper Austria.

10.1.2 Potential Challenges for the Host Country

The internationalisation of research, development and innovation can bring considerable benefits for host countries; the process, however, is associated with risks - which may provoke certain disadvantages for the host country. These risks mainly concern the well-functioning of the national innovation system and the way innovation is transferred into jobs and national welfare.

Loss of Control over Domestic Innovative Capacity

A main concern associated with the internationalisation of innovation is the loss of control over domestic innovative capacity. Foreign-owned enterprises could act in ways that are not in accordance with the best national interest -since decisions regarding research, development and innovation in foreign-owned enterprises are not made by local managers, but centrally at the parent enterprise. Faced with the need to cut cost in R&D, the management of an MNE may prefer to reduce R&D activities at a foreign subsidiary than at the parent enterprise in the home country.

The loss-of-control argument is based on the assumption that multinationals are "footloose", because they mainly pursue economic activities that can be easily transferred between countries (Görg and Strobl 2003). There is also reason to believe that political pressure on the enterprise but also felt solidarity may be stronger in the home country than in another location. Moreover, the MNE may benefit from a concentration of R&D and other innovative activities.

Foreign-owned subsidiaries, therefore, have only shallow roots with the host country. In a country perspective, a rising share of internationalisation may therefore lead to a situation where more and more decisions regarding corporate R&D are taken outside the country. As a consequence, domestic policy may gradually lose its ability to influence enterprise decisions when a rising share of the enterprise population is foreign-owned. Critical observers ask how policy-makers can avoid rent seeking and assess 'good citizenship' (Freeman and Soete 1997, p. 345) of MNEs.

Another aspect of this loss-of-control argument which has come up in recent months is associated with the activities of state-owned investment funds, so-called sovereign-wealth funds (DIE ZEIT 2007a, 2007b; The Economist 2007). Some observers fear that these funds, contrary to other financial investors, could invest in an enterprise not only for financial, but also for political and strategic reasons as well – in order to gain access to technological competences.

How real are threats from a loss of control over domestic innovative capacity? At first, studies on the differences in performance between foreign-owned and domestically owned enterprises (reviewed in 8.1) and the empirical analysis of this study, give only little indication of an inferior performance of foreign-owned enterprises and therefore does not support the loss-of-control argument. Enterprise characteristics and strategies are more decisive for innovative behaviour than the ownership status.

Additional empirical evidence on the loss-of-control argument can be found in the literature on mergers and acquisitions. If a domestically owned enterprise is acquired by a foreign-owned multinational, this may lead to a downsizing of R&D activity as part of the integration of the new subsidiary in the MNE. Empirical evidence shows that this is only the case when R&D activities of the acquired and the acquiring enterprise are competing (Cassiman et al. 2005). If R&D activities of both enterprises are complementary, the acquired enterprise may even do more, instead of less R&D. This is in sharp contrast to the loss-of-control argument, but supports the view that enterprise strategies are more important than the ownership status as such. We can add that reductions of R&D activity at the subsidiary are also less likely if the subsidiary is strongly embedded in the host country and benefits from spillovers.

Potential losses at the subsidiary may also be outweighed by the fact that multinational enterprises are less vulnerable to economic fluctuations. New jobs generated in MNE subsidiaries appear to be more persistent than jobs generated in domestically owned plants (Görg and Strobl 2003). Even if the *potential* danger of downsizing is higher in the case of foreign-owned enterprises, the *actual* danger is lower because employment is more persistent and growth perspectives are brighter.

One can also question the assumption that decisions of foreign-owned subsidiaries are usually made by the parent enterprise. Decision processes in corporate R&D of multinational enterprises become more and more decentralized, and R&D activity requires a certain degree of autonomy at the subsidiary level (Zanfei 2000; Criscuolo and Narula 2005). Moreover, subsidiary autonomy, and the assignments the subsidiary receives from the head office co-evolve with dynamic, self-enforcing and self-containing feedback effects (Birkinshaw and Hood 1998); a higher degree of subsidiary choice and autonomy granted by the head office may lead to a build-up of capabilities and a more entrepreneurial behaviour at the subsidiary, which, in turn may foster the decentralisation tendencies in the enterprise group. Some examples for this process and the degree of autonomy of foreign-owned subsidiaries in Austria are given in chapter 9.

Discussions of the loss-of-control argument should also consider concentration. Chapter 3 has shown that the current high level of R&D internationalisation in Austria is the result of the strategies and choices of a very limited number of enterprises. If some of these enterprises change their strategies, this may result in severe changes in overall R&D funding in Austria. In this perspective, the heart of the loss-of-control argument is not foreign ownership, but concentration.

To sum up, we cannot say that countries in general are better off if a large share of R&D capacity is under domestic control. Very much depends on enterprise strategies and the degree to which R&D activities of the subsidiary and parent enterprise complement or substitute each other. In the case of Austria, the problem of concentration of R&D activity is more severe than the loss-of-control argument.

Separation of R&D and Production

Another concern regarding internationalisation is the effectiveness of technology policy in a country with a share of foreign-controlled R&D activities. The final goal of technology policy as a field of economic policy is to foster economic growth and job creation (Metcalfe 1995; Freeman and Soete 1997). It builds on the finding that research, development and innovation are main contributors to economic growth at the enterprise and the aggregate level (OECD 2004c). Governments employ a number of instruments to overcome hampering factors, such as a lack of capital, low appropriability, or a high degree of uncertainty - which may prevent enterprises from performing R&D.

The existence of multinational enterprises influences the effectiveness of economic policy because MNEs have means to shift economic activity between subsidiaries located in various countries (Caves 1996, chapter 10; Haaland 2004). Internationalisation, therefore, also affects the effectiveness of R&D funding, since these policies are, in many cases, based on the implicit assumption that research, development, design and production of a certain good take place in the same country. If an MNE concentrates R&D at one location and the production at another, the country that hosts foreign-controlled R&D may end up in a situation where it supports the creation of new technologies, but does not benefit from their application. As a consequence, R&D subsidies and other measures to support R&D of the foreign-owned subsidiary would have no effect on growth and employment in the host country. This is, in some respect, the other side of the benefits for host countries from spillovers to domestic enterprises.

To our knowledge, there is no empirical analysis that studies the extent of the separation of innovation and production for a particular industry or country so far. An obvious candidate for such a study would be the pharmaceutical industry. It is a sector where a considerable share of enterprises are multinational or global; pharmaceuticals is an R&D intensive sector where a high share of enterprises purse competence-creating strategies and operate centres of excellence with a mandate for one specific group of products; the results of R&D activity can be codified and easily transferred and put into products anywhere.

Less Radical Innovations, more Adapting

A third concern regarding foreign-owned enterprises and innovation addresses the relationship between basic research and radical innovations. Foreign ownership, some observers fear, may lead to less radical innovation and more adaptation of foreign technologies than in the case of domestic ownership. The strongest argument that supports such a position is the observation that multinational enterprises still mostly purse competence-exploiting strategies abroad that restrict their foreign-owned enterprises to adaptive activities (le Bas and Sierra 2002; von Zedtwitz and Gassmann 2002).

Multinational enterprises may also prefer to locate the most basic, forward-looking R&D activities in their home country – since these activities require the strongest linkages to the home country innovation system. Moreover, since the outcome of basic research is often uncertain and future applications are difficult to predict, it may increase the appropriability of the results if basic research is located in proximity to corporate headquarters where knowledge and information exchange is not hampered by distance. A strategy of foreign-owned enterprises that focuses on adaptive R&D may also produce more firm-specific knowledge that is less likely to spill over to the host country innovation system. Finally, multinational enterprises may reduce basic research at newly acquired enterprises outside their home countries to avoid a duplication of R&D activities.

What is the relevance of the argument for Austria? Based on the results of this study, we believe it is limited. The empirical analysis of this study neither found a lower dedication of foreign-owned enterprises to permanent R&D, nor decreased co-operation with domestic universities that may indicate a lower orientation towards more basic R&D activity. Moreover, we have seen that significantly more foreign-owned than domestically owned enterprises introduced market novelties at international markets. This finding does not refute the assumption that foreign-owned enterprises would mainly focus on adapting existing technologies for local markets; however, it demonstrates that an adaptive strategy is even more frequently found among domestically owned than foreign-owned enterprises.

Less Interaction of Foreign-owned Enterprises with Local Organisations

An important determinant of the performance of innovation systems is the degree of interaction and exchange of information and knowledge between its actors (Edquist 2005b). If one group in the innovation system decides to restrict their interactions with other groups, this may have negative consequences for all actors. John Cantwell (1989) has referred to such an occurrence of foreign-owned enterprises mainly relying on internal superior knowledge for their innovative activities. As a consequence, knowledge flows in the innovation systems would be limited and spillovers would be weaker than in the case of domestic ownership. However, it could also be that domestic organisations lack the necessary absorptive capacity, or foreign-owned enterprises are active in different technologies and sectors than domestic organisations. This may be the case when the home and host country of the foreign-owned enterprise differ in terms of technological capabilities.

It is difficult to come to a definite judgement on the extent of spillovers between foreign-owned enterprises and their host country innovation systems. Finding evidence that supports or refutes the claim that a high share of foreign-owned enterprises leads to a lower degree of interaction in an innovation system is even more difficult, though, because such comparisons have to correct for a number of firm-specific and country-specific factors that all influence co-operation. A lower willingness to co-operate by foreign-owned enterprises, for example, may be outweighed by sectoral affiliation to high-tech industries that more frequently co-operate.

One study that compared co-operation behaviour of foreign-owned and domestically owned enterprise is Dachs, Eberberger and Lööf (2008a). They show that subsidiaries of foreign multinationals show a similar or even a higher propensity to co-operate with domestic partners than domestically owned enterprises in the Nordic countries. This study also found only limited evidence for a different behaviour of foreign-owned enterprises in Austria and in 15 countries of comparison. There is no significant effect from foreign ownership if all domestically owned enterprises are compared with all foreign-owned enterprises. From the results of the empirical analysis in the preceding chapters, we conclude that sectoral affiliation, size or the dedication to permanent R&D activity is a more reliable predictor for co-operative behaviour than the ownership status of the enterprise.

10.2 The Policy Framework of the Internationalisation of Innovation

National policies in the field of internationalisation can act freely only to a limited degree. They are embedded in – and, some would say, limited by - transnational regulations that considerably shape the range of policy measures countries can employ to influence the process of internationalisation. These regulations include EU legislation - in particular regulation concerning state aids and R&D funding - as well as international trade agreements and regulations established under the World Trade Organisation (WTO). We will discuss this international framework in the following section.

10.2.1 Policies of the European Union

Two aspects of the common policies of the European Union (EU) are relevant in the context of this chapter. First, regulations in competition policy prohibit state aids which may lead to distortions of the Single Market and the free movement of goods, capital, persons and services within the member countries - this also includes investment incentives to a certain degree. Second, the common research policy of the EU aims at promoting transnational co-operation and coherence in science and technology in Europe.

EU Competition Policy

The treaty establishing the European Communities prohibits all measures of the member states that result in the prevention, restriction or distortion of competition within the common market (Art 85-89). Special reference is given to 'dissimilar conditions to equivalent transactions with other trading parties, thereby placing them at a competitive disadvantage' (Art 85d). This regulation does not only refer to financial treatment but to a variety of state interventions such as grants, interest and tax relieves, guarantees, or the provision of goods and services on preferential terms.

EU competition policy has some important implications for the topic of this study. First, it removed most restrictions to market entry and the set-up of subsidiaries within the EU by ensuring free movement of capital within the Single Market. Second, all kinds of unequal treatment between domestically owned and foreign-owned enterprises (such as exclusion from R&D funding for foreign-owned enterprises, performance requirements like compulsory technology transfer) are prohibited as they may distort competition. Third, since movement of persons within the EU is unlimited, there are also no legal restrictions for employment of scientists and engineers abroad, as long as they are citizens of an EU or EEA member.

Furthermore, the EU has settled a political Code of Conduct to eliminate harmful business tax regimes in 1997 (European Commission 1999). The report lists tax measures, some of them related to research and development, which are regarded as harmful features. The Code is not a legally binding instrument but clearly does have political force because by adopting this Code, the EU member states have guaranteed to take back harmful measures and refrain from introducing such measures in the future.

The rules for state aids in the EU are strict, but there exist a number of exceptions. Two important exceptions with respect to innovation are state aids for the promotion of economic development of underdeveloped regions and for research and development. Moreover, a number of temporary exceptions for the new EU member states exist for free movement of people, but also for financial incentives to attract foreign investment.

EU Science and Technology Policy

Research and development is one of the most important exceptions from the general ban of state aids in the Single Market. The European Commission itself is actively promoting R&D with its Framework Programmes for Research and Technological Development (Caracostas and Muldur 2001). This promotion scheme is open to organisations and persons from the EU member states (including subsidiaries located in the EU). Moreover, the programmes are also open to participants from a number of countries outside of the EU. As a principle, the Framework programmes only support transnational projects; proposals are only accepted from consortia with partners from different countries. The FWP also offers support for trans-border researcher mobility at different stages (undergraduate, postgraduate, experienced researchers).

Facing a widening gap between Europe and the US and Japan in science and technology, the European Union, has launched an initiative toward supporting the creation of an "European Research Area" (ERA) in 2000 (European Commission 2000, 2007). The main goal of ERA is to reduce fragmentation and stimulate transnational interactions in European research by creating a border-free zone for research in Europe. In this respect, ERA is a continuation of the policy of integration already pursed by the FWP. A second task of ERA is to improve cohesion in European research by bringing together scientific communities, companies and researchers from all over Europe. This also includes networking of existing centres of excellence and support for the formation of 'critical masses' and the combination of complementary expertise. Third, ERA aims at an improved coordination of national policies which still account for most of the public funds available for S&T in Europe. ERA is expected to increase scientific specialisation among organisations and countries in Europe, which, in turn, may considerably affect location decisions for R&D units of MNEs.

10.2.2 International Investment Agreements

As a second important factor in the regulation of the internationalisation of innovation is the international policy framework with respect to cross-border investment. The purpose of Bilateral Investment Treaties (BITs) and Multilateral Investment Agreements (MIAs) is to protect investments abroad and grant them national or most favoured nation treatment. This includes several rights such as the right to make investment-related transfers, the right to hire personnel in a foreign country without taking into consideration nationality, regulation concerning dispute settlement and in some cases rules regarding access to funding. These regulations are also intended to prevent an unequal treatment of foreign-owned and domestically owned enterprises – for example in public R&D funding. Moreover, limits are imposed to financial and non-financial investment incentives by national treatment clauses in a number of cases. Since the effectiveness of general FDI incentives (regardless of their wide spread) is disputed among economists (Blomström 2001), BITs and similar regulations are an important step to overcome 'negative-sum' dynamics between countries competing for FDI (Oman 2000).

As for the treaties that concern themselves with economic regions, such as the Treaty of the European Community or the NAFTA treaty, most include the regulations of a BIT or even go far beyond them. It should be noted that their importance has diminished with the accession of the Central and Eastern European states to the European Union. BITs, however, do remain an important instrument for international protection of investment for non-EU member states as well as between the EU and developing countries. UNCTAD (2000a) reports more than two thousand of these treaties around the world.

Finally, the WTO agreements, although dealing with trade of goods and services, include rules on investment and competition protection which may affect internationalisation policies of the WTO members. The Agreement on Trade-Related Investment Measures ("TRIMs") prohibits measures that impose certain performance requirements to investors such as local content requirements (e.g. mandatory local sourcing of supplies to integrate local enterprises into the supply chains of foreign-owned subsidiaries or mandatory technology transfer) or joint venture requirements. The Agreement on Trade-Related Aspects of Intellectual Property Rights (TRIPS) sets minimum standards for the protection of intellectual property rights (IPRs) national legislation must meet. TRIPS could considerably promote the internationalisation of innovation - since weak protection of IPRs is a major disincentive for doing R&D abroad (see, for example, Thursby and Thursby 2006). TRIPS, however, is also heavily criticized by the anti-globalization movement for its negative consequences from a stronger IPR protection on drugs, in particular for the treatment of HIV. Moreover, the GATS Agreement on trade in services also affects investment as it regards FDI ("commercial presence") as one mode of supply of services.

EU as well as bi- and multilateral regulation towards equal treatment of foreign-owned and domestically owned enterprises have a huge effect on national science and technology policies. A recent review of policies in OECD countries towards the internationalisation of innovation reveals that non-discrimination is indeed the guiding principle in the OECD (see below). Foreign-owned enterprises are granted national treatment in all OECD countries (OECD 2004a) and both, foreign-owned and domestically owned enterprises are eligible for national innovation funding to the same conditions.

10.3 Building Blocks for Policy

Benefits and costs associated with the internationalisation of innovation as well as international regulations both shape the range of policy measures countries can employ to influence the process of internationalisation. Within this framework, we will now discuss some principles or building blocks for a policy to maximise the benefits from the presence of foreign-owned enterprises in a country. The chapter draws, on the one hand, on the results of a survey on measures in OECD countries (Dachs et al. 2005a). On the other hand, we will consider theoretical and empirical insights on the effectiveness and efficiency of various policy measures from the literature.

10.3.1 Economic Fundamentals vs. Financial Incentives

First, if countries want to attract foreign R&D, it is essential to look at the economic fundamentals. The development of technological capabilities of subsidiaries is an evolutionary process which does not start from scratch. R&D and design units are an extension of existing production and marketing activities in most cases (Birkinshaw and Hood 1998; Birkinshaw et al. 1998; Archibugi and Iammarino 1999). Investment in innovative activities becomes advantageous for the MNE when subsidiary operations on a particular location exceed a certain threshold. Only a few locations in the world are able to attract inward investment in innovative activities without prior production activities. These locations do not need much promotion by the government to further increase their international attractiveness.

As a consequence, factors which have been identified as influential for FDI also co-determine inward investment in innovative activities to a high degree. There is an extensive literature (reviewed by Ekholm and Midelfart 2004; Blonigen 2005) that has explored these factors. Determinants for inward investment include relative market size, political stability, public infrastructure, tax rates, a stable legal system including the protection of intellectual property rights, labour market conditions or relative production cost. To provide and secure a 'healthy business environment' (OECD 2003a) is therefore not only essential if policy wants to attract inward FDI, but also for attracting overseas innovative activity.

Empirical studies on the location decisions of R&D activities of MNEs have confirmed this relationship (Cantwell and Mudambi 2000; Kumar 2001; Cantwell and Piscitello 2002; Thursby and Thursby 2006). Jerry and Marie Thursby (2006), for example, examine factors that influence R&D location both in developed and emerging countries. They find that the strongest attractors in developed countries are the quality of R&D personnel and the level of IPR protection, followed by factors related to university research and output markets. For emerging economies, growth of output markets is first, followed by the quality of R&D personnel and the personnel costs of researchers. Financial incentives such as tax breaks play no role in both country groups. Cantwell and Mudambi (2000) come to a very similar conclusion and show that R&D units are more attracted by low economic risk, local experience and infrastructure than by special incentives. They find that only "locations that have reached MNE location short-lists can gain from the provision of incentives" (Cantwell and Mudambi 2000, p. 127). The choice of location for overseas R&D of MNEs depends on the internal strategies of MNEs at first, and secondly on location characteristics such as adequate infrastructure, public research facilities, educational system and science base of location (Molero and Alvarez 2004).

From a theoretical and empirical perspective, investment incentives to attract foreign R&D therefore have no substantial effect in the long run and are just triggering 'negative-sum' dynamics between countries competing for FDI (Oman 2000). Countries should avoid these measures and concentrate on offering favourable economic fundamentals to both, foreign-owned and domestically owned enterprises.

10.3.2 Non-Discrimination as a Guiding Principle

A well-developed promotional system for R&D open to both, domestically owned and foreign-owned enterprises is one of the strongest incentives a government can offer to attract R&D investment of MNEs. There are a number of reasons why countries should follow such a policy:

First, the empirical results of this study have showed that differences between foreign-owned and domestically owned enterprises with respect to research, development and innovation are related to enterprises characteristics (size, sector …) rather than to the ownership status. Foreign-owned enterprises do not exhibit a superior performance either after controlling for enterprise characteristics. Similar results are delivered by other studies on this topic. Rather, our results suggest to concentrate promotional activities on enterprises or industries regardless of ownership and to help enterprises to develop their innovative capabilities through human capital and investment.

Second, as discussed above, a positive or negative discrimination of foreign-owned or domestically owned enterprises with respect to funding and other incentives is not legally possible in a number of cases. EU competition law as well as national and international regulations on investment agreements set limits to monetary and non-monetary investment incentives.

A third objection vis-à-vis discrimination are the inconclusive results on the effectiveness of investment incentives discussed above. Moreover, a government that invests large amounts to attract R&D labs of MNEs may also be challenged by the domestic business community whether money is better invested in domestically owned enterprises which produce and create jobs within borders of the country.

Non-discrimination is indeed the guiding principle in the treatment of foreign-owned enterprises in all OECD countries (Koyama and Golub 2006). Foreign-owned enterprises are granted "national treatment" in all OECD countries with respect to R&D funding (see also OECD 2004a; Dachs et al. 2005a). They may apply for national R&D funding schemes just like domestically-owned organisations. Exemptions can be found in some countries for funding in sectors such as defence and energy.

R&D policies do not differentiate with respect to the ownership (foreign-owned vs. domestically owned), but with respect to location of the enterprise (locally domiciled vs. non-domiciled). Non-domiciled foreign-owned enterprises are mostly excluded from R&D funding. Some countries (for example Austria, New Zealand, Australia, and the Scandinavian countries), however, even open up national support schemes for non-domiciled organisations. Australia justifies this strategy with the argument that "Australia does not have all the necessary R&D expertise and facilities to meet industry needs, and that Australian companies should not be disadvantaged in seeking world class R&D wherever it may be located" (AusIndustry 2004, p. 2). In a number of countries, the purchase of R&D services and intellectual property from abroad is also regarded as expenditure eligible for tax deduction schemes and most jurisdictions do not differentiate between locally domiciled and non-domiciled organisations with respect to tax deductibility (IBFD 2004). Exceptions are Belgium, France, Japan, the Netherlands, Spain and the United States. Some countries are also trying to remove non-legal barriers such as language issues. Japan, for example, has facilitated access to its public R&D assistance schemes by allowing foreign-located researchers to submit their proposals in English.

10.3.3 The Importance of Non-Monetary Incentives

If countries try to actively recruit foreign direct investment in R&D, they rather use non-financial than financial measures (Table 26). Such incentives include, for example, advertisement and active recruitment of enterprises abroad, administrative support for establishing the subsidiary, assistance in creating links to the local business community etc. According to Guimon (2007), this strategy is most promising to attract foreign-owned R&D, in particular if emphasis is placed on "after-care" services and the provision of support through a longer period of time. He argues that foreign R&D centers rarely emerge overnight but are the result of an evolutionary process whereby existing subsidiaries are progressively gaining production and technology mandates from the parent enterprise. Hence, a one-time promotion would be less successful than providing constant services to overcome problems that emerge in this process. Moreover, a constant interaction with foreign-owned enterprises also increases their embeddedness in the host country and hence makes foreign-owned R&D less footless.

Table 26: Specific measures to support the location of new R&D activities through foreign direct investment in OECD countries

Country	Direct financial support	Administrative support	Provision of infrastructure	Public procurement	Active recruitment	Advertising
Australia	×				×	
Austria		×			×	×
Denmark					×	×
Finland					×	×
France			×			
Germany		×			×	×
Italy		×				
Japan						
Netherlands		×			×	
N. Zealand						
Norway						
Poland				×		

Source: Dachs et al. 2005a

Another non-monetary measure is the provision of infrastructure to foreign-owned enterprises in science and business parks. Science parks, in particular, are an important part of policies in countries outside the OECD (Appold 2004). An example is China; a current review by the OECD (2007c) discusses the role of science parks and incubators in detail.

In addition to the measures discussed here, there may be some additional benefits negotiated between MNEs and inward investment agencies to influence investment decisions on the margin, but such negotiated cases cannot be regarded as general rules.

10.3.4 The Role of Research, Innovation and Technology Policy

Measures to build an innovation-friendly environment and increase the scientific and technological capacities of a country will also help to attract foreign R&D. Like in the case of economic fundamentals, such a policy is not dedicated to foreign-owned enterprises alone, but supports all enterprises regardless of ownership status.

The literature usually distinguishes between various types of research, innovation and technology policy measures. Mowery (1995) identifies three types of measures: 'supply policies' that stimulate the creation of novelty, 'adoption policies' that encourage enterprises to take up new knowledge and technologies, and 'competition policy' that puts pressure on enterprises for continuous improvements. All three types of policies are important in the context of foreign-owned enterprises, although we will lay the emphasis of our discussion on the first two.

The literature provides a number of examples that illustrate how 'supply policies' influence location decisions of multinational enterprises. Foreign-owned enterprises are attracted by and benefit from these policies - since they operate in science-based sectors to a higher degree. MNEs are, for example, attracted by external local sources of knowledge in the host country (Cantwell and Janne 1999; Cantwell and Piscitello 2002) and agglomerations, which can be potential sources of knowledge spillovers (Barry et al. 2001). Other 'supply' factors that attract investment include the industrial specialisation of a country (Braunerhjelm and Svensson 1996), R&D intensity at the sectoral level (Neven and Siotis 1996), or skill differences between the home and the host country (Carr et al. 2001). The importance of the quality of scientific research as a locational factor has also been confirmed by Cantwell and Mudambi (2000), Kuemmerle (1999a), Kumar (2001; 2003) or Belderbos et al. (2007), who relate the number of foreign-located patent inventions to the number of cited publications in different scientific fields.

Supply policies, therefore, have a fundamental role in innovation-related FDI. They can create locational advantages in science and technology that attract MNE investments. Measures to create and foster these advantages include education and training, the promotion of scientific excellence and technological specialisation, or the provision of an excellent infrastructure, in particular ICT infrastructure (Edler and Mayer-Krahmer 2003). Universities and public research institutions play an important role in this context. They do not only develop new knowledge, which may stimulate innovation in the private sector, but also contribute to the training of scientists and engineers, promote the development of innovation networks and support the diffusion of technology among a variety of actors (Appold 2004; OECD 2004b).

Supply policies, together with providing a healthy business environment, can also help to face some threats associated with the internationalisation of innovation discussed above. Governments are worried that internationalisation may lead to less strategic research, less radical innovations, and more adapting than in the case of domestic ownership. It is obvious that governments have only little means to prevent such a strategy of MNEs. However, such a decision is less likely if countries provide good supply policies and attractive framework conditions for doing R&D.

10.3.5 Raising Absorptive Capacity

Various authors argue that domestically owned enterprises must have some types of knowledge (absorptive capabilities) in order to be able to receive and utilize spillovers (e.g. Blomström and Kokko 2003; Kumar 2003). R&D investment of domestically owned enterprises is crucial for enabling them to understand and evaluate new technological trends and innovations and eventually to acquire foreign technologies. We can therefore conclude that the benefits for the host country from the presence of foreign-owned enterprises are higher if countries promote improvements in the technological capabilities of domestically owned enterprises.

Governments take an active role in helping domestic organisations to improve their absorptive capabilities. These policies, however, are predominantly found under the more general heading of "adoption policies" (Mowery 1995), which aim to encourage the transfer of new knowledge and technologies, regardless if the source is foreign-owned or domestically owned. The INNO-Policy TrendChart project, a EU funded initiative to describe and analyse innovation policy trends, lists 160 policy measures throughout Europe and some other countries that target technology transfer[14]. Measures to improve absorptive capacities address small and medium sized enterprises (SMEs). 47 of the measures listed by TrendChart are only open to SMEs. Some programmes also target the diffusion of specific technologies (Nanotechnologies, ICT, ...) or focus on specific sectors. There is also a great variety with respect to the instrument mix – grants, (preferential) loans, provision of guarantees, assumption of liabilities and the like – and with respect to eligible R&D activities.

We could not identify programmes that are tailored to increase the ability to absorb spillovers from foreign-owned enterprises in the TrendChart database. Some of the new member states of the EU have installed measures to help domestic organisations to participate in the EU Framework programmes, for example, by providing additional funding. On a more general level, all OECD countries have measures in place to promote international co-operative research projects (see Allen Consulting Group 2003 for a recent overview).

10.3.6 Increasing Embeddedness of Foreign-owned Enterprises

Finally, measures seeking to maximise the benefits from the internationalisation of innovations should not only attract innovative subsidiaries of MNEs by improving framework conditions, but also foster the linkages between domestically

[14] http://www.proinno-europe.eu/index.cfm?fuseaction=page.display&topicID=262&parentID=52, information retrieved 07/12/2007

owned organisations and foreign-owned subsidiaries. The likelihood of spillovers can be improved if foreign-owned and domestically owned enterprises are in constant interaction with each other in supplier, customer or competitive relationships. We have called this a situation where foreign-owned enterprises show a high degree of local embeddedness. Kokko (1994; 1996; Blomström and Kokko 2003) argues that the scope for learning would be the greatest when foreign-owned subsidiaries and domestically owned enterprises are in direct competition with each other. Competition policy as a means of science, technology and innovation policy is therefore a third component of a policy to maximize the benefits from the presence of foreign-owned enterprises. Conversely, spillovers are less likely to occur when foreign-owned enterprises operate in "enclaves", where neither products nor technologies have much in common with those of local enterprises (Kokko 1996).

Linkages between domestically owned organisations and foreign-owned enterprises may occur 'by chance' without governmental intervention. Most governments follow a more proactive strategy and have programmes in place to promote R&D joint ventures and co-operative innovation projects. These measures, like measures to increase absorptive capacity, are only rarely associated with policies towards internationalisation, but pursue the general goal of increasing co-operation and exchange in the national innovation system.

An effective way to link foreign to domestically owned enterprises is to support the building of clusters, *i.e.* networks of enterprises, universities and other organisations. Clusters can be formed among enterprises in the same sector, specialized suppliers, service providers, and associated research and educational institutes, all at the regional, national, or even cross-border level. Cluster and co-operation policies are even more frequently found than policies to promote technology transfer. TrendChart lists more than 230 measures in Europe that pursue this goal[15]. An example of such a policy initiative in Austria is the structural programme of the *Forschungsförderungsgesellschaft* (FFG). The FFG supports temporary joint research centres between academia and enterprises with the 'Kplus' and the 'K-ind/K-net' programme, research co-operations with the *Fachhochschulen* (universities of applied sciences) in 'FHplus', and provides also special incentives for SMEs to co-operate in innovation programmes.

Spillovers may also occur via supplier-customer-relationships between foreign-owned (buyer) and domestically owned (supplier) enterprises. Technological learning via subcontracting and supplier-customer-relationships proved to be extremely successful in some catching-up economies such as Taiwan, South

---

15 http://www.proinno-europe.eu/index.cfm?fuseaction=page.display&topicID=262&parentID=52 information retrieved 07/12/2007

Korea, and most recently, China (Hobday 2000; Fagerberg and Godinho 2005). One way to prompt such objectives would be to establish performance requirements, *e.g.*, technology transfers to subcontracting local enterprises could be declared as mandatory, or foreign-owned enterprises could be forced to make use of local intermediate inputs, or to employ local staff (so-called local content provisions). However, today such practice is hardly an option since such provisions must be compatible with the TRIMs Agreement ruling out not only prescriptive measures such as local content requirement, but also such measures whose compliance is necessary in order to obtain an advantage (UNCTAD 2001, p. 165 ff).

10.3.7 The Role of Accompanying Policies

Science and technology are cross-cutting issues that touch a range of policy areas. Therefore, there are also other policies outside science, technology and economic policy that influence the attractiveness of countries as locations for MNE R&D. A policy area with a high relevance for the topics discussed in this study is immigration, in particular policies towards foreign highly-skilled labour. Knowledge within multinational enterprises is often bound to individuals; an exchange of knowledge within the MNE therefore depends, to a certain extent, on the possibility to move these individuals between countries. Moreover, the mobility of researchers and locating R&D units abroad may be substitutes, when the main motives for internationalisation is personnel shortage in the home country.

National legislation can facilitate or hinder this mobility. Across OECD countries, governments have been changing or modifying national immigration and income taxation policies as well as higher education structures in recent years to make them more compatible to each other. A variety of policy actions have been taken aiming at removing barriers to the international conduct of science and technology (Dumont and Lemaître 2004; Mahroum 2005). These have targeted two broad categories of impediments: Cultural/structural barriers and political/technical barriers. Technical barriers, such as immigration laws, income taxation for foreigners, regulations concerning the accreditation of qualifications etc. tend to fall directly under the influence of government. Cultural-structural barriers such as the image of the country abroad of the population's attitudes towards foreigners are harder to change, as they do not fall under the influence of any particular authority in society, but are rather more pervasive and organic. They require more time to change.

A comprehensive discussion of political and cultural barriers for the mobility of researchers and government action to remove them would go beyond the scope of this study. A survey on the status in different countries is provided by Sami Mahroum in Dachs et al. (2005a). From this overview, it seems that countries with a long tradition of immigration, such as Canada, the US or Australia or New Zealand have less problems in recruiting researchers from abroad. They all have higher shares of migrants among the total employed professionals and technicians than any European country (OECD 2007d, p. 53). Within Europe, only Ireland and Switzerland are at equal levels with these countries. Austria is at OECD average.

10.4 Chapter Conclusions

Countries can reap considerable benefits from the internationalisation of innovation, but can also run into the risk of loosing technological capabilities due to the process. In the case of Austria, we have shown in this study that advantages prevail over disadvantages.

Does this significant role of foreign-owned enterprises justify specific measures tailored for this type of enterprises?

The findings of the empirical parts of this study support a policy approach that does not discriminate between foreign-owned and domestically owned enterprises. Special investment incentives to foreign-owned enterprises are indeed only rarely in place in OECD countries and mostly prohibited by EU competition law and international agreements. Rather, governments should try to maintain good economic fundamentals and provide a "healthy business environment" to attract foreign R&D. This is supported by empirical studies which show that R&D units of multinational enterprises are more attracted by high income, growing market size, political stability, a well developed public infrastructure, favourable tax rates and the quality of the science base than by special incentives. Special investment incentives, however, can play a decisive role when the MNE chooses between two similar locations.

A positive or negative discrimination of foreign-owned enterprises is not an appropriate instrument to promote innovation and increase the technological capabilities of Austria. Innovation policy should instead try to foster innovative capabilities of both, foreign-owned and domestically owned enterprises. This includes 'supply policies' intended to support the *creation* of knowledge (funding, basic research and education at universities, public infrastructure), as well as the 'adoption policies' that foster the capabilities of enterprises to *absorb and utilize* new technology (information services, technology transfer, standards, promotion of technology diffusion). A key determinant of attractiveness is the quality and specialisation of the knowledge base of the host country. Hence, all measures to improve the scientific and technological capabilities of an economy are also increasing the country's attractiveness for MNE R&D investment. Policies that aim to strengthen the ties between different actors in the innovation system further increase the embeddedness of foreign-owned enterprises and therefore the possibility of knowledge spillovers to the domestic economy.

The promotion of research, development and innovation, however, is not a goal in itself, but a means of economic policy to achieve economic growth, stability and high levels of employment. Innovative activities of foreign-owned enterprises in Austria will only contribute to achieving these goals if they are accompanied by production activities that transform the outcomes of innovation into employment and growth.

11. References

Aitken, B. J., and A. E. Harrison (1999). Do Domestic Firms Benefit from Direct Foreign Investment? Evidence from Venezuela. *American Economic Review*, 89(3): 605-618.

Allen Consulting Group (2003). A study of International Science and Technology Policies and Programs. Melbourne: Report to the Department of Education, Science and Training, Australia.

Almeida, P. (1999). Knowledge Sourcing by Foreign Multinationals: A Patent Citation Analysis in the U.S. Semiconductor Industry. In J. Cantwell (ed.), *Foreign direct investment and technological change*: 421-431. Cheltenham, UK and Northampton, MA, USA: Edward Elgar.

Almeida, P., and A. Phene (2004). Subsidiaries and knowledge creation: the influence of the MNC and host country on innovation. *Strategic Management Journal*, 25(8-9): 847-864.

Appold, S. J. (2004). Research parks and the location of industrial research laboratories: An analysis of the effectiveness of a policy intervention. *Research Policy*, 33(2): 225-243.

Archibugi, D., and S. Iammarino (1999). The Policy Implications of the Globalisation of Innovation. *Research Policy*, 28: 317-336.

Artmäuer, A., M. Bauer, and J. Böheimer (2003). *Der Fall Semperit. Ohne jede Chance.* Vienna: ÖGB-Verlag.

Arundel, A., and H. Hollanders (2005). EXIS: An Exploratory Approach to Innovation Scoreboards. Maastricht: MERIT.

Asheim, B. T., and M. S. Gertler (2005). The Geography of Innovation. Regional Innovation Systems. In J. Fagerberg, D. C. Movery, & R. R. Nelson (eds.), *The Oxford Handbook of Innovation*: 290-317. Oxford: Oxford University Press.

Audretsch, D., and Z. Acs (1991). Innovation and Size at the Firm Level. *Southern Economic Journal*, 57(3): 739-744.

Audretsch, D., and M. Feldman (1996). R&D Spillovers and the Geography of Innovation and Production. *American Economic Review*, 86(3): 630-640.

AusIndustry (2004). Industry Research and Development Board (Overseas Research and Development Activities) Guidelines 2004.

Balcet, G., and R. Evangelista (2005). Global Technology: Innovative Strategies of Multinational Affiliates in Italy. *Transnational Corporations*, 14(2): 53-92.

Barba Navaretti, G. (2004). Host Country Effects: Conceptual Framework and the Evidence. In G. Barba Navaretti, & A. J. Venables (eds.), *Multinational Firms in the World Economy*: 151-182. Princeton and Oxford: Princeton University Press.

Barba Navaretti, G., and A. J. Venables (eds., 2004). *Multinational Firms in the World Economy*. Princeton and Oxford: Princeton University Press.

Barry, F. (2004). FDI and the Host Economy: a Case Study of Ireland. In G. Barba Navaretti, & A. J. Venables (eds.), *Multinational Firms in the World Economy*: 187-215. Princeton and Oxford: Princeton University Press.

Barry, F., H. Görg, and E. Strobl (2001). Foreign Direct Investment, Agglomerations and Demonstration Effects: An Empirical Investigation, *CEPR Discussion Paper*, Vol. 2907. London.

Barry, F., and C. van Egeraat. 2005. *The Eastward Shift of Computer Hardware Production: How Ireland Adjusted.* Paper presented at the Conference "Relocation of Production and Jobs to CEECs: Who gains and who loses?" 16 - 17 September 2005, Hamburg.

Belderbos, R. (2001). Overseas Innovations by Japanese Firms: An Analysis of Patent and Subsidiary Data. *Research Policy*, 30(2): 313-332.

Belderbos, R., M. Carree, and B. Lokshin (2004). Cooperative R&D and firm performance. *Research Policy*, 33: 1477-1492.

Belderbos, R., B. Leten, and S. Suzuki. 2007. *Does Excellence in Scientific Research attract foreign R&D?* Paper presented at the Conference "Knowledge for Growth", 8 - 9 October, 2007, Seville.

Bellak, C. (2004). How Domestic and Foreign Firms Differ and Why Does It Matter? *Journal of Economic Surveys*, 18(4): 483-514.

Bellandi, M. (2001). Local Development and Embedded Large Firms. *Entrepreneurship & Regional Development*, 13(3): 189-210.

Bertrand, O., and P. Zuniga (2006). R&D and M&A: Are cross-border M&A different? An investigation on OECD countries. *International Journal of Industrial Organization*, 24: 401-423.

Birkinshaw, J. M., and N. Hood (1998). Multinational Subsidiary Evolution: Capability and Charter Change in Foreign-Owned Subsidiary Companies. *Academy of Management Review*, 23(4): 773-795.

Birkinshaw, J. M., and N. Hood (2000). Characteristics of Foreign Subsidiaries in Industry Clusters. *Journal of International Business Studies*, 31(1): 141-154.

Birkinshaw, J. M., N. Hood, and S. Jonsson (1998). Building Firm-specific Advantages in Multinational Corporations: the Role of Subsidiary Initiative. *Strategic Management Journal*, 19: 221-241.

Bleaney, M., and K. Wakelin (2002). Efficiency, Innovation and Exports. *Oxford Bulletin of Economics and Statistics*, 64(1): 3-15.

Bloch, C. (2007a). Assessing recent developments in innovation measurement: the third edition of the Oslo Manual. *Science and Public Policy*, 34(1): 23-34.

Bloch, C. (2007b). Innovation indicators – some proposals based on the NIND project. Aarhus: mimeo, University of Aahus.

Blomström, M. (2001). The Economics of International Investment Incentives, *Paper prepared for the OECD, Committee for International Investment and Multinational Enterprises (CIME).* Paris: OECD, Committee for International Investment and Multinational Enterprises (CIME).

Blomström, M., S. Globerman, and A. Kokko (2000). The Determiants of Host Country Spillovers from Foreign Direct Investment, *CEPR Discussion Paper*, Vol. 2350. London.

Blomström, M., and A. Kokko (1998). Multinational Corporations and Spillovers. *Journal of Economic Surveys*, 12(3): 247-277.

Blomström, M., and A. Kokko (2003). The Economics of foreign direct investment incentives, *NBER Working Paper*, Vol. 9489. Cambridge, MA.

Blonigen, B. A. (2005). A Review of the Empirical Literature on FDI Determinants, *NBER Working Paper*, Vol. 11299. Cambridge, Mass.

Braunerhjelm, P., and R. Svensson (1996). Host Country Characteristics and Agglomeration in Foreign Direct Investment. *Applied Economics*, 28(7): 833-840.

Breschi, S., and F. Lissoni (2001a). Knowledge Spillovers and Local Innovation Systems: A Critical Survey. *Industrial and Corporate Change*, 10(4): 975-1005.

Breschi, S., and F. Lissoni (2001b). Localized knowledge spillovers vs. innovative milieux: Knowledge "taciteness" reconsidered. *Papers in Regional Science*, 80: 255-273.

Bresnahan, T., and A. Gambardella (eds., 2004). *Building High-Tech Clusters*. Cambridge, MA: Cambridge University Press.

Buckley, P. J. (2000). Cross-border Governance in Multinational Enterprises. In P. J. Buckley (ed.), *Multinational Firms, Cooperation and Competition in the World Economy*: 289-304. Basingstoke: Macmillan Press.

Burke, P. (2001). *A Social History of Knowledge. From Gutenberg to Diderot*. Cambridge: Polity Press.

Calhoun, M. A. (2002). Unpacking liability of foreignness: identifying culturally driven external and internal sources of liability for the foreign subsidiary. *Journal of International Management*, 8(3): 301-321.

Caloghirou, Y., S. Ioannides, and N. S. Vonortas (2003). Research Joint Ventures. *Journal of Economic Surveys*, 17(4): 541-570.

Cantner, U., and A. Pyka (1998). Absorbing Technological Spillovers: Simulations in an Evolutionary Framework. *Industrial and Corporate Change*, 7(2): 369-397.

Cantwell, J. (1989). *Technological Innovation and Multinational Corporations*. Oxford: Basil Blackwell.

Cantwell, J. (1995). The Globalisation of Technology: What Remains of the Product Cycle Model? *Cambridge Journal of Economics*, 19: 155-174.

Cantwell, J., and S. Iammarino (2000). Multinational Corporations and the Location of Technological Innovation in the UK Regions. *Regional Studies*, 34(4): 317-332.

Cantwell, J., and O. Janne (1999). Technological Globalisation and Innovative Centres: The Role of Corporate Technological Leadership and Locational Hierarchy. *Research Policy*, 28: 119-144.

Cantwell, J., and R. Mudambi (2000). The location of MNE R&D activity; the role of investment incentives. *Management International Review*, 40(1): 127-148.

Cantwell, J., and R. Mudambi (2005). MNE competence-creating subsidiary mandates. *Strategic Management Journal*, 26(12): 1109-1128.

Cantwell, J., and L. Piscitello (2002). The location of technological activities of MNCs in European regions: The role of spillovers and local competencies. *Journal of International Management*, 8: 69–96.

Caracostas, P., and U. Muldur (2001). The Emergence of a New European Union Research and Innovation Policy. In P. Larédo, & P. Mustar (eds.), *Research and Innovation Policies in the New Global Economy*. Cheltenham, UK and Northampton, MA, USA: Edward Elgar.

Carr, D. L., J. R. Markusen, and K. E. Maskus (2001). Estimating The Knowledge-Capital Model of the Multinational Enterprise. *American Economic Review*, 91(3).

Cassiman, B., M. G. Colombo, P. Garrone, and R. Veugelers (2005). The impact of M&A on the R&D process. An empirical analysis of the role of technological- and market-relatedness. *Research Policy*, 34: 195–220.

Cassiman, B., and R. Veugelers (2002). R&D Cooperation and Spillovers: Some Empirical Evidence from Belgium. *American Economic Review*, 92(4): 1169-1184.

Castellani, D., and A. Zanfei (2002). Multinational experience and the creation of linkages with local firms. Evidence from the electronics industry. *Cambridge Journal of Economics*, 26: 1-25.

Castellani, D., and A. Zanfei (2003). Technology Gaps, Absorptive Capacity and the Impact of Inward Investments on Productivity of European firms. *Economics of Innovation and New Technology*, 12(6): 1.

Castellani, D., and A. Zanfei (2004). Multinationals, innovation and productivity. Evidence from Italian manufacturing firms, *mimeo*. Urbino: Universita di Urbino.

Caves, R. (1996). *Multinational Enterprises and Economic Analysis*. Cambridge: Cambridge University Press.

Chesbrough, H. W. (2003a). The Era of Open Innovation. *Sloan Management Review*(Summer): 35-41.

Chesbrough, H. W. (2003b). *Open Innovation: The New Imperative for Creating and Profiting from Technology*. Boston, MA: Harvard Business School Press.

Christensen, J. F. (2006). Whither Core Competency for the Large Corporation in an Open Innovation World? In H. W. Chesbrough, W. Vanhaverbeke, & J. West (eds.), *Open Innovation: Researching a New Paradigm*: 35-61. Oxford: Oxford University Press.

Cohen, W. M. (1995). Empirical Studies of Innovative Activity. In P. Stoneman (ed.), *Handbook of Innovation and Technological Change*: 182-264. Oxford: Blackwell.

Cohen, W. M., and R. C. Levin (1989). Empirical Studies of Innovation and Market Structure. In R. Schmalensee, & R. D. Willig (eds.), *Handbook of Industrial Organization*, Vol. 2: 1059-1107. Amsterdam; Oxford and Tokyo: North-Holland; distributed in the U.S. and Canada by Elsevier Science, New York.

Cohen, W. M., and D. Levinthal (1989). Innovation and Learning: the Two Faces of R&D. *Economic Journal*, 99(September): 569-596.

Cohen, W. M., and D. Levinthal (1990). Absorptive Capacity: A New Perspective on Learning and Innovation. *Administrative Science Quarterly*, 35: 128-152.

Cohendet, P., and W. E. Steinmueller (2000). The Codification of Knowledge: A Conceptual and Empirical Exploration. *Industrial and Corporate Change*, 9(2): 195-209.

Coombs, R. (1996). Core Competencies and the Strategic Management of R&D. *R&D Management*, 31(4): 361-380.

Cowan, R., P. A. David, and D. Foray (2000). The Explicit Economics of Knowledge Codification and Tacitness. *Industrial and Corporate Change*, 9(2): 211-253.

Crepon, B., E. Duguet, and J. Mairesse (1998). Research, Innovation and Productivity: An Econometric Analysis at the Firm Level. *Economics of Innovation and New Technology*, 7(2): 115-158.

Criscuolo, P., and R. Narula (2005). Using multi-hub structures for international R&D: Organizational inertia and the challenges of implementation, *MERIT-Infonomics Research Memorandum series*, Vol. 025-2005: 37. Maastricht.

Dachs, B. (2008). Case Study Infineon. In H. M. Meijers, B. Dachs, & P. J. J. Welfens (eds.), *Internationalisation of European ICT Activities*. Berlin: Springer.

Dachs, B., B. Ebersberger, and H. Lööf (2008a). The Innovative Performance of Foreign-owned Enterprises in Small Open Economies. *Journal of Technology Transfer*, forthcoming.

Dachs, B., B. Ebersberger, and A. Pyka (2008b). Why do Firms Co-operate for Innovation? A comparison of Austrian and Finnish CIS 3 results. *International Journal of Foresight and Innovation Policy*, 4(3).

Dachs, B., R. Falk, S. Mahroum, B. Nones, and A. Schibany (2005a). Policies to benefit from the Internationalisation of R&D. Vienna: TIP report. www.tip.ac.at

Dachs, B., K. Friesenbichler, B. Nones, and M. Falk (2005b). Innovationsaktivitäten österreichischen Unternehmen im Ausland. Umfang, Motive und Auswirkungen auf Österreich und deren Auswirkungen auf Österreich. Vienna: TIP report. www.tip.ac.at

Dachs, B., and A. Pyka (2007). Is R&D still "an important case of non-globalisation"? Evidence from European Patent Data. Vienna: mimeo.

Dekimpe, M. G., P. M. Parker, and M. Sarvary (2000). "Globalization" - Modeling Technology Adoption Timing Across Countries. Technological Forecasting and Social Change, 61(1): 25-42.

Dell'mour, R. (2007). Direktinvestitionen 2005. Österreichische Direktinvestitionen im Ausland und ausländische Direktinvestitionen in Österreich. Wien: Oesterreichische Nationalbank.

DIE PRESSE (1997). Semperit darf wieder ein bißchen forschen. 17. 06 1997

DIE ZEIT (2007a). Angst vorm Chinesen. 12.07.2007

DIE ZEIT (2007b). Mit der Macht von zwölf Billionen Dollar. *12. 07. 2007*

Dimsdale, N., and M. Prevezer (eds., 1994). *Capital markets and corporate governance*. Oxford: Oxford University Press.

Disdier, A.-C., and K. Head (2004). The Puzzling Persistence of the Distance Effect on Bilateral Trade, *UBC Economics Department Discussion Paper*, Vol. 21. Vancouver.

Djellal, F., and F. Gallouj (1999). Services and the search for relevant innovation indicators: a review of national and international surveys. *Science and Public Policy*, 26(4): 218-232.

Dogson, M., and R. Rothwell (1994). Innovation and the Size of the Firm. In M. Dogson, & R. Rothwell (eds.), *The Handbook of Industrial Innovation*: 310-325. Cheltenham, UK and Northampton, MA, USA: Edward Elgar.

Doms, M. E., and J. B. Jensen (1998). Comparing Wages, Skills, and Productivity between Domestically and Foreign-Owned Manufacturing Establishments in the United States. In R. E. Baldwin, R. E. Lipsey, & J. D. Richardson (eds.), *Geography and ownership as bases for economic accounting. NBER Studies in Income and Wealth, vol. 59*: 235-255. Chicago and London: University of Chicago Press.

Dosi, G. (1982). Technological Paradigms and Technological Trajectories: A Suggested Interpretation of the Determinants and Directions of Technical Change. *Research Policy*, 11(3): 147-162.

Dosi, G. (1988). Sources, Procedures, and Microeconomic Effects of Innovation. *Journal of Economic Literature*, 26(3): 1120-1171.

Drejer, I. (2000). Comparing Patterns of Industrial Interdependence in National Systems of Innovation - A Study of Germany, the United Kingdom, Japan and the United States. *Economic Systems Research*, 12(3): 377-399.

Driffield, N. L., and K. Taylor (2000). FDI and the labour market: a review of the evidence and policy implications. *Oxford Review of Economic Policy*, 16: 90-103.

Dumont, J.-C., and G. Lemaître (2004). Counting Immigrants and Expatriates: A New Perspective, *Directorate for Employment Labour and Social Affairs, DELSA*.

Dunning, J. (1973). The Determinants of International Production. *Oxford Economic Papers*, 25: 289-336.

Dunning, J. (1981). *International Production and the Multinational Enterprise*. London: Allen and Unwin.

Dunning, J. (1995). Reappraising the Eclectic Paradigm in an Age of Allicance Capitalism. *Journal of International Business Studies*, 26(3): 461-492.

Dunning, J., and R. Narula (1995). The R&D activities of foreign firms in the United States. *International Studies of Management & Organization*, 25(1-2): 39-72.

Ebersberger, B., and H. Lööf (2004). Multinational Enterprises, Spillovers, Innovation and Productivity., *CESIS Working Paper*, Vol. 22. Stockholm.

Ebersberger, B., and H. Lööf (2005). Corporate Innovation Activities, Does Ownership Matter? Oslo: STEP.

Ebersberger, B., H. Lööf, and J. Oksanen (2005). Does foreign ownership matter for the innovation activities of Finnish firms? *VTT Working Paper*, Vol. 26. Espoo.

Eden, L., and S. Miller (2004). Distance Matters: Liability of foreignness, institutional distance and ownership strategy. In M. A. Hitt, & J. L. C. Cheng (eds.), *The Evolving Theory of the Multinational Firm. Advances in International Management.*, Vol. 16. Amsterdam: Elsevier.

Edler, J., and F. Mayer-Krahmer (2003). How International are National (and European) Science and Technology Policies? mimeo, Karlsruhe: Fraunhofer ISI.

Edquist, C. (ed.). 1997). *Systems of Innovation - Technologies, Institutions and Organizations*. London: Pinter.

Edquist, C. (2005a). Systems of Innovation: Perspectives and Challenges. In J. Fagerberg, D. Mowery, & R. R. Nelson (eds.), *The Oxford Handbook of Innovation*. Oxford: Oxford University Press.

Edquist, C. (2005b). Systems of Innovation: Perspectives and Challenges. In J. Fagerberg, D. Mowery, & R. R. Nelson (eds.), *The Oxford Handbook of Innovation*: 182-208. Oxford: Oxford University Press.

Ekholm, K., and K. H. Midelfart (2004). Determinants of FDI: the Evidence. In G. Barba Navaretti, & A. J. Venables (eds.), *Multinational Firms in the World Economy*: 127-150. Princeton and Oxford: Princeton University Press.

European Commission (1999). Code of Conduct (Business Taxation) / Primarolo Group. Brussles.

European Commission (2000). Towards a European research area. Communication from the Commission to the Council, the European Parliament, the Economic and Social Committee and the Committee of the Regions - COM(2000) 6. Brussles:

European Commission (2007). Green Paper: The European Research Area: New Perspectives. COM(2007) 161 final. Brussles.

EUROSTAT (2004). *Innovation in Europe. Results for the EU, Iceland and Norway. Data 1998-2000.* Luxembourg: Office for Official Publications of the European Communities.

EUROSTAT (2006). *The Third Community Innovation Survey (CIS3): Summary of the Anonymization Method.* mimeo, Luxemburg: Eurostat.

Fagerberg, J., and M. M. Godinho (2005). Innovation and Catching Up. In J. Fagerberg, D. Mowery, & R. R. Nelson (eds.), *The Oxford Handbook of Innovation*: 514-542. Oxford: Oxford University Press.

Fagerberg, J., D. Mowery, and R. R. Nelson (eds., 2005). *The Oxford Handbook of Innovation.* Oxford: Oxford University Press.

Falk, M., and R. Falk (2006). Do Foreign-Owned Firms Have a Lower Innovation Intensity Than Domestic Firms? *WIFO Working Paper*, Vol. 275. Vienna.

Florida, R. (1997). The globalization of R&D: Results of a survey of foreign-affiliated R&D laboratories in the USA. *Research Policy*, 26(1): 85-103.

Foray, D. (2004). *The Economics of Knowledge.* Cambridge [Mass], London: MIT Press.

Freeman, C., and L. Soete (1997). *The Economics of Industrial Innovation* (3rd ed.). Cambridge [Mass.] and London: MIT Press.

Frenz, M., and G. Ietto-Gillies (2007). Does Multinationality Affect the Propensity to Innovate? An Analysis of the Third UK Community Innovation Survey. *International Review of Applied Economics*, 21(1): 99-117.

Frost, T. S. (2001). The geographic sources of foreign subsidiaries' innovations. *Strategic Management Journal*, 22(2): 101-123.

Geroski, P. A. (2000). Models of Technology Diffusion. *Research Policy*, 29(4-5): 603-625.

Gersbach, H., and A. Schmutzler (2006). Foreign Direct Investment and R&D Offshoring, *Socioeconomic Institute University of Zurich Working Paper*, Vol. 0606. Zürich.

Ghoshal, S., and C. Bartlett (1991). The multinational corporation as an interorganizational network. *Academy of Management Review*, 15: 603-625.

Giarratana, M., A. Pagano, and S. Torrisi (2004). Are multinational firms a source of knowledge spillovers for domestic firms? Evidence from the software industry in India, Ireland and Israel, *International Workshop "Public Research Institutions,*

International Business, and Technological and Economic Catch Up in Developing Regions", Faculty of Political Science. University of Catania, 19-20 March 2004.

Globerman, S., J. C. Ries, and I. Vertinsky (1994). The Economic Performance of Foreign Affiliates in Canada. *Canadian Journal of Economics*, 27(1): 124-149.

Görg, H., and E. Strobl (2001). Multinational Companies and Productivity Spillovers: A Meta-analysis. *Economic Journal*, 111(November): 723-739.

Görg, H., and E. Strobl (2003). 'Footloose' Multinationals? *The Manchester School*, 71(1): 1-19.

Görg, H., and E. Strobl (2005). Spillovers from Foreign Firms through Worker Mobility: An Empirical Investigation. *Scandinavian Journal of Economics*, 107(4): 693–709.

Granovetter, M. (1985). Economic Action and Social Structure: The Problem of Embeddedness. *American Journal of Sociology*, 91(3): 481-510.

Granstrand, O. (1998). Towards a Theory of the Technology-Based Firm. *Research Policy*, 27(5): 465-489.

Granstrand, O., and S. Sjölander (1994). Managing Innovation in Multi-Technology Corporations. In M. Dogson, & R. Rothwell (eds.), *The Handbook of Industrial Innovation*: 367-383. Cheltenham, UK and Northampton, MA, USA: Edward Elgar.

Greenhalgh, C. A., and P. Taylor (1990). Innovation and Export Volumes and Prices: A Disaggregated Study, *CEPR Discussion Papers*, Vol. 487.

Griffith, R., S. Redding, and H. Simpson (2004). Foreign Ownership and Productivity: New Evidence from the Service Sector and the R&D Lab, *CEP Discussion Paper*, Vol. 649. London.

Griliches, Z. (1990). Patent Statistics as Economic Indicators: A Survey. *Journal of Economic Literature*, 28(4): 1661-1707.

Griliches, Z. (1992). The Search for R&D Spillovers. *Scandinavian Journal of Economics*, 94(3): 529-547.

Griliches, Z. (1995). R&D and Productivity. In P. Stoneman (ed.), *Handbook of Innovation and Technological Change*: 52-90. Oxford: Blackwell.

Guellec, D., and B. van Pottelsberghe de la Potterie (2001). The Internationalisation of Technology Analysed with Patent Data. *Research Policy*, 30(8): 1253-1266.

Guellec, D., and B. van Pottelsberghe de la Potterie (2004). Measuring the Internationalisation of The Generation of Knowledge. In H. F. Moed, W. Glänzel, & U. Schmoch (eds.), *Handbook of Quantitative Science and Technology Research*: 645-662. Dordrecht: Kluwer Academic Publishers.

Guimon, J. 2007. *Government strategies to attract R&D-intensive FDI: The link between innovation policy and inward investment promotion.* Paper presented at the Atlanta Conference on Science Technology and Innovation Policy, Atlanta, GA.

Gupta, A. K., and V. Govindarajanan (1994). Organizing for knowledge flows within MNCs. *International Business Review*, 3(4): 443-457.

Gupta, A. K., and V. Govindarajanan (2000). Knowledge flows within multinational corporations. *Strategic Management Journal*, 21(4): 473-496.

Haaland, J. I. (2004). Policy Implications and Effects. In G. Barba Navaretti, & A. J. Venables (eds.), *Multinational Firms in the World Economy*: 241-277. Princeton and Oxford: Princeton University Press.

Hagedoorn, J. (2002). Inter-firm R&D Partnerships: An Overview of Major Trends and Patterns since 1960. *Research Policy*, 31(4): 477-492.

Hagedoorn, J., and J. Schakenraad (1989). Strategic Partnering and Technological Cooperation. In B. Dankbaar, J. Groenewegen, & H. Schenk (eds.), *Perspectives in Industrial Economics*. Dordrecht: Kluwer Academic Publishers.

Hall, B. A. (2005). Innovation and Diffusion. In J. Fagerberg, D. Mowery, & R. R. Nelson (eds.), *The Oxford Handbook of Innovation*: 495-485. Oxford: Oxford University Press.

Hanusch, H., and A. Pyka (2007). *Elgar Companion to Neo-Schumpeterian Economics*. Cheltenham, UK and Northampton, MA, USA: Edward Elgar.

Heckman, J. J. (1976). The Common Structure of Statistical Models of Truncation, Sample Selection and Limited Dependent Variables and a Simple Estimator for Such Models. *Annals of Economic and Social Measurement*, 5(4): 475-492.

Hipp, C. (2000). *Innovationsprozesse im Dienstleistungssektor*. Heidelberg: Physica.

Hobday, M. (2000). East versus Southeast Asian Innovation Systems: Comparing OEM- and TNC-led Growth in Electronics. In L. Kim, & R. R. Nelson (eds.), *Technology, Learning and Innovation. Experiences from Newly Industrializing Economies*. Cambridge [Mass.]: Cambridge University Press.

Hummels, D. (2007). Transportation Costs and International Trade in the Second Era of Globalization. *Journal of Economic Perspectives*, 21(3): 131-155.

IBFD (2004). Tax treatment of research and development expenditure. Brussles: European Commission.

Infineon Austria AG (2006). Infineon Austria Factsheet. Villach: http://www.infineon.com/upload/Document/Austria/ifat_broschuere_2006_e.pdf

Infineon Technologies AG (2006). Gaining Momentum. Infineon Technologies Annual Report 2005. Munich: Infineon Investors Relations. www.infineon.com

Jaffe, A. B., and M. Trajtenberg (2002). *Patents, citations, and innovations: A window on the knowledge economy*. MIT Press: Cambridge and London.

Jaffe, A. B., M. Trajtenberg, and R. Henderson (1993). Geographic Localization of Knowledge Spillovers as Evidenced by Patent Citations. *Quarterly Journal of Economics*, 108: 577-598.

Javorcik, S. B. (2004). Does Foreign Direct Investment Increase the Productivity of Domestic Firms? In Search of Spillovers Through Backward Linkages. *American Economic Review*, 94(3): 605-627.

Kathuria, V. (2002). Liberalisation, FDI, and Productivity Spillovers - an Analysis of Indian Manufacturing Firms. *Oxford Economic Papers*, 54: 688-718.

Keller, W. (2004). International Technology Diffusion. *Journal of Economic Literature*, 42(3): 752-758.

Keller, W., and S. R. Yeaple (2003). Multinational Enterprises, International Trade, and Productivity Growth: Firm-Level Evidence from the United States, *IMF Working Paper*, Vol. WP/03/248. Washington.

Kennedy, P. (2003). *A Guide to Econometrics*. 5th Edition, Blackwell Publishing: Oxford.

Kleinknecht, A. (1989). Firm size and Innovation. *Small Business Economics*, 3(2): 157-158.

Kleinknecht, A., K. Monfort, and E. Brouwer (2002). The non-trivial Choice between Innovation Indicators. *Economics of Innovation and New Technology*, 11: 109-121.

Kline, S., and N. Rosenberg (1986). An Overview of Innovation. In R. Landau, & N. Rosenberg (eds.), *The Positive Sum Strategy - Harnessing Technology for Economic Growth*: 275-305. Washington: National Academy Press.

Knoll, N. (2004). International orientierte Unternehmen in Österreich: Rahmenbedingungen für Steuerungsfunktionen und Forschungskompetenz. Vienna: WIFO.

Kokko, A. (1994). Technology, Market Characteristics, and Spillovers. *Journal of Development Economics*, 43: 279-293.

Kokko, A. (1996). Productivity Spillovers from Competition between Local Firms and Foreign Affiliates. *Journal of International Development*, 8: 517-530.

Koyama, T., and S. Golub (2006). OECD's FDI Regulatory Restrictiveness Index: Revision and Extension to More Economies., *OECD Papers on International Investment*, Vol. 2006/4. Paris.

Krugman, P. (1995). Technological Change in International Trade. In P. Stoneman (ed.), *Handbook of Innovation and Technological Change*: 342-365. Oxford: Blackwell.

Kuemmerle, W. (1999a). The Drivers of Foreign Direct Investment into Research and Development: An Empirical Investigation. *Journal of International Business Studies*, 30(1): 1-24.

Kuemmerle, W. (1999b). Foreign Direct Investment in Industrial Research in the Pharmaceutical and Electronics Industries - Results from a Survey of Multinational Firms. *Research Policy*, 28(2-3): 179-193.

Kumar, N. (2001). Determinants of Location of Overseas R&D Activity of Multinational Enterprises: The Case of US and Japanese Corporations. *Research Policy*, 30(1): 159-174.

Kumar, R. (2003). Changing Role of the Public Sector in the Promotion of Foreign Direct Investment. *Asia-Pacific Development Journal*, 10(2): 1-27.

Lachenmaier, S., and L. Wößmann (2004). Does innovation cause exports? Evidence from exogenous innovation impulses and obstacles using German micro data, *CESIFO Working Paper*, Vol. 1178. Munich.

Larédo, P., and P. Mustar (2001). *Research and Innovation Policies in the New Global Economy: An International Comparative Analysis*. Cheltenham, UK and Northampton, MA, USA: Edward Elgar.

le Bas, C., and C. Sierra (2002). 'Location versus Home Country Advantages' in R&D Activities: Some Further Results on Multinationals' Locational Strategies. *Research Policy*, 31(4): 589-609.

Leamer, E. E., and J. Levinsohn (1995). International Trade Theory: The Evidence. In G. E. Grossman, & K. Rogoff (eds.), *Handbook Of International Economics*, Vol. 3: 1339-1394. Amsterdam, New York and Oxford: Elsevier, North-Holland.

Leitner, K.-H. (2003). *Von der Idee zum Markt: Die 50 besten Innovationen Österreichs.* Wien: Böhlau.

Leonard-Barton, D. (1998). *Wellsprings of Knowledge: Building and Sustaining the Sources of Innovation.* Harvard: Harvard Business School Press.

Lipsey, R. E. (2002). Home and Host Country Effects of FDI, *NBER Working Paper*, Vol. 9293. Cambridge, MA.

Lipsey, R. G., K. I. Carlaw, and C. T. Bekar (2005). *Economic Transformations: General Purpose Technologies and Long Term Economic Growth.* Oxford: Oxford University Press.

Lonmo, C., and F. Anderson (2003). A Comparison of International R&D Performance: An Analysis of Countries that Have Significantly Increased Their GERD/GDP Ratios during the Period 1989-1999, *Statistics Canada*, Vol. 88F0006XIE2003001. Ottawa.

Lorenzen, M., and V. Mahnke (2002). Global strategy and the acquisition of local knowledge: how MNCs enter regional knowledge clusters, *DRUID Working Paper*, Vol. 02-08.

Lueghammer, W., and H. Schneider (2005). Leading Competence Units. Ihre Bedeutung für Wertschöpfung, Innovation und Strukturwandel in Österreich. Vienna: Institute for Industrial Research (IWI).

Lundvall, B.-A. (1988). Innovation as an Interactive Process: From User-Producer Interaction to the National System of Innovation. In G. Dosi, C. Freeman, R. Nelson, G. Silverberg, & L. Soete (eds.), *Technical Change and Economic Theory*: 349-369. London and New York: Pinter Publishers.

Lundvall, B.-A. (ed.). 1992). *National Systems of Innovation: Towards a Theory of Innovation and Interactive Learning.* London: Pinter.

Lundvall, B.-A. (1998). Why Study National Systems and National Styles of Innovation? *Technology Analysis & Strategic Management*, 10(4).

Mahroum, S. (2005). The International Policies of Brain Gain. *Technology Analysis & Strategic Management*, 17(2): 219-230.

Malerba, F. (2002). Sectoral Systems of Innovation and Production. *Research Policy*, 31(2): 247-264.

Malerba, F. (2005). Sectoral Systems of Innovation: A Framework for Linking Innovation to the Knowledge Base, Structure and Dynamics of Sectors. *Economics of Innovation and New Technology*, 14(1-2): 63–82.

Malerba, F., and L. Orsenigo (1996). Schumpeterian Patterns of Innovation are technology-specific. *Research Policy*, 25: 451-478.

Markusen, J. R. (1995). The Boundaries of Multinational Enterprises and the Theory of International Trade. *Journal of Economic Perspectives*, 9(2): 169-189.

Markusen, J. R. (2002). *Multinational Firms and the Theory of International Trade.* Cambridge [Mass.] and London: MIT Press.

Marsili, O. (2001). *The Anatomy and Evolution of Industries: Technological Change and Industrial Dynamics.* Cheltenham, UK and Northampton, MA, USA: Edward Elgar.

Marsili, O. (2002). Technological Regimes and Sources of Entrepreneurship. *Small Business Economics*, 19(3): 217-231.

Marsili, O., and A. Salter (2005). 'Inequality' of innovation: skewed distributions and the returns to innovation in Dutch manufacturing. *Economics of Innovation and New Technology*, 14(1-2): 83-102.

Marsili, O., and B. Verspagen (2002). Technology and the Dynamics of Industrial Structures: An Empirical Mapping of Dutch Manufacturing. *Industrial and Corporate Change*, 11(4): 791-815.

Metcalfe, S. (1995). The Economic Foundations of Technology Policy: Equilibrium and Evolutionary Perspectives. In P. Stoneman (ed.), *Handbook of Innovation and Technological Change*: 409-513. Oxford: Blackwell.

Meyer-Krahmer, F., and G. Reger (1999). New perspectives on innovation strategies of multinational enterprises: lessons for technology policy in Europe. *Research Policy*, 28: 751-776.

Miles, I. (2005). Innovation in Services. In J. Fagerberg, D. C. Movery, & R. R. Nelson (eds.), *The Oxford Handbook of Innovation*: 433-458. Oxford: Oxford University Press.

Molero, J., and I. Alvarez (2004). Multinational enterprises and national systems of innovation: Background and new insights, *Paper presented at the EIBA conference, Ljubljana.*

Mowery, D. (1995). The Practice of Technology Policy. In P. Stoneman (ed.), *Handbook of Innovation and Technological Change*: 513-557. Oxford: Blackwell.

Narula, R., and A. Zanfei (2005). Globalisation of Innovation: The Role of Multinational Enterprises. In J. Fagerberg, D. C. Movery, & R. R. Nelson (eds.), *The Oxford Handbook of Innovation*: 318-348. Oxford: Oxford University Press.

Navaretti Barba, G., and A. J. Venables (2004). *Multinational Firms in the World Economy.* Princeton and Oxford: Princeton University Press.

Nelson, R. R. (ed.). 1993). *National Systems of Innovation: A Comparative Analysis*. New York, Oxford: Oxford University Press.

Nelson, R. R., and S. G. Winter (1982). *An Evolutionary Theory of Economic Change*. Cambridge, Mass, London: Belknap Press.

Neven, D. J., and G. Siotis (1996). Technology Sourcing and FDI in the EC: An Empirical Evaluation. *International Journal of Industrial Organization*, 14(5): 543-560.

Nones, B. (2003). *Die Rollen ausländischer F&E-Einheiten in multinationalen Unternehmen und deren Einsatz moderner IuK-Technologien. Eine empirische Studie zu F&E-Einheiten multinationaler Unternehmen in Österreich.*, Dissertation, Linz.

O'Sullivan, M. (2005). Finance and Innovation. In J. Fagerberg, D. C. Movery, & R. R. Nelson (eds.), *The Oxford Handbook of Innovation*: 240-265. Oxford: Oxford University Press.

OECD (1992). *Technology and the Economy: The Key Relationships.* Paris: Organisation for Economic Co-operation and Development.

OECD (1996). *OECD Benchmark Definition of Foreign Direct Investment.* Paris: Organisation for Economic Co-operation and Development.

OECD (2002). *Frascati Manual 2002. Proposed Standard Practice for Surveys on Research and Experimental Development*. Paris: Organisation for Economic Co-operation and Development.

OECD (2003a). *Checklist for Foreign Direct Investment Incentive Policies*. Paris: Organisation for Economic Co-operation and Development.

OECD (2003b). *OECD Science, Technology and Industry Scoreboard*. Paris: Organisation for Economic Co-operation and Development.

OECD (2004a). *National treatment for foreign-controlled enterprises*. Paris: Organisation for Economic Co-operation and Development.

OECD (2004b). *OECD Science, Technology and Industry Outlook 2004*. Paris: Organisation for Economic Co-operation and Development.

OECD (2004c). *Understanding Economic Growth*. Paris: Organisation for Economic Co-operation and Development.

OECD (2005a). *Compendium of Patent Statistics 2005*. Paris: Organisation for Economic Co-operation and Development.

OECD (2005b). *OECD Science, Technology and Industry Scoreboard*. Paris: Organisation for Economic Co-operation and Development.

OECD (2005c). *Oslo Manual. Guidelines for Collecting and Interpreting Innovation Data* (Third Edition ed.). Paris: Organisation for Economic Co-operation and Development.

OECD (2006a). *OECD Information Technology Outlook 2006*. Paris: Organisation for Economic Co-operation and Development.

OECD (2006b). *OECD Science, Technology and Industry Outlook 2006*. Paris: Organisation for Economic Co-operation and Development.

OECD (2006c). *Research and Development Statistics: 2005 Edition*. Paris: Organisation for Economic Co-operation and Development.

OECD (2007a). *Main Science and Technology Indicators 1/2007*. Paris: Organisation for Economic Co-operation and Development.

OECD (2007b). *Main Science and Technology Indicators 2/2007*. Paris: Organisation for Economic Co-operation and Development.

OECD (2007c). *OECD Reviews of Innovation Policy - CHINA. Synthesis Report*. Paris: Organisation for Economic Co-operation and Development.

OECD (2007d). *OECD Science, Technology and Industry Scoreboard. Innovation and Performance in the Global Economy*. Paris: Organisation for Economic Co-operation and Development.

ÖGB (2003). Der Fall Semperit. Eine Familie zerbricht, Press release, August 28, 2003. Vienna: Österreichischer Gewerkschaftsbund.

Oman, C. (2000). Policy Competition for Foreign Direct Investment. A study of Competition among Governments to Attract FDI. Paris: OECD Development Center.

Patel, P., and K. Pavitt (1997). The Technological Competencies of the Wold's Largest Firms: Complex and Path-Dependent, But Not Much Variety. *Research Policy*, 26: 141-156.

Patel, P., and M. Vega (1999). Patterns of Internationalisation of Corporate Technology: Location vs. Home Country Advantages. *Research Policy*, 28(2-3): 145-155.

Pavitt, K. (1984). Sectoral Patterns of Technological Change: Towards a Taxonomy and a Theory. *Research Policy*, 13(6): 343-373.

Pavitt, K. (2005). Innovation Processes. In J. Fagerberg, D. C. Movery, & R. R. Nelson (eds.), *The Oxford Handbook of Innovation*: 86-114. Oxford: Oxford University Press.

Pavlínek, P. (2004). Regional Development Implications of Foreign Direct Investment in Central Europe. *European Urban and Regional Studies*, 11(1): 47-70.

Peneder, M. (2002). Intangible Investment and Human Resources. *Journal of Evolutionary Economics*, 12(1-2): 107-134.

Peneder, M. (2003). Industrial Structure and Aggregate Growth. *Structural Change and Economic Dynamics*, 14(4): 427-448.

Powell, W. P., and S. Grodal (2005). Networks of Innovators. In J. Fagerberg, D. Mowery, & R. R. Nelson (eds.), *The Oxford Handbook of Innovation*: 57-85. Oxford: Oxford University Press.

Pyka, A. (1997). Informal Networking. *Technovation*, 17(4): 207-220.

Pyka, A. (2002). Innovation networks in economics: from the incentive-based to the knowledge-based approaches. *European Journal of Innovation Management*, 5(3): 152-163.

Pyka, A. (2007). Innovation Networks. In H. Hanusch, & A. Pyka (eds.), *Elgar Companion to Neo-Schumpeterian Economics*: 360-376. Cheltenham, UK and Northampton, MA, USA: Edward Elgar.

Pyka, A., and H. Hanusch (2007). Principles of Neo-Schumpeterian Economics. *Cambridge Journal of Economics*, 31(2): 275-289.

Pyka, A., and G. Küppers (eds., 2002). *Innovation networks. Theory and Practice*. Cheltenham, UK and Northampton, MA, USA: Edward Elgar.

Reger, G. (2003). Linking corporate-wide global R&D activities. In J. Cantwell, & J. Molero (eds.), *Multinational Enterprises, Innovative Strategies and Systems of Innovation*: 81-105. Cheltenham, UK and Northampton, MA, USA: Edward Elgar.

Rosenberg, N. (1990). Why Do Firms Do Basic Research (With Their Own Money)? *Research Policy*, 9(2): 165-174.

Rossak, S. (2002). *Forschungs- und Innovationsprozesse in multinationalen Unternehmen.*, ARC Systems Research Report, Seibersdorf.

Sadowski, B. M., and G. Sadowski-Rasters (2006). On the innovativeness of foreign affiliates: Evidence from companies in The Netherlands. *Research Policy*, 35(3): 447-462.

Sadowski, B. M., and C. van Beers (2002). The Innovation Performance of Foreign Affiliates: Evidence from Dutch Manufacturing Firms, *ECIS Working Paper Series*. Eindhoven.

Salazar, M., and A. J. D. Holbrook (2004). A debate on innovation surveys. *Science and Public Policy*, 31(4): 254-266.

Sanna-Randaccio, F., and R. Veugelers (2003). Global Innovation Strategies of MNEs: Implications for Host Economies. In J. Cantwell, & J. Molero (eds.), *Multinational Enterprises, Innovative Strategies and Systems of Innovation*: 17-47. Cheltenham, UK and Northampton, MA, USA: Edward Elgar.

Schartinger, D., C. Rammer, M. Fischer, and J. Fröhlich (2002). Knowledge Interactions between Universities and Industry in Austria: Sectoral Patterns and Determinants. *Research Policy*, 31(3): 303-328.

Schibany, A., B. Nones, H. Gassler, and J. Schindler (2004). Die Attraktivität Österreichs als Forschungsstandort für internationale Unternehmen. Vienna: Joanneum Research.

Schiefer, A. (2006). Forschung und experimentelle Entwicklung (F&E) im Unternehmenssektor 2004. *Statistische Nachrichten*, 2006(11): 1019-1042.

Schiefer, A. (2007). Innovationsaktivitäten der Unternehmen im internationalen Vergleich. *Statistische Nachrichten*, 2007(4): 392-402.

Schumpeter, J. A. (1911). *Theorie der wirtschaftlichen Entwicklung* (8th ed.). Berlin: Dunckner & Humblot.

Schumpeter, J. A. (1942). *Capitalism, Socialism and Democracy*. London and New York: Routledge.

Smith, K. (2005). Measuring Innovation. In J. Fagerberg, D. Mowery, & R. R. Nelson (eds.), *The Oxford Handbook of Innovation*: 149-177. Oxford: Oxford University Press.

Statistik Austria (2002). *Innovation in österreichischen Unternehmen. Ergebnisse der Dritten Europäischen Innovationserhebung (CIS3)*. Vienna: Statistik Austria.

Statistik Austria (2005). *Leistungs- und Strukturstatistik 2003, Produktion & Dienstleistungen*. Vienna: Statistik Austria.

Statistik Austria (2007a). Forschung und experimentelle Entwicklung (F&E) im Unternehmenssektor 2006. *Statistische Nachrichten*, 2008(11): 1012-1042.

Statistik Austria (2007b). Österreichische Forschungsquote 2007 voraussichtlich 2,54% des BIP - F&E-Ausgaben steigen auf 6,83 Milliarden Euro. Vienna: Press Release, 16. 4. 2007.

Statistik Austria (2007c). *Statistisches Jahrbuch Österreichs 2007*. Vienna: Verlag Österreich.

Teece, D. J., G. Pisano, and A. Shuen (1997). Dynamic Capabilities and Strategic Management. *Strategic Management Journal*, 18(7): 509-533.

Tether, B. S. (2001). Identifying Innovation, Innovators and Innovative Behaviours: A Critical Assessment of the Community Innovation Survey (CIS), *CRIC Discussion Paper*, Vol. 48. Manchester.

Tether, B. S. (2002). Who Co-operates for Innovation, and Why: An Empirical Analysis. *Research Policy*, 31(6): 947-967.

The Economist (2007). Keep your T-bonds, we'll take the bank. *July 28th 2007*

Thursby, J., and M. Thursby (2006). Here or There? A Survey of Factors in Multinational R&D Location. Washington DC: National Academies Press. http://www.kauffman.org/pdf/thursby_final_1206.pdf

Tichy, G. (2001). What Do We Know about Success and Failure of Mergers? *Journal for Industry, Competition and Trade*, 1(4): 347-394.

Timmer, M. P., and A. Szirmai (2000). Productivity Growth in Asian Manufacturing: The Structural Bonus Hypothesis Examined. *Structural Change and Economic Dynamics*, 11(4): 371-392.

UNCTAD (2000a). Bilateral Investment Treaties 1959-1999. New York and Geneva: United Nations. http://www.unctad.org/en/docs/poiteiiad2.en.pdf

UNCTAD (2000b). World Investment Report 2000: Cross-border Mergers and Acquisitions and Development. New York and Geneva: United Nations.

UNCTAD (2001). World Investment Report 2001: Promoting Linkages. New York and Geneva: United Nations.

UNCTAD (2005). World Investment Report 2005: Transnational Corporations and the Internazionalisation of R&D. New York and Geneva: United Nations.

UNITED NATIONS (2006). Bridging the Technology Gap Between and Within Nations. Geneva: UN Economic and Social Council, Commission on Science and Technology for Development.

van Beers, C., E. Berghäll, and T. Poot (2004). Foreign Direct Investment and Science and Technology Infrastructure in Small Countries: Evidence from Finland and the Netherlands, *Paper presented at the Schumpeter Conference, Milan 2004*.

Vernon, R. (1966). International Investment and International Trade in the Product Cycle. *Quarterly Journal of Economics*, 80(2): 190-207.

Verona, G. (1999). A Resource-based View on Product Development. *Academy of Management Review*, 24: 132-142.

Veugelers, R. (1997). Internal R&D Expenditures and External Technology Sourcing. *Research Policy*, 26(3): 303-315.

Veugelers, R. (2005). Internationalisation of R&D:Trends, Issues and Implications for S&T policies. Background report for the OECD forum on the internationalization of R&D. Brussles: OECD.

von Zedtwitz, M., and O. Gassmann (2002). Market versus Technology Drive in R&D Internationalization: Four different Patterns of Managing Research and Development. *Research Policy*, 31(4): 569-558.

Wieser, R. (2005). Research and Development Productivity and Spillovers: Empirical Evidence at the Firm Level. *Journal of Economic Surveys*, 19(4): 587-621.

Wooldridge, J. M. (2002). *Introductory Econometrics: A Modern Approach. 2nd Edition*. Mason: South-Western College Publishers.

Xu, D., and O. Shenkar (2002). Institutional Distance and the Multinational Enterprise. *Academy of Management Review*, 27(4): 608-618.

Young, S., N. Hood, and E. Peters (1994). Multinational Enterprises and Regional Economic Development. *Regional Studies*, 28(7): 657-677.

Zaheer, S. (1995). Overcoming the Liability of Foreignness. *Academy of Management Journal*, 38(2): 341-364.

Zaheer, S. (2002). The liability of foreignness, redux: a commentary. *Journal of International Management*, 8(3): 351-358.

Zaheer, S., and E. Mosakowski (1997). The Dynamics of the Liability of Foreignness: A Global Study of Survival in Financial Services. *Strategic Management Journal*, 18(6): 439-463.

Zander, I. (1999). Where to the Multinational? The Evolution of Technological Capabilities in the Multinational Network. *International Business Review*, 8: 261-291.

Zander, I. (2002). The formation of international innovation networks in the multinational corporation: an evolutionary perspective. *Industrial and Corporate Change*, 11(2): 327-353.

Zanfei, A. (2000). Transnational Firms and the Changing Organisation of Innovative Activities. *Cambridge Journal of Economics*, 24(5): 515-542.

Zitt, M., and E. Bassecoulard (2004). Internationalisation in Science in the Prism of Bibliometric Indicators. In H. F. Moed, W. Glänzel, & U. Schmoch (eds.), *Handbook of Quantitative Science and Technology Research*: 407-436. Dordrecht: Kluwer Academic Publishers.

12. Annex

12.1 List of Abbreviations

CEEC	Central and Eastern European Countries
CIS	Community Innovation Survey
EU	European Union
FDI	Foreign Direct Investment
FP	Framework Programme for Research and Technology Development
GDP	Gross Domestic Product
GERD	Gross Domestic Expenditure on Research and Development
IPRs	Intellectual Capital Rights
LOF	Liability of Foreignness
MNEs	Multinational Enterprises
OECD	Organisation for Economic Co-operation and Development
R&D	Research and Development
SMEs	Small and Medium sized Enterprises

12.2 Tables

Table 27: Correlation matrix of the independent variables

	rd	co	lnipc	seos	sekis	selt	semlt	semht	growth	markti	marktn	marktl	fund	est	lninvest	tertshr	lnemp
lnemp	0.34	0.24	0.08	-0.31	-0.16	0.08	0.16	0.3	0.07	0.34	-0.07	-0.32	0.33	-0.04	0.13	0.03	1
tertshr	0.21	0.22	0.29	-0.03	0.27	-0.17	-0.11	0	0.13	0.07	0.08	-0.16	0.08	0.12	-0.04	1	
lninvest	0.15	0.14	0.32	-0.21	-0.11	0.14	0.19	0.06	-0.01	0.11	-0.09	-0.04	0.24	-0.01	1		
est	0.07	0.05	0.03	0.05	-0.07	0.03	-0.06	0.05	0.01	0.02	0.03	-0.06	0.07	1			
fund	0.43	0.26	0.37	-0.16	-0.37	0.15	0.14	0.32	0.08	0.38	-0.06	-0.36	1				
marktl	-0.44	-0.15	-0.26	-0.07	0.41	-0.01	-0.15	-0.24	-0.04	-0.54	-0.38	1					
marktn	-0.09	-0.12	-0.09	0.23	0.01	-0.01	-0.03	-0.23	-0.08	-0.57	1						
markti	0.47	0.25	0.31	-0.15	-0.37	0.02	0.16	0.42	0.11	1							
growth	0.06	0.14	0.11	-0.01	0.15	-0.16	-0.07	0.07	1								
semht	0.33	0.11	0.24	-0.28	-0.28	-0.22	-0.18	1									
semlt	0.22	0.09	0.05	-0.23	-0.23	-0.18	1										
selt	0.07	-0.08	-0.07	-0.27	-0.27	1											
sekis	-0.32	-0.06	-0.07	-0.34	1												
seos	-0.2	-0.05	-0.12	1													
lnipc	0.36	0.2	1														
co	0.26	1															
rd	1																

Source: Community Innovation Survey 3, Statistics Austria

Table 28: Differences and their significance between groups of foreign-owned and domestically owned enterprises

Difference between:	Employment, persons	Turnover, 1.000 Euro	Share of exports on turnover	Tertiary employment as % of total employment	Propensity to innovate
Domuni-domgroup	- 244 ***	- 81,031 ***	-8% ***	-3% ***	-34% ***
domuni-for	- 116 ***	- 51,824 ***	-19% ***	-7% ***	-15% ***
domuni-gls	- 264 ***	- 75,175 ***	-19% ***	-3% ***	-22% ***
domgroup-for	129 *	29,206	-11% ***	-4% ***	19% ***
domgroup-gls	- 20	5,856	-11% ***	0%	12% **
for-gls	- 149 **	- 23,351	0%	4% **	-7%

Difference between:	High and medium high technology	Medium low technology	Low technology	Knowledge intensive services	Other services
domuni-domgroup	-4% **	-1%	14% ***	-40% ***	30% ***
domuni-for	-8% ***	3%	12% ***	-6% **	-1%
domuni-gls	-16% ***	1%	17% ***	-6% **	4%
domgroup-for	-5%	5%	-3%	34% ***	-31% ***
domgroup-gls	-13% ***	3%	2%	34% ***	-26% ***
for-gls	-8%	-2%	5%	0%	5%

Difference between:	Innovative expenditure as % of turnover	Innovative expenditure per employee, Euro	Innovative expenditure, 1.000 Euro	Number of R&D personnel	R&D personnel as % of total employment
domuni-domgroup	5% **	836	- 1,888 ***	-14 *	2%
domuni-for	5%	1,314	- 1,330 ***	-15 *	2%
domuni-gls	4%	- 1,605	- 4,200 ***	-37 ***	0%
domgroup-for	0%	478	557	0	1%
domgroup-gls	-1%	- 2,441	- 2,313 *	-23 *	-2%
for-gls	-1%	- 2,919	- 2,870	-23	-3%

Difference between:	Propensity to introduce products new to the market	Share of turnover from new products	Propensity for innovation co-operation	Propensity for domestic innovation co-operation	Propensity for co-operation with domestic universities
domuni-domgroup	-5%	7.1 **	-13% ***	0%	-30% ***
domuni-for	-19% **	0.1	-8%	35%	-6%
domuni-gls	-26% ***	0.7	-17% **	-1%	-30% **
domgroup-for	-14%	-7.0	5%	35% ***	24%
domgroup-gls	-21% **	-6.4	-5%	-1%	0%
for-gls	-6%	0.6	-9%	-36% **	-24%

Notes: Domuni: domestically owned non-group enterprise; domgroup: domestically owned group enterprise; for: foreign-owned enterprise with a parent enterprise in Germany, Liechtenstein or Switzerland; for: all other foreign-owned enterprises

* significant at 10%; ** significant at 5%; *** significant at 1%, % pts are percentage points.

Source: Community Innovation Survey 3, Statistics Austria

Table 29: Determinants of the propensity to innovate, probit estimates

Case	(1)	(2)	(3)	(4)
	innov	innov	innov	innov
domuni		-0.389	-0.451	-0.451
		(3.81)***	(4.17)***	(4.17)***
euro			-0.495	
			(2.37)**	
as			-0.362	
			(1.69)*	
gls			-0.227	-0.228
			(1.43)	(1.43)
others				-0.431
				(2.64)***
forown	-0.039	-0.252		
	(0.32)	(1.89)*		
lnemp	0.271	0.234	0.231	0.232
	(8.14)***	(6.74)***	(6.64)***	(6.65)***
growth	0.357	0.355	0.353	0.353
	(4.37)***	(4.32)***	(4.30)***	(4.30)***
tertshr	0.351	0.342	0.519	0.539
	(0.70)	(0.69)	(1.04)	(1.08)
exshr	0.717	0.647	0.649	0.645
	(4.45)***	(3.97)***	(3.98)***	(3.96)***
lninvest	0.095	0.108	0.107	0.106
	(3.37)***	(3.80)***	(3.74)***	(3.71)***
invCo	0.004	0.005	0.005	0.005
	(2.38)**	(2.58)**	(2.75)***	(2.74)***
est	0.520	0.469	0.453	0.445
	(2.36)**	(2.13)**	(2.05)**	(2.02)**
semht	0.400	0.363	0.365	0.368
	(2.26)**	(2.03)**	(2.04)**	(2.05)**
semlt	0.018	-0.047	-0.051	-0.048
	(0.11)	(0.30)	(0.33)	(0.31)
sekis	0.504	0.239	0.180	0.178
	(3.56)***	(1.52)	(1.12)	(1.11)
seos	-0.322	-0.389	-0.393	-0.393
	(2.75)***	(3.27)***	(3.30)***	(3.30)***
Constant	-1.270	-0.751	-0.688	-0.691
	(6.69)***	(3.22)***	(2.92)***	(2.94)***
Observations	1261	1261	1261	1261
McFadden r2	0.2071	0.2164	0.2184	0.2184
Prob > chi2	0.0000	0.0000	0.0000	0.0000

Absolute value of z statistics in parentheses, * significant at 10%; ** significant at 5%; *** significant at 1%

Source: Community Innovation Survey 3, Statistics Austria

Table 30: Determinants of innovation expenditure intensity, Heckman probit estimates

Case	(1)	(2)	(3)	(4)
	lnipc	lnipc	lnipc	lnipc
domuni		-0.218	-0.184	-0.180
		(1.43)	(1.16)	(1.13)
euro			-0.142	
			(0.50)	
as			0.253	
			(0.89)	
gls			-0.092	-0.093
			(0.49)	(0.49)
others				0.053
				(0.25)
forown	-0.057	-0.139		
	(0.37)	(0.84)		
lnemp	-0.126	-0.127	-0.133	-0.132
	(2.21)**	(2.39)**	(2.44)**	(2.41)**
growth	0.064	0.093	0.083	0.086
	(0.48)	(0.72)	(0.63)	(0.65)
est	-0.148	-0.130	-0.136	-0.150
	(0.57)	(0.51)	(0.53)	(0.59)
rd	0.731	0.749	0.752	0.752
	(5.45)***	(5.58)***	(5.60)***	(5.59)***
fund	0.676	0.690	0.688	0.697
	(4.97)***	(5.07)***	(5.05)***	(5.13)***
exshr	0.702	0.716	0.691	0.690
	(3.04)***	(3.19)***	(3.03)***	(3.02)***
lninvest	0.336	0.352	0.353	0.346
	(7.45)***	(7.69)***	(7.59)***	(7.50)***
invCo	0.009	0.010	0.010	0.009
	(3.32)***	(3.56)***	(3.35)***	(3.32)***
semht	0.578	0.578	0.568	0.574
	(2.97)***	(2.99)***	(2.92)***	(2.95)***
semlt	0.146	0.111	0.116	0.123
	(0.74)	(0.55)	(0.58)	(0.61)
sekis	0.762	0.691	0.703	0.707
	(3.64)***	(3.25)***	(3.29)***	(3.31)***
seos	0.432	0.358	0.375	0.368
	(2.19)**	(1.79)*	(1.85)*	(1.81)*
Constant	3.756	3.789	3.837	3.799
	(7.49)***	(8.32)***	(8.16)***	(8.07)***
Observations	1227	1227	1227	1227
Uncensored obs	515	515	515	515
Wald Chi2 and sig.	199.17***	204.65***	205.1***	203.3***

Absolute value of z statistics in parentheses, * significant at 10%; ** significant at 5%; *** significant at 1%

Source: Community Innovation Survey 3, Statistics Austria

Table 31: Determinants of R&D personnel intensity, Heckman probit estimates

Case	(1)	(2)	(3)	(4)
	rdyrs	rdyrs	rdyrs	rdyrs
domuni		0.026	0.023	0.023
		(1.71)*	(1.48)	(1.48)
euro			-0.016	
			(0.52)	
as			-0.020	
			(0.68)	
gls			0.031	0.031
			(1.70)*	(1.70)*
others				-0.018
				(0.80)
forown	0.015	0.023		
	(0.94)	(1.36)		
lnemp	-0.030	-0.027	-0.026	-0.026
	(6.11)***	(5.05)***	(5.01)***	(5.01)***
growth	0.004	0.004	0.006	0.006
	(0.34)	(0.29)	(0.43)	(0.43)
est	0.009	0.013	0.015	0.015
	(0.37)	(0.51)	(0.61)	(0.62)
fund	0.045	0.041	0.043	0.043
	(3.41)***	(3.16)***	(3.28)***	(3.28)***
exshr	0.049	0.055	0.057	0.057
	(2.43)**	(2.69)***	(2.78)***	(2.78)***
lninvest	0.015	0.013	0.014	0.014
	(2.91)***	(2.65)***	(2.84)***	(2.85)***
invCo	0.000	0.000	0.000	0.000
	(1.06)	(1.01)	(1.17)	(1.17)
semht	0.010	0.011	0.008	0.008
	(0.55)	(0.62)	(0.47)	(0.47)
semlt	-0.014	-0.010	-0.013	-0.013
	(0.78)	(0.56)	(0.73)	(0.73)
sekis	0.130	0.140	0.138	0.138
	(5.58)***	(5.83)***	(5.80)***	(5.80)***
seos	0.088	0.094	0.092	0.092
	(4.41)***	(4.64)***	(4.52)***	(4.52)***
Constant	0.213	0.179	0.179	0.179
	(5.68)***	(4.31)***	(4.32)***	(4.33)***
Observations	999	999	999	999
Uncensored obs	287	287	287	287
Wald Chi 2 and sig.	138.02***	139.80***	145.40***	145.35***

Absolute value of z statistics in parentheses, * significant at 10%; ** significant at 5%; *** significant at 1%

Source: Community Innovation Survey 3, Statistics Austria

Table 32: Determinants of the propensity to introduce market novelties, Heckman probit estimates

Case	(1)	(2)	(3)	(4)
	InMar	InMar	InMar	InMar
domuni		-0.268	-0.189	-0.208
		(1.55)	(0.74)	(0.85)
euro			0.072	
			(0.18)	
as			0.310	
			(0.60)	
gls			0.086	0.067
			(0.31)	(0.25)
others				0.151
				(0.39)
forown	0.147	0.000		
	(0.72)	(0.00)		
lnemp	0.312	0.313	0.302	0.307
	(4.14)***	(6.33)***	(4.39)***	(5.06)***
growth	0.384	0.438	0.408	0.421
	(2.18)**	(3.15)***	(2.27)**	(2.54)**
est	0.551	0.554	0.555	0.558
	(1.63)	(1.85)*	(1.69)*	(1.75)*
rd	0.696	0.612	0.697	0.676
	(3.54)***	(2.87)***	(2.96)***	(2.71)***
fund	-0.242	-0.186	-0.218	-0.205
	(1.35)	(1.19)	(1.18)	(1.14)
exshr	0.300	0.467	0.333	0.376
	(0.84)	(1.59)	(0.79)	(0.93)
lninvest	-0.016	0.018	0.004	0.005
	(0.24)	(0.30)	(0.06)	(0.07)
invCo	-0.000	0.002	0.000	0.001
	(0.08)	(0.47)	(0.03)	(0.11)
semht	0.032	0.111	0.050	0.068
	(0.13)	(0.48)	(0.18)	(0.25)
semlt	0.255	0.188	0.213	0.208
	(1.04)	(0.85)	(0.87)	(0.87)
sekis	-0.299	-0.246	-0.308	-0.286
	(0.91)	(0.90)	(0.93)	(0.89)
seos	-0.166	-0.336	-0.230	-0.273
	(0.56)	(1.36)	(0.65)	(0.83)
lnipc	0.039	0.027	0.033	0.031
	(0.67)	(0.52)	(0.57)	(0.55)
Constant	-2.653	-2.713	-2.584	-2.664
	(3.40)***	(6.32)***	(3.65)***	(4.54)***
Observations	1105	1105	1105	1105
Uncensored obs	393	393	393	393
Wald Chi 2 and sig.	97.81***	180.88***	124.08***	139.78***

Absolute value of z statistics in parentheses, * significant at 10%; ** significant at 5%; *** significant at 1%

Source: Community Innovation Survey 3, Statistics Austria

Table 33: Determinants of the share of innovations on turnover, Heckman probit estimates

Case	(1) TurnIn	(2) TurnIn	(3) TurnIn	(4) TurnIn
domuni		5.559	6.470	6.626
		(1.60)	(1.84)*	(1.87)*
euro			-4.964	
			(0.78)	
as			10.306	
			(1.54)	
gls			3.431	3.376
			(0.80)	(0.79)
others				2.260
				(0.46)
forown	-2.042	-0.035		
	(0.57)	(0.01)		
lnemp	-1.477	-1.351	-1.548	-1.490
	(1.09)	(1.16)	(1.37)	(1.30)
growth	0.577	-0.134	-0.511	-0.332
	(0.18)	(0.05)	(0.17)	(0.11)
est	8.996	8.777	8.015	8.119
	(1.50)	(1.49)	(1.36)	(1.38)
rd	-5.095	-5.776	-5.909	-5.810
	(1.50)	(1.69)*	(1.74)*	(1.70)*
fund	5.073	4.558	4.455	4.760
	(1.56)	(1.40)	(1.37)	(1.46)
exshr	10.597	10.072	9.230	9.276
	(1.92)*	(1.97)**	(1.83)*	(1.83)*
lninvest	0.327	-0.020	0.182	-0.096
	(0.30)	(0.02)	(0.16)	(0.09)
invCo	0.124	0.106	0.098	0.100
	(1.99)**	(1.73)*	(1.60)	(1.61)
semht	3.006	3.121	2.547	2.659
	(0.68)	(0.72)	(0.59)	(0.61)
semlt	-3.478	-2.309	-2.434	-2.194
	(0.78)	(0.51)	(0.54)	(0.48)
sekis	-0.810	0.874	0.987	1.056
	(0.16)	(0.18)	(0.20)	(0.21)
seos	1.230	3.159	4.210	3.419
	(0.24)	(0.64)	(0.86)	(0.69)
lnipc	4.443	4.485	4.447	4.467
	(4.24)***	(4.30)***	(4.28)***	(4.28)***
Constant	12.885	11.785	14.269	12.465
	(0.96)	(1.08)	(1.36)	(1.17)
Observations	1105	1105	1105	1105
Uncensored obs	393	393	393	393
Wald Chi 2 and sig.	65.62***	68.49***	72.72***	69.12***

Absolute value of z statistics in parentheses, * significant at 10%; ** significant at 5%; *** significant at 1%

Source: Community Innovation Survey 3, Statistics Austria

Table 34: Determinants for the importance of internal information sources, Heckman probit estimates

Case	(1) sorint	(2) sorint	(3) sorint
euro		0.792	
		(2.72)***	
as		0.148	
		(0.58)	
gls		0.287	0.290
		(1.60)	(1.62)
others			0.436
			(2.26)**
forown	0.417		
	(2.62)***		
lnemp	-0.017	-0.032	-0.035
	(0.24)	(0.49)	(0.52)
growth	0.089	0.065	0.054
	(0.60)	(0.44)	(0.37)
est			
rd	0.220	0.227	0.227
	(1.67)*	(1.74)*	(1.75)*
fund	0.130	0.133	0.124
	(1.00)	(1.06)	(0.99)
exshr	-0.077	-0.126	-0.130
	(0.32)	(0.53)	(0.55)
lninvest	-0.000	-0.010	-0.000
	(0.00)	(0.22)	(0.01)
invCo	0.001	-0.000	0.000
	(0.26)	(0.02)	(0.04)
semht	0.195	0.196	0.181
	(0.96)	(0.97)	(0.90)
semlt	0.173	0.190	0.174
	(0.87)	(0.96)	(0.89)
sekis	0.378	0.366	0.356
	(1.60)	(1.54)	(1.49)
seos	0.353	0.367	0.374
	(1.90)*	(2.05)**	(2.11)**
Constant	-0.044	0.072	0.142
	(0.07)	(0.12)	(0.23)
Observations	1227	1227	1227
Uncensored obs	515	515	515
Wald Chi 2 and sig.	16.85*	19.64	17.31

Note: Reference case is the group of domestically owned enterprises

Absolute value of z statistics in parentheses, * significant at 10%; ** significant at 5%; *** significant at 1%

Source: Community Innovation Survey 3, Statistics Austria

Table 35: Determinants for the importance of external information sources, Heckman probit estimates

Case	(1)	(2)	(3)	(4)
	sorext	sorext	sorext	sorext
domuni		0.114	0.062	0.050
		(0.65)	(0.31)	(0.25)
euro			-0.046	
			(0.15)	
as			-0.318	
			(1.08)	
gls			-0.292	-0.296
			(1.42)	(1.44)
others				-0.196
				(0.81)
forown	-0.225	-0.171		
	(1.39)	(0.94)		
lnemp	0.083	0.067	0.081	0.085
	(1.14)	(0.92)	(1.05)	(1.08)
growth	0.016	-0.025	-0.002	0.004
	(0.10)	(0.16)	(0.01)	(0.02)
est	-0.087	-0.122	-0.110	-0.093
	(0.32)	(0.46)	(0.40)	(0.34)
rd	0.226	0.212	0.213	0.216
	(1.66)*	(1.54)	(1.54)	(1.56)
fund	0.186	0.179	0.184	0.178
	(1.35)	(1.32)	(1.34)	(1.30)
exshr	0.340	0.293	0.347	0.357
	(1.32)	(1.12)	(1.26)	(1.29)
lninvest	0.053	0.038	0.037	0.044
	(1.09)	(0.71)	(0.67)	(0.80)
invCo	0.002	0.001	0.001	0.002
	(0.65)	(0.40)	(0.48)	(0.54)
semht	0.192	0.174	0.203	0.205
	(0.92)	(0.84)	(0.97)	(0.97)
semlt	0.118	0.135	0.136	0.131
	(0.57)	(0.66)	(0.65)	(0.63)
sekis	0.122	0.133	0.135	0.137
	(0.54)	(0.59)	(0.60)	(0.61)
seos	0.364	0.425	0.407	0.398
	(1.76)*	(2.02)**	(1.80)*	(1.71)*
Constant	-0.650	-0.499	-0.636	-0.657
	(0.96)	(0.75)	(0.90)	(0.90)
Observations	1227	1227	1227	1227
Uncensored obs	515	515	515	515
Wald Chi 2 and sig.	26.31**	25.50**	27.67**	27.45**

Absolute value of z statistics in parentheses, * significant at 10%; ** significant at 5%; *** significant at 1%

Source: Community Innovation Survey 3, Statistics Austria

Table 36: Determinants of the propensity for innovation co-operation, Heckman probit estimates

	(1)	(2)	(3)	(4)
COEFFICIENT	co	co	co	co
domuni		-0.119	-0.260	-0.280
		(0.188)	(0.200)	(0.198)
euro			0.0145	
			(0.340)	
as			-1.109***	
			(0.412)	
gls			-0.00379	-0.0120
			(0.229)	(0.229)
others				-0.492*
				(0.274)
forown	0.176	0.131		
	(0.178)	(0.195)		
lnemp	0.0652	0.0674	0.0915	0.0974
	(0.0661)	(0.0668)	(0.0685)	(0.0674)
rd	0.396**	0.418**	0.401**	0.410**
	(0.173)	(0.179)	(0.182)	(0.180)
fund	0.387**	0.408**	0.454***	0.422***
	(0.156)	(0.162)	(0.166)	(0.163)
tertshr	1.447**	1.492**	2.130***	1.884**
	(0.728)	(0.741)	(0.815)	(0.791)
sorext	0.223*	0.229*	0.229*	0.232*
	(0.130)	(0.132)	(0.136)	(0.136)
exshr	0.357	0.369	0.496*	0.495*
	(0.270)	(0.274)	(0.286)	(0.281)
lninvest	0.123**	0.132**	0.143**	0.166***
	(0.0612)	(0.0633)	(0.0640)	(0.0618)
semht	-0.0334	-0.0225	-0.0260	-0.0128
	(0.232)	(0.236)	(0.243)	(0.243)
semlt	0.333	0.327	0.279	0.274
	(0.231)	(0.234)	(0.240)	(0.240)
sekis	0.524*	0.514*	0.485	0.484
	(0.295)	(0.297)	(0.299)	(0.295)
seos	0.729***	0.708***	0.671***	0.659**
	(0.231)	(0.240)	(0.257)	(0.259)
seutil	0.259	0.186	0.0449	-0.0135
	(0.474)	(0.499)	(0.519)	(0.518)
Constant	-2.386***	-2.489***	-2.738***	-2.883***
	(0.823)	(0.834)	(0.805)	(0.767)
Observations	1218	1218	1218	1218
Uncensored obs	549	549	549	549
Wald Chi2 and sig.	43.9***	45.18***	54.31***	54.5***

Absolute value of z statistics in parentheses, * significant at 10%; ** significant at 5%; *** significant at 1%

Source: Community Innovation Survey 3, Statistics Austria

Table 37: Determinants of the propensity for external domestic innovation co-operation, Heckman probit estimates

COEFFICIENT	(1) codom	(2) codom	(4) codom	(4) codom
domuni		0.411	0.463	0.232
		(0.348)	(0.349)	(0.404)
euro			-0.557	
			(0.502)	
gls			0.335	0.0607
			(0.418)	(0.433)
others				-1.268**
				(0.529)
forown	-0.137	-0.000340		
	(0.320)	(0.331)		
lnemp	-0.0321	-0.0266	-0.0495	0.0236
	(0.124)	(0.115)	(0.113)	(0.141)
growth	-0.609*	-0.599*	-0.675**	-0.691*
	(0.363)	(0.340)	(0.335)	(0.390)
exshr	-1.146**	-1.180***	-1.212***	-1.006**
	(0.459)	(0.425)	(0.402)	(0.497)
rd	0.725*	0.565	0.458	0.512
	(0.379)	(0.383)	(0.373)	(0.419)
tertshr	0.176	0.175	0.178	0.281
	(1.204)	(1.172)	(1.175)	(1.304)
sorext	0.187	0.184	0.196	0.272
	(0.175)	(0.169)	(0.170)	(0.192)
Constant	1.901**	1.956**	2.253***	1.730
	(0.942)	(0.806)	(0.779)	(1.089)
Observations	814	814	814	814
Uncensored obs	135	135	135	135
Wald Chi2 and sig.	12.84*	16.41**	20.63**	19.09**

Absolute value of z statistics in parentheses, * significant at 10%; ** significant at 5%; *** significant at 1%

Source: Community Innovation Survey 3, Statistics Austria

Table 38: Determinants of the propensity for international innovation co-operation, Heckman probit estimates

COEFFICIENT	(1) coint	(2) coint	(3) coint	(4) coint
domuni	-0.0735	-0.0837	-0.0973	
	(0.366)	(0.370)	(0.372)	
euro	0.559			
	(0.510)			
as	6.499			
	(29225)			
gls	-0.254	-0.270		
	(0.394)	(0.394)		
others		0.637		
		(0.490)		
forown			-0.0396	0.0000728
			(0.340)	(0.301)
lnemp	-0.0887	-0.0821	-0.0806	-0.0900
	(0.146)	(0.148)	(0.154)	(0.144)
exshr	0.668	0.709	0.672	0.602
	(0.598)	(0.602)	(0.609)	(0.527)
rd	0.616	0.631*	0.554	0.519
	(0.381)	(0.383)	(0.372)	(0.344)
tertshr	-0.417	-0.433	-0.368	-0.370
	(0.987)	(0.992)	(0.984)	(0.969)
sorext	0.282*	0.287*	0.282*	0.281*
	(0.157)	(0.158)	(0.156)	(0.153)
Constant	0.204	0.119	0.211	0.351
	(1.366)	(1.383)	(1.457)	(1.289)
Observations	814	814	814	814
Uncensored obs	135	135	135	135
Wald Chi 2 and sig.	13.36	14.67*	13.41*	12.21*

Absolute value of z statistics in parentheses, * significant at 10%; ** significant at 5%; *** significant at 1%

Source: Community Innovation Survey 3, Statistics Austria

Table 39: Structural indicators of the countries of comparison, 2000

Country	Total GDP, bn USD PPP	GDP per capita, USD PPP	GERD/GDP
BELGIUM	284	27,671	2.0
BULGARIA	48	6,026	0.5
CZECH REPUBLIC	161	15,654	1.2
ESTONIA	13	9,745	0.6
GERMANY	2,095	25,466	2.5
GREECE	194	17,682	0.5
HUNGARY	132	12,962	0.8
ICELAND	8	29,605	2.7
LATVIA	19	7,889	0.4
LITHUANIA	31	8,696	0.6
NORWAY	154	34,174	1.6
PORTUGAL	198	19,322	0.8
ROMANIA	132	5,974	0.4
SLOVAKIA	61	11,393	0.6
SPAIN	867	21,401	0.9
AUSTRIA	232	28,987	1.9

Notes: GDP and GDP per capita based on purchasing-power-parity (PPP) current international dollar; GERD/GDP for Norway and Greece: 2001

Source: Eurostat, Structural Statistics (GERD/GDP), IMF Financial World Economic Outlook Database (GDP)

Table 40: Description of the EUROCIS dataset

Country	Sample size	Share of high and medium-high tech enterprises	Share of exports on turnover, mean
BE	1,273	25%	33%
BG	10,279	11%	10%
CZ	3,300	14%	23%
DE	2,906	23%	15%
EE	2,384	8%	31%
ES	8,024	20%	13%
GR	1,543	21%	0%
HU	951	19%	36%
IS	680	18%	15%
LT	1,863	8%	35%
LV	1,993	8%	46%
NO	3,548	18%	79%
PT	1,804	18%	25%
RO	7,479	10%	21%
SK	1,734	19%	41%
Total	49,761	15%	23%

Source: EUROSTAT, EUROCIS database

Table 41: Propensity to introduce product and/or process innovations and significance of difference, means

Country	All enterprises	Foreign-owned enterprises	Domestically owned enterprises	Difference	Significance of difference, error level
		Propensity to introduce innovations			
BE	59%	68%	55%	12%	***
BG	12%	22%	11%	10%	***
CZ	41%	53%	38%	14%	***
DE	63%	74%	63%	11%	***
EE	37%	59%	34%	25%	***
ES	45%	66%	42%	24%	***
GR	30%	39%	29%	10%	***
HU	30%	36%	29%	7%	-
IS	53%	55%	53%	1%	-
LT	33%	51%	32%	19%	***
LV	25%	39%	24%	15%	***
NO	44%	53%	43%	11%	***
PT	46%	55%	45%	10%	***
RO	24%	46%	23%	23%	***
SK	27%	41%	25%	16%	***
Total	33%	54%	31%	23%	***

* significant at 10%; ** significant at 5%; *** significant at 1%, % pts are percentage points

Source: Community Innovation Survey 3, EUROSTAT database

Table 42: Determinants of the propensity to innovate, probit estimates, 15 countries and Austria

	15 countries	Austria
	innov	innov
forown	-0.146	-0.305
	(5.07)***	(2.40)**
domuni	-0.233	-0.448
	(10.36)***	(4.05)***
lneturn	0.071	0.122
	(14.95)***	(3.25)***
EST	-0.021	0.450
	(0.57)	(2.11)**
lnemphi	0.174	0.186
	(30.56)***	(3.78)***
lninvest	0.075	0.122
	(16.69)***	(4.47)***
semht	0.344	0.466
	(16.26)***	(2.72)***
semlt	0.126	-0.027
	(5.83)***	(0.17)
sekis	0.147	0.057
	(6.06)***	(0.39)
seos	-0.404	-0.463
	(20.30)***	(4.00)***
seutil	-0.481	-0.974
	(10.29)***	(4.63)***
ro	0.953	
	(19.22)***	
baltic	0.736	
	(28.20)***	
cz	0.979	
	(29.87)***	
sk	0.566	
	(13.37)***	
hu	0.714	
	(13.11)***	
gr	1.400	
	(24.77)***	
no	0.769	
	(23.88)***	
pt	1.237	
	(30.00)***	
is	1.338	
	(23.23)***	
es	1.215	
	(43.83)***	
be	1.290	
	(28.87)***	
de	1.104	
	(31.90)***	
Constant	-1.795	-0.491
	(26.97)***	(1.35)
Observations	41348	1253
McFadden R2	0.1776	0.2009
Prob > chi2	0.0000	0.0000

Absolute value of z statistics in parentheses, * significant at 10%; ** significant at 5%; *** significant at 1%

Source: Community Innovation Survey 3 EUROSTAT and Statistics Austria

Table 43: Determinants of innovation expenditure intensity, Heckman probit estimates, 15 countries and Austria

	15 countries			Austria	
Case	(1)	(2)	(3)	(1)	(2)
domuni		-0.164	-0.164		-0.120
		(2.95)***	(2.96)***		(0.60)
forown	0.060	-0.043		0.009	-0.037
	(1.09)	(0.65)		(0.05)	(0.19)
EU			-0.071		
			(1.02)		
non_EU			0.069		
			(0.62)		
lneturn	0.026	0.025	0.025	-0.538	-0.548
	(3.69)***	(3.59)***	(3.59)***	(8.12)***	(8.02)***
lnemphi	-0.007	0.002	0.001	0.341	0.349
	(0.37)	(0.10)	(0.08)	(4.51)***	(4.54)***
fund	0.441	0.443	0.443	0.665	0.672
	(10.46)***	(10.52)***	(10.51)***	(3.91)***	(3.94)***
exshr	0.232	0.231	0.227	0.283	0.263
	(3.82)***	(3.82)***	(3.75)***	(1.07)	(0.99)
lninvest	0.504	0.510	0.510	0.390	0.395
	(44.60)***	(45.03)***	(44.99)***	(7.09)***	(7.08)***
semht	0.676	0.703	0.699	0.502	0.498
	(11.89)***	(12.29)***	(12.22)***	(2.03)**	(2.01)**
semlt	0.161	0.173	0.173	-0.031	-0.055
	(2.78)***	(2.95)***	(2.96)***	(0.12)	(0.21)
sekis	1.200	1.206	1.205	0.058	0.003
	(19.19)***	(19.10)***	(19.10)***	(0.24)	(0.01)
seos	-0.398	-0.442	-0.441	-0.000	-0.028
	(5.65)***	(6.27)***	(6.26)***	(0.00)	(0.12)
seutil	-1.127	-1.169	-1.169	0.490	0.426
	(7.67)***	(7.93)***	(7.93)***	(1.06)	(0.90)
rd	-0.263	-0.248	-0.249	0.080	0.086
	(6.26)***	(5.93)***	(5.94)***	(0.47)	(0.50)
rdintensity	0.239	0.237	0.236		
	(5.34)***	(5.24)***	(5.23)***		
lngdp	-0.035	-0.023	-0.023		
	(1.72)*	(1.12)	(1.15)		
Constant	-3.481	-3.623	-3.610	1.583	1.724
	(9.45)***	(10.64)***	(10.59)***	(2.30)**	(2.36)**
Observations	40027	40027	40027	1253	1253
Uncensored obs	13889	13889	13889	547	547
Wald chi2 and sig	3018.06***	2996.04***	2997.98***	232.13***	235.29***

Absolute value of z statistics in parentheses, * significant at 10%; ** significant at 5%; *** significant at 1%

Source: Community Innovation Survey 3 EUROSTAT and Statistics Austria

Table 44: Determinants the propensity to introduce market novelties, Heckman probit estimates, 15 countries and Austria

	15 countries			Austria	
Case	(1)	(2)	(3)	(1)	(2)
domuni		-0.193	-0.193		-0.353
		(7.21)***	(7.22)***		(2.57)**
forown	0.146	0.015		0.111	-0.098
	(5.14)***	(0.45)		(0.72)	(0.70)
EU			0.002		
			(0.07)		
non_EU			0.064		
			(1.15)		
lneturn	-0.050	-0.050	-0.050	0.018	0.084
	(12.34)***	(12.71)***	(12.72)***	(0.24)	(1.65)*
lnemphi	0.192	0.187	0.187	0.146	0.215
	(28.22)***	(28.19)***	(28.16)***	(1.98)**	(3.82)***
fund	0.052	0.051	0.051	-0.231	-0.190
	(2.37)**	(2.39)**	(2.39)**	(1.52)	(1.71)*
exshr	0.016	0.009	0.007	0.004	-0.005
	(0.51)	(0.30)	(0.24)	(0.02)	(0.03)
lninvest	0.020	0.021	0.021	-0.049	0.045
	(3.58)***	(3.89)***	(3.88)***	(0.88)	(1.10)
semht	0.299	0.307	0.306	-0.043	0.215
	(10.75)***	(11.34)***	(11.29)***	(0.19)	(1.24)
semlt	0.082	0.086	0.086	0.124	0.063
	(2.75)***	(2.95)***	(2.96)***	(0.59)	(0.36)
sekis	0.043	0.043	0.043	-0.450	-0.390
	(1.30)	(1.34)	(1.34)	(2.01)**	(2.01)**
seos	-0.229	-0.246	-0.246	-0.144	-0.478
	(7.00)***	(7.81)***	(7.80)***	(0.59)	(3.05)***
seutil	-0.913	-0.904	-0.904	-0.708	-1.150
	(10.66)***	(10.84)***	(10.84)***	(1.40)	(3.13)***
rd	0.371	0.357	0.357	0.864	0.712
	(17.48)***	(17.41)***	(17.40)***	(4.81)***	(6.04)***
lnipc	0.017	0.016	0.016	0.071	0.063
	(3.80)***	(3.82)***	(3.81)***	(1.78)*	(2.02)**
rdintensity	-0.019	-0.029	-0.029		
	(0.81)	(1.26)	(1.27)		
lngdp	0.048	0.053	0.052		
	(5.17)***	(5.99)***	(5.94)***		
Constant	-1.307	-1.228	-1.222	-0.709	-1.596
	(9.41)***	(9.52)***	(9.46)***	(0.76)	(3.23)***
Observations	40027	40027	40027	1253	1253
Uncensored obs	13889	13889	13889	547	547
Wald chi2 and sig	2360.33***	2605.31***	2603.46***	54.54***	250.01***

Absolute value of z statistics in parentheses, * significant at 10%; ** significant at 5%; *** significant at 1%

Source: Community Innovation Survey 3 EUROSTAT and Statistics Austria

Table 45: Determinants of the share of innovations on turnover, Heckman probit estimates, 15 countries and Austria

	15 countries			Austria	
Case	(1)	(2)	(3)	(1)	(2)
domuni		-0.036***	-0.036***		0.093*
		(0.008)	(0.008)		(0.05)
forown	0.020***	-0.0015		0.024	0.072
	(0.008)	(0.009)		(0.03)	(0.05)
EU			-0.0033		
			(0.010)		
non_EU			0.0054		
			(0.02)		
lneturn	-0.00054	-0.00100	-0.00099	-0.030**	-0.035**
	(0.0010)	(0.0010)	(0.0010)	(0.01)	(0.02)
lnemphi	0.020***	0.023***	0.023***	0.019	0.0013
	(0.003)	(0.003)	(0.003)	(0.01)	(0.02)
fund	0.0095	0.0094	0.0094	0.068**	0.060*
	(0.006)	(0.006)	(0.006)	(0.03)	(0.03)
exshr	0.048***	0.048***	0.047***	0.12***	0.13***
	(0.008)	(0.008)	(0.008)	(0.05)	(0.05)
lninvest	0.0055***	0.0061***	0.0061***	0.0027	-0.0071
	(0.002)	(0.002)	(0.002)	(0.01)	(0.01)
semht	0.066***	0.073***	0.072***	0.021	-0.012
	(0.008)	(0.008)	(0.008)	(0.05)	(0.05)
semlt	0.0071	0.0096	0.0096	-0.041	-0.028
	(0.008)	(0.008)	(0.008)	(0.05)	(0.05)
sekis	0.080***	0.082***	0.082***	0.029	0.038
	(0.009)	(0.009)	(0.009)	(0.05)	(0.05)
seos	-0.053***	-0.061***	-0.061***	0.054	0.13*
	(0.010)	(0.010)	(0.010)	(0.05)	(0.07)
seutil	-0.14***	-0.15***	-0.15***	0.021	0.16
	(0.02)	(0.02)	(0.02)	(0.1)	(0.1)
rdintensity	-0.040***	-0.039***	-0.039***		
	(0.007)	(0.007)	(0.007)		
lngdp	0.026***	0.028***	0.028***		
	(0.003)	(0.003)	(0.003)		
rd	0.048***	0.049***	0.049***	-0.015	-0.026
	(0.006)	(0.006)	(0.006)	(0.03)	(0.03)
lnipc	0.016***	0.015***	0.015***	0.017**	0.017**
	(0.001)	(0.001)	(0.001)	(0.008)	(0.007)
Constant	-0.22***	-0.24***	-0.24***	0.53***	0.64***
	(0.04)	(0.04)	(0.04)	(0.2)	(0.2)
Observations	38437	38437	38437	1125	1125
Uncensored obs	12299	12299	12299	419	419
Wald chi2 and sig	4680.82***	5355.93***	5108.86***	272.00***	343.81***

Absolute value of z statistics in parentheses, * significant at 10%; ** significant at 5%; *** significant at 1%

Source: Community Innovation Survey 3 EUROSTAT and Statistics Austria

Table 46: Determinants of the propensity for external domestic innovation co-operation, Heckman probit estimates, 15 countries and Austria

	15 countries			Austria	
Case	(1)	(2)	(3)	(1)	(2)
domuni		-0.375	-0.376		-0.275
		(11.58)***	(11.58)***		(1.23)
forown	-0.018	-0.236		-0.226	-0.335
	(0.50)	(5.94)***		(1.26)	(1.71)*
EU			-0.243		
			(5.71)***		
non_EU			-0.209		
			(2.99)***		
lneturn	0.031	0.028	0.028	0.050	0.053
	(6.55)***	(6.11)***	(6.11)***	(0.63)	(0.68)
lnemphi	0.136	0.155	0.155	0.129	0.157
	(11.42)***	(15.30)***	(15.29)***	(1.60)	(1.90)*
fund	0.635	0.619	0.619	0.364	0.393
	(22.13)***	(21.35)***	(21.35)***	(2.09)**	(2.22)**
exshr	0.056	0.049	0.048	0.514	0.486
	(1.31)	(1.18)	(1.15)	(2.03)**	(1.90)*
lninvest	0.057	0.065	0.065	0.127	0.157
	(6.93)***	(8.39)***	(8.38)***	(1.94)*	(2.41)**
semht	0.275	0.329	0.328	0.354	0.402
	(7.20)***	(9.08)***	(9.04)***	(1.31)	(1.49)
semlt	0.191	0.206	0.206	0.619	0.588
	(4.71)***	(5.25)***	(5.25)***	(2.35)**	(2.19)**
sekis	0.338	0.338	0.338	0.973	0.930
	(7.97)***	(8.20)***	(8.20)***	(3.06)***	(2.98)***
seos	0.233	0.131	0.131	1.321	1.226
	(4.84)***	(2.76)***	(2.76)***	(4.76)***	(3.67)***
seutil	0.286	0.177	0.176	0.620	0.395
	(3.02)***	(1.91)*	(1.91)*	(1.22)	(0.71)
rd	0.450	0.452	0.452	0.556	0.589
	(14.92)***	(15.69)***	(15.69)***	(2.92)***	(3.13)***
lnipc	0.007	0.005	0.005	0.034	0.033
	(1.10)	(0.82)	(0.82)	(0.71)	(0.68)
rdintensity	0.091	0.082	0.082		
	(3.10)***	(2.90)***	(2.89)***		
lngdp	-0.154	-0.124	-0.124		
	(12.19)***	(9.24)***	(9.24)***		
Constant	-0.126	-0.448	-0.445	-2.237	-2.319
	(0.57)	(2.18)**	(2.16)**	(2.35)**	(2.75)***
Observations	40027	40027	40027	1253	1253
Uncensored obs	13889	13889	13889	547	547
Wald chi2 and sig	1580.20***	2251.15***	2250.03***	53.89***	72.24***

Absolute value of z statistics in parentheses, * significant at 10%; ** significant at 5%; *** significant at 1%

Source: Community Innovation Survey 3 EUROSTAT and Statistics Austria

Table 47: Determinants of the propensity for innovation co-operation with domestic science, Heckman probit estimates, 15 countries and Austria

	15 countries			Austria	
Case	(1)	(2)	(3)	(1)	(2)
domuni		-0.305	-0.306		-0.595
		(7.94)***	(7.96)***		(2.24)**
forown	-0.081	-0.252		-0.192	-0.395
	(2.04)**	(5.58)***		(0.90)	(1.78)*
EU			-0.296		
			(6.02)***		
non_EU			-0.107		
			(1.39)		
lneturn	0.008	0.006	0.007	0.159	0.161
	(1.36)	(1.15)	(1.19)	(1.59)	(1.72)*
lnemphi	0.168	0.190	0.190	0.146	0.174
	(11.96)***	(14.94)***	(14.88)***	(1.47)	(1.76)*
fund	0.752	0.760	0.760	0.744	0.830
	(23.84)***	(24.39)***	(24.39)***	(3.27)***	(3.50)***
exshr	0.165	0.160	0.153	0.412	0.341
	(3.43)***	(3.30)***	(3.16)***	(1.38)	(1.12)
lninvest	0.035	0.044	0.044	0.125	0.173
	(3.69)***	(4.70)***	(4.66)***	(1.51)	(2.14)**
semht	0.292	0.349	0.345	0.215	0.280
	(6.67)***	(8.10)***	(7.99)***	(0.74)	(0.94)
semlt	0.222	0.243	0.244	0.279	0.184
	(4.77)***	(5.23)***	(5.25)***	(0.93)	(0.59)
sekis	0.156	0.168	0.169	0.734	0.681
	(3.19)***	(3.43)***	(3.45)***	(1.86)*	(1.73)*
seos	0.143	0.064	0.063	1.214	1.067
	(2.47)**	(1.07)	(1.06)	(3.61)***	(2.57)**
seutil	0.369	0.287	0.286	0.152	-0.199
	(3.58)***	(2.72)***	(2.72)***	(0.21)	(0.27)
rd	0.570	0.587	0.587	0.913	0.990
	(15.09)***	(16.01)***	(16.00)***	(3.12)***	(3.32)***
lnipc	0.023	0.022	0.022	0.076	0.083
	(3.13)***	(2.94)***	(2.92)***	(1.07)	(1.14)
rdintensity	0.008	0.004	0.002		
	(0.25)	(0.11)	(0.06)		
lngdp	-0.072	-0.050	-0.051		
	(5.25)***	(3.45)***	(3.51)***		
Constant	-1.184	-1.506	-1.490	-3.893	-3.916
	(4.73)***	(6.19)***	(6.12)***	(3.22)***	(3.98)***
Observations	40027	40027	40027	1253	1253
Uncensored obs	13889	13889	13889	547	547
Wald chi2 and sig	1159.60***	1602.03***	1602.07***	45.51***	84.14***

Absolute value of z statistics in parentheses, * significant at 10%; ** significant at 5%; *** significant at 1%

Source: Community Innovation Survey 3 EUROSTAT and Statistics Austria

Table 48: Determinants of the propensity for international innovation co-operation, Heckman probit estimates, 15 countries and Austria

	15 countries			Austria	
Case	(1)	(2)	(3)	(1)	(2)
domuni		-0.383	-0.383		-0.218
		(10.56)***	(10.56)***		(0.79)
forown	0.500	0.262		0.091	0.015
	(14.03)***	(6.32)***		(0.50)	(0.07)
EU			0.260		
			(5.89)***		
non_EU			0.271		
			(3.86)***		
lneturn	0.033	0.029	0.030	-0.109	-0.109
	(6.39)***	(6.02)***	(6.02)***	(1.24)	(1.18)
lnemphi	0.150	0.169	0.169	0.351	0.377
	(11.57)***	(15.53)***	(15.52)***	(3.42)***	(3.61)***
fund	0.429	0.414	0.414	0.014	0.038
	(13.31)***	(12.97)***	(12.97)***	(0.07)	(0.19)
exshr	0.510	0.486	0.486	1.097	1.107
	(11.45)***	(11.22)***	(11.20)***	(3.91)***	(3.98)***
lninvest	0.058	0.067	0.067	0.135	0.159
	(6.26)***	(7.63)***	(7.63)***	(1.80)*	(1.98)**
semht	0.190	0.246	0.246	-0.121	-0.094
	(4.54)***	(6.16)***	(6.14)***	(0.45)	(0.34)
semlt	0.071	0.094	0.094	0.417	0.404
	(1.57)	(2.12)**	(2.12)**	(1.56)	(1.48)
sekis	0.234	0.240	0.240	-0.048	-0.074
	(4.99)***	(5.27)***	(5.27)***	(0.14)	(0.21)
seos	0.092	0.000	0.000	0.964	0.909
	(1.70)*	(0.01)	(0.01)	(3.41)***	(2.80)***
seutil	0.021	-0.068	-0.068	0.148	-0.009
	(0.18)	(0.63)	(0.63)	(0.24)	(0.01)
rd	0.367	0.372	0.372	0.412	0.444
	(10.60)***	(11.34)***	(11.34)***	(1.78)*	(1.89)*
lnipc	0.027	0.025	0.025	-0.002	-0.001
	(3.83)***	(3.63)***	(3.63)***	(0.03)	(0.02)
rdintensity	-0.044	-0.052	-0.052		
	(1.34)	(1.63)	(1.63)		
lngdp	-0.188	-0.160	-0.160		
	(13.55)***	(10.86)***	(10.86)***		
Constant	0.105	-0.171	-0.170	-0.891	-0.956
	(0.44)	(0.76)	(0.76)	(0.87)	(0.91)
Observations	40027	40027	40027	1253	1253
Uncensored obs	13889	13889	13889	547	547
Wald chi2 and sig	1589.23***	2135.71***	2135.53***	53.91***	61.76***

Absolute value of z statistics in parentheses, * significant at 10%; ** significant at 5%; *** significant at 1%

Source: Community Innovation Survey 3 EUROSTAT and Statistics Austria

Strukturwandel und Strukturpolitik

Herausgegeben von Wolfram Elsner

Band 1 Karsten Seidel: Maritime Netzwerke und europäische Industriepolitik. 2000.

Band 2 Dieter Bögenhold (Hrsg.): Kleine und mittlere Unternehmen im Strukturwandel – Arbeitsmarkt und Strukturpolitik. 2000.

Band 3 Thomas Knogge: Umweltschocks und langfristige regionale Wirtschaftsentwicklung. Eine integrative Analyse reginalökonomischer Folgen des globalen Klimawandels. Mit dem Fallbeispiel der nordwestdeutschen Küstenregion. 2002.

Band 4 Wolfram Elsner (Hrsg.): Neue Alternativen des Länder-Finanzausgleichs. Modellrechnungen und Gutachten unter besonderer Berücksichtigung der Stadtstaaten-Problematik. 2002.

Band 5 Stefan Meyer: Strukturerneuerung und Regionalentwicklung durch Kooperationen und Netzwerke. Mit einer Fallstudie zum Autorecycling in Bremen. 2002.

Band 6 Martin Wrobel: Flughäfen in der Region. Regionale Gravitationszentren vor dem Verkehrsinfarkt? Eine Strukturanalyse und Prognose der landseitigen Verkehrssituation – am Beispiel des Airport Bremen. 2002.

Band 7 Martin Heinlein: Innovationen kleiner Unternehmen in regionalen Netzwerken. Die Förderung von Forschung und Entwicklung durch aktive Vermittlung im Wissens- und Technologietransfer. 2004.

Band 8 Martin Wrobel: Die Logistik als Motor regionaler Strukturentwicklung. Sektorale Clusterstrukturen und Netzwerkpotentiale am Beispiel Bremen und Hamburg. 2004.

Band 9 Sabine Bruns-Vietor: Logistik, Organisation und Netzwerke. Eine radikal konstruktivistische Diskussion des Fließsystemansatzes. 2004.

Band 10 Ernst Mönnich: Erklärungsansätze regionaler Entwicklung und politisches Handeln. Kritik und regionalökonomische Konsequenzen. 2004.

Band 11 Jost Bartkowiak: Stadtzentren im Umbruch. Zur *Revitalisierung* von Großstadtzentren, deren Bedeutung für Stadtökonomie, Städtebau und Stadtgesellschaft. Am Beispiel zentralstädtischer Bahnhofsareale. 2004.

Band 12 Wolfram Elsner / Christoph Otte / Inhi Yu: Klimawandel und regionale Wirtschaft. Vermögensschäden und Einkommensverluste durch extreme Klimaereignisse sowie Kosten-Nutzen-Analysen von Schutzmaßnahmen. Am Beispiel der nordwestdeutschen Küstenregion. 2005.

Band 13 Wolfram Elsner / J. Andreas Hübscher / Manfred Zachcial: Regionale Logistik-Cluster. Statistische Erfassung, Stärken und Schwächen, Handlungspotentiale. 2005.

Band 14 Marion Salot: Konkurrenz und Kooperation in Hightech-Branchen. Das Beispiel der internationalen Flugzeugbauindustrie. 2006.

Band 15 Maya Behrens-Schablow: Unternehmensinterne Netzwerke in der Informationsgesellschaft. Prozesse und Gestaltung der Vernetzung, Netzwerkkultur und Social Learning am Beispiel der Einführung von DC eLife in der DaimlerChrysler AG. 2007.

Band 16 Stefan Reiter: Wettbewerb und Monopolisierung in der Luft- und Raumfahrtindustrie. Analyse und Bewertung des Unternehmenszusammenschlusses Daimler-Benz/MBB aus Sicht der modernen Industrieökonomik. 2007.

Band 17 Lorraine Frisina: Understanding Regional Development. Absorption, Institutions and Socioeconomic Growth in the Regions of the European Union. A Case Study on Italy. 2008.

Band 18 Gero Hocker: Market – Hierarchy – Networking: Cooperation in Times of Globalization, Fragmentation, and Uncertainty. 2008.

Band 19 Bernhard Dachs: Innovative Activities of Multinational Enterprises in Austria. 2009.

www.peterlang.de

Peter Lang · Internationaler Verlag der Wissenschaften

Gero Hocker

Market – Hierarchy – Networking: Cooperation in Times of Globalization, Fragmentation, and Uncertainty

Frankfurt am Main, Berlin, Bern, Bruxelles, New York, Oxford, Wien, 2008.
XIII, 229 pp., num. tab., graph.
Strukturwandel und Strukturpolitik. Edited by Wolfram Elsner. Vol. 18
ISBN 978-3-631-57526-0 · pb. € 42.50*

Due to globalization and increased competition, many international firms have been adopting outsourcing strategies in order to cut costs by decreasing their degree of vertical integration. However, this strategy causes new problems. For instance, fragmentation of the company's value chain causes uncertainty with respect to the quality and availability of resources and the reliability of transaction partners. Further, the number of potential transaction partners has increased with the abolishment of trade barriers, which not only increases uncertainty, but also the complexity of the processes. International firms are managing these problems with different organizational structures and contractual arrangements with their transaction partners, while others have been evolutionary emerging.

Contents: The World of Rational Choice and Isolated Maximizing Individuals · The World of Direct Interdependencies and Complexity · Empirical Appearances of Networks Distinctive to 'Market' and 'Hierarchy' – Mercedes as a 'Closed Shop'-Structure · Openness, Shared Information and the Willingness to Reciprocate: Different Institutions in the Internet Economy · Possible Learning Effects – is the Open Source Model a Chance for Traditional Industries to Deal with Uncertainty?

Frankfurt am Main · Berlin · Bern · Bruxelles · New York · Oxford · Wien
Distribution: Verlag Peter Lang AG
Moosstr. 1, CH-2542 Pieterlen
Telefax 00 41 (0) 32 / 376 17 27

*The €-price includes German tax rate
Prices are subject to change without notice

Homepage http://www.peterlang.de

FSC
www.fsc.org
MIX
Papier | Fördert
gute Waldnutzung
FSC® C083411

Kolibri 360 GmbH
Ferdinand-Jühlke-Straße 7
99095 Erfurt, Deutschland
produktsicherheit@kolibri360.de